We Don't Play It For Fun

DON MOSEY

We Don't Play It For Fun

A Story of Yorkshire Cricket

Methuen London

First published in Great Britain 1988
by Methuen London Ltd
11 New Fetter Lane, London EC4P 4EE
Copyright © 1988 Don Mosey

British Library Cataloguing in Publication Data

Mosey, Don
    We don't play it for fun: a story of
    Yorkshire cricket.
    1. Cricket—England—Yorkshire
    —History
    I. Title
    796.35'8'09428   GV928.G7

    ISBN 0 413 60480 2

Printed in Great Britain
by
Redwood Burn Ltd,
Trowbridge, Wiltshire

Contents

Illustrations

The photographs in this book are reproduced by kind
permission of the following: *Illustrated London News* Picture
Library: 1a, 1b; Press Association Ltd: 1c, 2a, 3a, 3b, 4a, 5d,
6b; S & G Press Agency Ltd: 1d, 5a, 5b, 7a, 7b, 8a, 8b;
Popperfoto: 2b, 3c, 4b, 4c; J. Wardle: 5c; K. Kelly: 6a;
R. Bagnall: 8c

Acknowledgements

I am grateful to Mrs Ann Heap in the Local History section of Leeds Reference Library, to Joe Lister (the Yorkshire CCC Secretary) and to my friend Jack Wainwright for their help in tracing books which are either out of print or very difficult to obtain.

It has been useful – no, invaluable – to refresh my memory in certain areas by re-reading a number of publications: *The History of Yorkshire County Cricket, 1833–1903* by the Rev. R. S. Holmes (Archibald and Constable, 1904); *Recollections and Reminiscences of Lord Hawke* (Williams and Norgate, 1924); *Talks with Old Yorkshire Cricketers* by Old Ebor, first printed in the *Yorkshire Evening Post* and published in book form in 1898; *For Yorkshire and England* by Herbert Sutcliffe (Edward Arnold and Co., 1935); *Cricket is my Life* by Len Hutton (Hutchinson, 1949), *Express Deliveries* by Bill Bowes (Stanley Paul, 1949); *Thanks to Cricket* by J. M. Kilburn (Stanley Paul, 1972); *The Roses Matches, 1919–1939* (Neville Cardus's reports from the *Manchester Guardian* published by Souvenir Press, 1982); *Yorkshire's Pride* by John Callaghan (Pelham Books, 1984); *Hedley Verity* by Alan Hill (Kingswood Press, 1986); and, of course, the indispensable Yorkshire CCC handbooks and the *Wisden Book of Cricket Records* by Bill Frindall (Queen Anne Press, 1985).

Introduction

A whole generation of Yorkshiremen and women has grown up without seeing the county side play *great* cricket. The period since 1971 has been the blackest in the county's modern history of more than a hundred years, plagued by controversy, resigned to failure, torn by revolution. When I started the planning of this book in October 1986 I intended to dedicate it to the current Yorkshire side with a gentle hint that they were the heirs to the greatest tradition in English cricket, a reminder that they were the descendants of very special people. After watching them in three games at the start of 1987 I realised that those hints and reminders were not necessary. Yorkshire cricket was, after all, *all reight*.

Nevertheless, a whole generation *has* grown up without experiencing the triumphs and achievements which were commonplace to those of us in more advanced stages of antiquity, and as the Renaissance of Yorkshire cricket begins it is perhaps the right time to offer a glimpse of the past to those of the present and the future in the hope that they will be able to ensure that the horrors of the last two decades never occur again. It is written with unashamed sentiment, natural pride and the most enormous affection and I admit readily and happily that I wrote much of it with a great lump in my throat.

Morecambe (otherwise known as Bradford-by-the-Sea,
a Yorkshire colony in Lancashire)
1 June, 1987

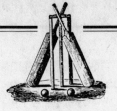

I
'Vive La Différence'

On the last day of February 1978 I was commentating on New Zealand *v.* England at Lancaster Park, Christchurch, when Derek Randall of Nottinghamshire, the non-striking batsman, was run out without warning by the bowler, Ewen Chatfield, as Randall backed up rather incautiously. Consternation immediately swept through the crowd and for a moment there was stunned silence amongst my colleagues. Such things are simply not done in the best circles and, in terms of sportsmanship, there are no better circles than New Zealand cricket.

During the tea interval I was asked by a television interviewer for my views on the incident and I replied, airily: 'All I can say is that in the part of the world where I learned my cricket such things are commonplace.' It was, if you like, an act of unbridled cowardice on my part but the reply was not wholly cynical. I have played in games where the non-striker has been run out and I have seen it happen in matches where I have been a spectator. And even if it is a trifle unusual to see it happen in a Test, my honest reaction would have to be, in American parlance, 'It's no big deal.' Probably only a Yorkshireman would take that view; it certainly would find no echo amongst my 'Test Match Special' commentary colleagues (with the notable exception of F. S. Trueman) and it would not meet with universal enthusiasm in many circles outside the Broad Acres.

But surely the issue is simple? The batsman was taking an unfair advantage. The Laws say that he may be run out in those circumstances; they don't say anything about giving him a warning. Those who want to conduct their cricket in an atmosphere of Corinthian purity are most welcome to do so but they must not expect *us* always

to take the same view. Because *we* don't play it for fun (or 'laik' it –
to use our vernacular). When the last ball has been bowled and the
last run struck, then is the time to congratulate the opposition on a
well-timed cover drive or a beautifully flighted leg break which
materially affected the course of the game. But not until we are all
back in the pavilion and the game is won or lost. Oh my word, no.
So on that occasion in Christchurch, Chatfield had a good deal of
my sympathy as the wrath of his countrymen descended upon him.
I had a sneaking bit of sympathy for Randall, too – not for being
dismissed in such a fashion but because he looked a right Charlie!
There has always been a certain gaucheness about Derek's cricket –
a sort of schoolboy naiveté which is, in its way, an engaging quality.
There the poor chap stood, looking like a kid who has been caught
with his fingers in the jam-pot, shifting from one leg to the other
with the most sheepish of grins on his face, before realising that
there was nothing for it but to return whence he had come: Randall,
run out 13. It would have to be 13, wouldn't it? History would
record, solemnly: 'It was only the third instance of this type of
dismissal in Test cricket and the first between New Zealand and
England.' But as pandemonium reigned in the ground and my Kiwi
colleagues generously and decently sought for words to apologise I
swear I could hear in my head a hundred Yorkshire voices,
individual voices around the grounds of Halifax and Huddersfield
and Holbeck and Hull, pronouncing a single verdict: 'Serves t'silly
bugger reight.'

It would not matter a twopenny damn that the incident had
provoked the most almighty row because almighty rows are part and
parcel of Saturday afternoon in Yorkshire. I love 'em. There is
something about the passion, the grandeur, the sheer majesty of a
Yorkshire cricket row which transcends just about everything except
the outbreak of war. And even then your average Yorkie would
have to be convinced that the war was of special personal concern to
him. If lesser mortals, unfortunate enough to be born on less
hallowed ground, do not really understand our point of view, then
that's their problem. Because *we know* that it is right. It doesn't
really matter how this came about. Almost certainly the Good Lord
decided one day as He watched His flock down below developing
this quaint pastime of bat and ball, that it was altogether too gentle
an occupation as initiated on Broad Ha'penny Down, developed on

the playing fields of Eton and refined in the committee rooms of Lord's. It needed a catalyst, something to breathe fire and brimstone into the game. And so He looked with favour upon His chosen people for this role: Yorkshiremen.

Not everyone outside the county has always understood this. Even fewer have appreciated it. Nevertheless, just a handful have recognised it. When I was about to embark on my cricket broadcasting career I sought the advice of John Arlott, on the basis that he really should have been a Yorkshireman (just as Trevor Bailey should, for the way he *played* his cricket). John considered for a moment, then growled: 'Undo the top button of your trousers, make yourself comfortable, then *explain* the game to the listeners with a lordly Yorkshire air.' And so, just as the players have always been different (what other county could have produced a Sutcliffe or a Hutton, a Trueman, a Close or an Illingworth – and certainly a Boycott?), the spectators have always been different, the county members different, the reporters and commentators different. We don't play it or think it or write it or talk it for fun. Thus, as our cricketing character has developed differently, so has the gap widened between the cricketing philosophies of what is broadly termed North and South (for the purposes of sorting out the Effete South we occasionally are willing to enlist Lancashire as an ally but it is, at best, a tenuous relationship). The South has overwhelming superiority in administrative fire-power. The game is run from London NW8; its roots go deep into public school and Oxbridge soil. It is difficult, if not impossible, to beat The System other than by asserting superiority on the field of play and for an unacceptable length of time now we have not been able to do that. Life has been hard to bear since Yorkshire last won the County Championship in 1968. The plain fact is that 'they' do not like us overmuch and for nearly twenty years now 'they' have been able to crack the whip.

Just what are the manifestations of this North *v.* South schism? The game as evolved by the bucolic yeomen of Hambledon was taken up in London at a high – socially speaking – level. The Duke of Dorset, the Duke of Hamilton, the Earls of Winchelsea and Tankerville were members of the White Conduit Club, soon to become the MCC, when the rules in the late eighteenth Century decreed: 'None but gentlemen ever to play.' In Yorkshire, after a little initial dabbling by gentleman-farmers (who had the space to provide cricket grounds) and the odd parson, it was taken up with enthusiasm by the working-class population. Some of the best of our earlier players were cottage-weavers in the Huddersfield area and the steel-grinders of Sheffield. Thomas Lord, whose name for 200 years has been synonymous with the Establishment of cricket, might well have been a Yorkshireman but he was neither a peer nor even a successful businessman who had gone to London in search of his fortune, Dick Whittington style. It is really by accident that this particular Yorkie happens to have given his name to all that is traditional in the game.

Thomas Lord was born in 1755 in Thirsk, that pleasant market town in North Yorkshire which was later to be the birthplace of George Macaulay and Joe Lister, the present Yorkshire secretary. His was a Catholic family and thus supporters of the lost cause of Bonnie Prince Charlie ten years before the birth of young Thomas. From being a country landowner at the time of the Jacobite Rising, his father was reduced to agricultural labouring and it was, in fact, after the family had moved to Norfolk that Thomas learned his cricket. It helped him to a position as an *attendant* (no gentleman, young Lord) at the White Conduit Club and he was occasionally called upon to act as what would now be called a net bowler to the peers who were members. It was in this capacity (and because he was a bright and enterprising 21-year-old) that he was asked if he would care to set up a private ground – with the support of Club members. This undoubtedly helped him to establish his own business, which was selling wine, and in due course he made a lot of money, but we can't really claim by any stretch of the imagination to have sent a Yorkshire missionary to London to get the game going. Until Lord Hawke came on the scene there was little, if any, connection between the peerage and cricket in Yorkshire.

It is all very well for G. M. Trevelyan, the historian, to claim that if the French nobility had been capable of playing cricket with their peasantry their châteaux would never have been burned. That might have been a fair analogy as far as cricket in the Home Counties was concerned, but it had no relevance to the way it developed in the North of England. Country-house cricket, with the squire mingling with his tenantry, might have helped the progress of egalitarianism in some quarters but I doubt if it has ever had much impact in Yorkshire. Cricket, once taken up, swept like a moorland fire through the working-class areas of the county and there its roots (at least in the most fiercely competitive terms) have remained. The social structure of southern counties has largely prevented any parallel development; the strength of Yorkshire cricket has always rested firmly in its leagues, and our attitudes to the game as well as each other in North and South have progressed accordingly. For East and West, read North and South and Kipling had it right: never the twain shall meet.

Peter May, chairman of the England Selectors from 1982, is the most charming and urbane of men; it is difficult to think of any organisation more Establishment-orientated than the BBC, at least in the context of cricket. Yet during my period as BBC cricket correspondent I never once had a conversation with P. B. H. in which I felt either of us was completely at ease. It was always as if Peter was poised lightly on his toes awaiting the delivery of a verbal beneath-the-belt blow. I cannot recall ever meeting the late Bill Edrich without a snarled greeting: 'Ah! The bloody Yorkshireman.' And even amongst my BBC colleagues (perhaps I should say *especially* amongst them) it is difficult to recall an occasion when I have waxed wrathful about something without hearing the muttered comment, 'Look out. He's doing his Joe Champion act again.' I expect all this; I even look forward to it. For the first conscious feeling a Yorkie must learn to recognise is that he is *different*. And nowhere is this more ostentatiously manifested than in the game of cricket. Historically, we have always been the awkward squad; in cricket, coming relatively late in our history, we have steadfastly followed the same tradition. There has always been 'them' and they have never liked 'us'. It goes back more than a hundred years but let us look for a moment, at a few post-war examples.

In 1948 Alec Coxon played in his first and only Test against the most powerful of Australian sides. Rumour had it that he swopped punches with Denis Compton after a personal North–South row in the England dressing-room. Coxon, who hadn't done badly against tough opposition, never played for England again and we did not trouble ourselves overmuch about the rights and wrongs of the story; it became another injustice to be avenged in due course. In 1967 Brian Close was deprived of the England captaincy for reasons far removed from Test cricket and the leadership went to Colin Cowdrey (Tonbridge and Oxford). In 1970–1 Raymond Illingworth had a most acrimonious passage through Australia as captain with his manager David Clark (who subsequently became President of MCC). Geoffrey Boycott bitterly resented being passed over for the England captaincy for, successively, Mike Denness, Tony Greig, Mike Brearley and – heaven help us! – Bob Willis. Even Len Hutton, after winning the Ashes at home and retaining them abroad, could not escape the stage whispers that his methods were not exactly cricket as it was understood in the Long Room. (There has, of course, long been a discrepancy between the views of, say, the Cross Arrows dressing-room and that of Pudsey St Lawrence, on what exactly does constitute cricket.) Fred Trueman's battles with almost every conceivable form of authority from the early fifties to mid-sixties now seem like Enid Blyton stories beside the adventures of Ian Botham but at the time Fred was the *enfant terrible* of the game, the like of which had never been known. It cannot be without significance that Fred has never been honoured either on the Queen's birthday or at New Year for his haul of 307 Test wickets in only sixty-seven matches spread over thirteen years – an infinitely more remarkable achievement than taking more wickets in more Tests closely following each other. It is scandalous and can only be explained by, shall we say, a lack of enthusiasm for Fred at Lord's, from where any recommendation would come. Herbert Sutcliffe was never honoured either, and there was a man who by his patrician approach to a plebeian role did more to increase the stature of the cricket mercenary than any professional before or since his time.

On a purely personal note, and very much more modest scale, in 1965 I was called upon to lead the BBC North team in an inter-regional tournament at Edgbaston. Our innings closed at ten past one and the Midlanders' captain – who wore one of those coloured, hooped caps long since identified by Cardus as the original red rag to any northern bull – genially asked if I was ready to join him for lunch. Reasoning that he wouldn't want to lose a wicket before the break and we could therefore dispose of three or four of his limited overs without the risk of conceding many runs, I gently suggested that after the pitch had been rolled we would still have time for another ten minutes' play. His face reddened and he snapped: 'That's a right bloody Yorkshire trick.' I replied, 'Exactly,' and felt inordinately pleased with myself. Oh yes. We are different.

So while we can certainly make out a case for a brooding

resentment against 'The South', as we generically dismiss those not
lucky enough to have been born between the Tees and the Humber,
should we not ask ourselves if 'they' have not reasonable grounds
for regarding us with suspicion, with distaste and even active
dislike? 'They', too, may have a case of sorts.

It is a thought we may, perhaps, pursue in the following pages,
for this is by no means a formal history of Yorkshire cricket. It is
more an exploration of our native character as seen through the
careers of some of our cricketing giants, and one or two others.
They will certainly not emerge as coming from the same mould.
What greater contrast could there be, for instance, between captains
like Lord Hawke and Brian Sellers? Could there be more dissimilar
personalities than batsmen like George Ulyett and Herbert Sutcliffe,
bowlers like Bobby Peel and Hedley Verity? And at the same time
is it not possible to find a link, a common denominator, which
touches all of them? Some may find it, others may search in vain. In
that case we must switch our argument and claim that it is the sum
of so many differing styles, personalities, foibles, prejudices, tem-
peraments, strengths and weaknesses which makes up the whole
character of the Yorkshire cricketer. Some – indeed, a lot of them –
may have found fun in playing the game but most assuredly no
individual, no team throughout the ages, has played it simply for
fun. The pleasure has come from being the best, from knowing that
the opposition has always regarded Yorkshire as different and tried
that bit harder in consequence. Quixotic declarations to achieve a
result may have had a place in games between any two other
counties, but they have not often come Yorkshire's way. Second
and third place in the county championship may have looked good
to counties who have struggled for years in the lower reaches of the
table, but for Yorkshire it has spelled failure. That has always been
our burden, and our pride.

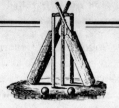

2
The Beginning

In some ways the wheel of cricket has turned full circle in the past 150 years or so. The emphasis today is very much on money: prize-money, merit-money, man-of-the-match awards, even the individual stipends of star players in what has always been regarded as essentially a team game. It's not new, merely different. The earliest competitive cricket was almost always played for a 'purse', the term no doubt derived from the contemporarily popular prize-fighting. Indeed, England's champion boxer, Bendigo, got himself involved in single-wicket matches, as we shall shortly see. Bendigo was a Nottingham man and the rivalry between that city and Sheffield had been manifest in cricket fixtures going back to 1771. George III was on the throne and Captain Cook was exploring the South Pacific when W. North, a Nottingham player and chronicler, solemnly recorded that in the first match between the cities 'Nottingham gave in'. Their backers would not be too pleased about that because a purse of 500 guineas was not unusual and within a few years it had increased to 1,000 sovereigns on occasions.

Single-wicket matches were popular and quite often originated with a challenge being thrown out in the columns of such newspapers as existed at the start of the nineteenth century. This is how Tom Marsden, of Sheffield, offered through the *Sheffield Independent* to meet any man in England for the sum of £50 and found no one to take up the challenge. Marsden, who flitted briefly across the cricketing scene of South Yorkshire, was perhaps the first of our highly individual characters. In 1826 he had played an innings of eight hours, scoring 227 against Nottingham, and this was clearly an attempt to cash in on his fame. He was immortalised in verse and, though his career was short, twenty years later a presentation breastpin given to the treasurer of the Leeds Club incorporated two hairs from Tom Marsden's head! A few country gentlemen at this stage played matches on their estates and no doubt enjoyed competing for a side-stake, but the most fiercely competitive cricket was that which took place in the Sheffield area. It was not, as yet, a spectator-sport to challenge cock-fighting in popularity, but clubs were beginning to be formed in other parts of the county and it was the opening in 1822 of a ground at Darnall, in Sheffield, which seems to have established the greatest popular appeal up to this point.

George Steer, of Darnall Hall, was the man who prepared the land, built a stand and opened the ground with a match between fifteen of Sheffield versus eleven of Notts but a temporary stand collapsed, injuring twenty-three people, to give the spectator-sport in South Yorkshire an unfortunate send-off. Undismayed, Mr Steer opened a new ground in 1824 and crowds as large as 30,000 watched cricket there, establishing Sheffield as the foremost centre in the country for the support of competitive cricket. It was at Darnall that the first of three 'test matches' was staged between Sussex and England, really to decide whether the new, round-arm style of bowling (recently introduced by the Sussex men, Lillywhite and Broadbridge) was superior to the old underhand style, so Yorkshire certainly played its part in the first major technical revolution of the game. Somehow this new style of bowling appealed to Yorkshiremen, for now clubs began to spring up all over the county, particularly in the West Riding: Leeds, Harewood, Huddersfield, Dewsbury, Wakefield, Halifax, Armley, Knaresborough, Otley, Keighley, Rotherham, Mexborough, and – further afield within the county – Redcar, Scarborough, Bedale. The latter is worth dwelling on for a moment – a tiny Wensleydale township of fewer than 1,500 people today, obviously much smaller in the reigns of George IV and William IV. Yet by the time a 'Yorkshire' side had been formed to play Sheffield in 1861, Bedale contributed no fewer than four players – George Anderson, Roger Iddison, John and George Morton. Anderson and Iddison were in the official county side which played Surrey two years later – six months after the Yorkshire CCC had been formally constituted – and the two of them were in the group of five who refused to play against Surrey in 1865 in what was, perhaps, the earliest manifestation of North–South 'feeling'. The rebels took a poor view of the no-balling of a bowler called Edgar Willsher, suspecting that the umpire had been 'got at'. Oh yes, we were standing no nonsense from the southerners as far back as that!

But stepping back in time to the earlier half of the nineteenth century, single-wicket challenge matches for 'purses' were very much in vogue and the story I like best from this age concerns one of these challenges between Bendigo, the aforementioned champion pugilist of England, and Andrew Dalton of Dalton (Huddersfield), a village which produced four early Yorkshire cricketers. The match was not going well for Bendigo and he seems not to have been too happy about the situation. The last straw came when a dog pinched the ball and dashed off the ground, whereupon the boxer-bowler stamped off with the snarled comment that he was there to play against men, not dogs. Bendigo – he seems to have had no other name, at least for prize-fighting and cricketing purposes – was a colourful character and a good friend of Richard Daft, the great Nottinghamshire player and no mean boxer himself. Bendigo earned himself a bob or two after retiring from the fight-game by challenging anyone to land a blow on his face or head during luncheon intervals at Trent Bridge while he defended himself simply by bobbing and weaving (no other form of defence allowed). The ex-champion seems to have gone steadily downhill as the years rolled by because I remember that while working in Nottingham in the early 1950s I looked up references to Bendigo in the files of a local newspaper. He developed the engaging hobby of standing at the bar of local pubs and *spitting* into the pint of anyone who happened to be drinking there. The unfortunate drinker, if he recognised Bendigo, felt it impolitic to take any action other than walking away and leaving behind his drink and so the crafty old boy was left with a buckshee pint which he apparently had no qualms about drinking despite his personal contribution to the contents of the glass!

These years were what we might reasonably call the dawn of Yorkshire cricket history. Details of matches were imprecisely recorded; folklore and legend must certainly have played a major part in any attempt to record those early days of the game in Yorkshire. It is only with the establishment of the county club on an official footing in the second half of the nineteenth century that records become more trustworthy and, more importantly to us, players begin to emerge as clearly defined personalities. We shall look at a selection of them shortly, but first it is very well worthwhile taking a look at the original constitution of Yorkshire County Cricket Club as adopted in 1863. It was drawn up by a dozen Sheffield men but to their eternal credit they did not seek for one moment to 'hog' the glory that was to come. This was to be a *Yorkshire* county club and the rules they laid down form the broad base of the county club today:

> A central or any fixed ground shall not be considered requisite and matches shall be played at various localities in the county as the Management Committee may arrange.
>
> The County Club will not offer, and it entirely disclaims the right or desire of interference with the particular concerns of any local clubs, their only object being to develop the cricketing power of the County and promote the game generally. They earnestly invite recommendations from all local clubs of any young players who may be considered likely to add to the strength of the County in any department of the game.
>
> The Management Committee shall duly consider propositions from any part of the county for the choice of its particular neighbourhood as the locality for one county match in any year and that it may be publicly understood that the Yorkshire County Club invites such propositions from every neighbourhood having a cricket ground in first-rate playing condition.

That has to be seen as a particularly enlightened start to the history of cricket in a county where parochialism has always been rife and rivalry intense. Consider, for instance, this delightful exchange which took place in August 1826 in the columns of the *Bradford Courier*: (1) 'A cricket match was played at Huddersfield on Monday between the Huddersfield and Dewsbury Clubs which was won by the former with four wickets to go down. Dewsbury got 46 at the first innings and 55 at the second; Huddersfield 75 at the first innings and 31 at the unfinished innings which terminated the game.' (2) 'We are authorised to contradict a paragraph which appeared in the Bradford Courier of the 3rd inst. stating a cricket match was played between Dewsbury and Huddersfield, no such match having taken place. Some gentlemen from Dewsbury certainly went to Huddersfield by invitation to play with their club upon an express understanding that it should be considered no match but merely for practice and improvement.' (3) 'Last week, by special request, we stated that the paragraph relating to a cricket match played at Huddersfield was incorrect and this week, on equally good authority, we are requested to say that it was perfectly correct. Having told the story on both sides we hope we shall be excused from any further notice on the subject.' Isn't that beautiful?

Knowing that tribal warfare of that kind was regularly raging throughout the county without, perhaps, the same sort of indulgence from the local press, the first Yorkshire Committee set out to make it clear from the start that this was to be a *county* club in every sense of the word. And so it has remained. The first official Yorkshire County Cricket Club team was composed of three Sheffield players – Joe Rowbottom, Edwin Stephenson and William Slinn; three from Huddersfield – John Thewliss (Lascelles Hall), John Berry and Edwin Dawson (Dalton); two from Bedale – Roger Iddison and George Anderson; George Atkinson from Ripon, Ike Hodgson from Bradford and Brian Waud from Leeds. Three from the north of the county, three from the south and five from the middle – what could have been more democratic?

And so, before we look at some of these earliest of our heroes, let's consider the conditions under which they played and travelled to their games. Today we may perhaps divide ourselves roughly into two groups – those who used to drive about the country every Tuesday and Friday evenings (in the days of the 'old' county championship before limited-overs competition gave us a fixture list of a very different nature) before there were any motorways; and those who have grown up in the last twenty-five years and had to endure torture (despite motorways) like: Saturday, *v.* Middlesex at Middlesbrough; Sunday, *v.* Kent at Canterbury; Monday and Tuesday, *v.* Middlesex at Middlesbrough. In 1863 the railway system was by no means complete and many journeys had to be undertaken by horse-drawn coach. On one trip between Wisbech and Sleaford a player had to climb a sign-post and strike a light to determine which way to go. The legendary Norfolk player, Fuller Pilch, went to Glasgow to play a single-wicket match on a ground where the grass had to be *scythed* before it could start. In Truro, a fieldsman disturbed a covey of partridges as he chased a ball into the well-named longfield. It was coarse cricket with a vengeance.

So who were some of those earlier Yorkshire cricketers?

George Anderson, one of the Bedale men in Yorkshire's original 'official' team, played cricket from the age of sixteen until he was fifty. At that point, after scoring 114 not out for Constable Burton *v.* Darlington he announced that he was so tired he would never play again. And he didn't. In one way, Anderson might be said to have been a direct predecessor of Brian Close (capped by England before being so honoured by Yorkshire) for he was a member of the original Old England XI before the county club was founded. He was described by Grace as 'a punishing hitter' and was certainly one of the leading batsmen in the country when he, with Anderson, Atkinson, Iddison, Rowbotham and Stephenson, refused to play against Surrey (because of the no-balling of Willsher) in 1865. The Club had been founded and, as we have seen, had been constituted with pragmatic delicacy, yet here we were in the middle of a full-scale row after only two years. In April of that year, Anderson was offered the Yorkshire captaincy but he refused without hesitation and let it be known, with towering indignation, that 'he would not play against those who have combined to sweep us from the cricket field altogether if they could'.

His fellow-villager, Iddison (who was Yorkshire's first official captain), had refused to get together a North side to play the South the previous year because the no-balling of Willsher, which had occurred as far back as 1862 at The Oval (before, remember, Yorkshire was officially in existence) still rankled. The southern feathers were ruffled, and they in turn then refused to play a fixture arranged with the North at Newmarket which presumably was regarded as neutral ground. Yorkshire's Committee, seeking a reasonable solution, issued a statement refusing to take sides in the North *v.* South argument but reminding the striking players of their obligations as professionals. That brought no response from the now infamous five. The Committee, having decided it had done all that could be expected, now decreed that, having been forced either 'to bow to the will of the players or play the matches with such talent as they could bring together at the risk of almost certain failure and pecuniary loss, the latter course would be taken'. In 1865 Yorkshire did not win a single match, and in 1866 no matches were arranged at all. It had been a sad beginning for a Club so bravely launched.

Anderson, a tall, burly man with his inevitable drooping moustache supplemented by a Hapsburg beard, was clearly a man of strong principle – in some ways his direct descendant has to be Ray Illingworth. Every reference book comments upon his powerful hitting, one going so far as to say he was the hardest-hitter ever to play for the county, though that was published just after the turn of the twentieth century. His reputation was largely made before Yorkshire CCC came into official existence. He went to Australia with George Parr's team in 1863–4, for instance and the poetic pen-picture drawn for the benefit of Australian cricket enthusiasts ran like this:

> Next Anderson, of Yorkshire the pride
> Whose bat's a mighty help to any side;
> His county of him always has been proud.
> And greets his play with acclamation loud.
> No doubt the bowlers, to their cost, will find
> To drive the ball he's 'mazingly inclined.

Unfortunately, illness prevented Anderson from living up to his reputation. He was ill during most of the six-week voyage and for the greater part of the tour, once the party had landed, as well. But so stubbornly did he hold to his principle when the 'no-balling' dispute split North and South that one wonders if he was perhaps influenced by two factors: (1) George Parr, his captain in 1863–4, had refused to accompany the 1861–2 tour, the first ever to Australia, because he regarded a fee of £150 as inadequate; (2) during his tour, the Australian professionals went on strike for greater pay. True, Anderson's dispute with his club had nothing to do with money but he had been a fringe observer of what may well have been the first two rebellions against established authority in cricket. Iddison, his fellow Bedalian, was coaxed back to the fold and was, in fact, the Yorkshire captain until 1870.

If George Anderson must be seen as a stubborn and uncompromising individual, Tom Emmett of Halifax was a horse of a very different colour. He learned to play in a road with one of the stone gateposts at the home of a local tradesman as the wicket. This meant frequent interruptions to the game because of non-sportingminded policemen. At a ripe old age he still recalled a schoolboy match ('I turned out in a beautiful white smock and clogs') in which he hit a ball through the window of a wool-combing shed and was horrified to see a man emerge, with blood streaming from a cut head, threatening to wheel them all in front of the magistrates – a threat calculated to inspire a good deal more fear and respect than it would today. The injured man was ultimately 'bought off' by a whip-round to pay for the window, but the game was ruined. Mercifully, this did not kill off Emmett's sense of humour, which was legendary throughout the game during his lifetime and has left us with a series of drolleries which represent, perhaps, the first recorded epigrams in cricket. We shall look at them shortly but, first, let us consider the finest bowler of his day, a man who took 1,269 wickets at 12.68, a bowler of whom Grace said, 'When they [Emmett and Freeman] were on together I realised that a hundred runs against them was something to be proud of.'

He was a quickish bowler who very quickly learned that irrespective of pace his deliveries were played easily by batsmen of ability and he started to experiment. He developed an away swinger but never knew how he bowled it. He did, however, master the earliest-known leg-cutter: 'My best ball was one which pitched between the legs and wickets and broke enough to take the off bail.' It was this ball which impressed Grace, who described it in exactly the same terms as Emmett and added, 'I have had occasional balls from him which would have beaten any batsman.' Tom's first professional engagement was in his native Halifax, where, on his way to a game (two shillings and sixpence a match) in clogs and carrying his cricket boots wrapped in a copy of the local newspaper as usual, he encountered the Keighley team in their wagonette, *en route* to a game, and hitched a lift with them. They asked him to join the club and Tom replied, 'Find me something to do in winter and I will.' He was professional at Keighley for the next three years and it was during this time that he was asked to turn out for Todmorden against George Parr's All England XI. His demand for a fee of seven and sixpence and his train fare was turned down as exorbitant. He was invited to play for Yorkshire in 1866 and promptly demanded £5 as his fee, which shook the county secretary. However, as he was expected to pay his own expenses and the game was away to

Nottinghamshire, it was agreed to pay him what was a very high fee indeed for a beginner and Emmett's first-class career was launched.

He did not at first find it easy to make his mark because Yorkshire's opening pair, George Freeman and Luke Greenwood, usually bowled out the opposition. However, in his second season he got his chance against Surrey and promptly returned figures of 12-8-7-6. Tom Emmett had arrived. The Oval was a happy hunting-ground for him. At the age of forty he skippered Yorkshire there, and after Ulyett, Peate and Bates had failed to make an impression Tom bowled himself and took eight for 22. He feigned to despise batting, preferring to bowl and to excel in the field. Nevertheless, he enjoyed telling the dressing-room that he was the best player of lobs in the game. That was until a game against Gloucs in 1878 when he encountered the redoubtable Frank Townsend. In his own words, he then 'played forward, went back, decided to let it go; it hit something and bowled me'. Tom replaced the dislodged bail and called down the wicket, 'Hey, Mr Townsend, just let me have that one over again, please.'

He had a marvellous on-the-field relationship with the great W. G. At Cheltenham, in 1876 (Grace's great year), Tom announced before the game that, 'I'll shoot him before he makes a hundred against us.' Grace made 318 not out. In 1870, at Lord's, Grace faced Freeman and Emmett on 'one of the roughest, bumpiest wickets' on which the ball hit all batsmen about the body, occasionally shot along the ground but was just as likely to fly about their ears. Emmett, with whimsical admiration, remarked, 'I don't believe W. G. had a square inch of sound flesh on his body after that innings.' After Grace had qualified as a doctor he played in a game against Yorkshire and slipped on the field, leaving a distinct mark on his flannels. It was Emmett who drily commented, 'Aye, Mr Grace. I see you've got your diploma.' Emmett it was, when suffering from a rough passage across the Bay of Biscay, who remarked to Lord Harris that 'the groundsman ought to be sacked if he can't provide a better wicket than this'. He was – perhaps apart from his geniality towards the opposition – the ancestor of F. S. Trueman.

In some ways, so was George Ulyett, though again his sunny nature belies the claim. Ulyett, a Sheffield man, was known throughout the game as Happy Jack, which certainly has the same cadence and syllabic rhythm as Fiery Fred if not the same significance, and was a splendid all-round cricketer who played for twenty seasons from 1873. Like Emmett, his earliest cricket was played on a road with fieldsmen posted in adjoining fields, and the side-stake was a ha'penny a man.

He was refused membership of the Pitsmoor Club because he was too young at sixteen, but two months later the club relented and included him in a game against the Derbyshire village of Staveley. Ulyett took seven wickets in the first innings and five in the second, and his career was under way. By the time he was twenty he was a professional in Bradford. He had a memorable encounter with Grace when he first went to London with the North team to play the South. One can only wonder whether the crafty northerners were 'trying it on', but they turned out with twelve men – which W. G. promptly pointed out. Someone had to stand down, and just how this came to be George Ulyett is not clear. But the following dialogue then ensued:

Grace: Can you stand as umpire? Do you know anything about it?

Ulyett: Certainly.

He then gave out the great man lbw playing forward. Afterwards the dialogue resumed.

Grace: You made a great mistake, you know.

Ulyett: No sir. The ball pitched on your foot. The bowler hadn't told me whether he was going to turn it or not.

Long pause. Then, Grace: You'll do.

In his good-humoured way, Ulyett was a tilter at windmills of authority. On a visit to play Sussex he found himself locked out of his digs after a bit of a night on the town. By knocking up the proprietor of a tobacconist's shop next door to his lodgings he managed to get through to the back and climb up a ladder to his room. Inevitably the story leaked out and George was carpeted before the Committee. He did not deny the allegations but blandly pointed out that he was late to bed because he had been in the company of two gentlemen, Mr Crowther of The New Inn, Bradford, and Mr Dawson of The Unicorn, and it would have been impolite to leave earlier. Both Mr Crowther and Mr Dawson were Yorkshire Committee members. For some reason which is not quite clear, Ulyett was in the habit of carrying about with him a surgical lance; perhaps he was a frustrated surgeon. But he certainly frightened to death a young doctor in Australia by offering to 'bleed' him.

When he toured South Africa with the first party to go there in 1888 (he was, in fact, called up by cable to join the party) he took with him a gallon jar of whisky which he got past the ship's officers and the Customs and Excise by blithely telling them it was linseed oil for the bats of the entire party. But let us not lose sight of the fact that Ulyett was a very serious and accomplished cricketer. He joined Yorkshire – and England, too – primarily as a bowler but gradually developed his batting until he became the best all-rounder Yorkshire were to see until the arrival of George Hirst. Ulyett scored 16,063 runs for the county and took 484 wickets. When the Hon. M. B. Hawke took over the Yorkshire captaincy, Ulyett was very much his right-hand man. He made five tours of Australia and, with the dawn of official Test cricket, he played in twenty-five of them, scoring 949 runs and taking fifty wickets. Against New South Wales, in Sydney on the 1878–9 tour he took four wickets in four balls. After his retirement, in contrast to so many of his contemporaries who took up coaching, Ulyett kept a pub in Sheffield. His friendly nature was probably more at home there.

If Ulyett shows us one side of the Yorkshire character, how about George Harrison (1883–92) for a glimpse of an entirely different personality? He took 88 wickets in his first season, 72 of them clean-bowled, and if his subsequent rate of success was not quite so spectacular he had gathered together 295 first-class wickets at 14.48 when Grace took him apart in a Gents v. Players match. Harrison took to his bed and was never any use to Yorkshire again!

Billy Bates (1877–88) was a fine batsman who was noted as a snappy dresser, which earned him the dressing-room title of The Duke. When his son, William Edric Bates, followed him into the side twenty years later with much the same sartorial presence, the Yorkshire team promptly showed (as well they might with Lord Hawke as captain) a proper appreciation of the hereditary peerage by christening him The Marquis.

Ephraim Lockwood, one of the great Huddersfield contingent, was a dour type of individual despite his reputation as the finest cutter of the ball in his time. Known as Old Mary Ann within the ranks, he dismissed his first glimpse of the Niagara Falls with the comment that he'd rather be at Lascelles Hall ('It's quite as pretty there'). Lockwood took no chance with his batting, and none with his life either. At Scarborough he went into the sea only with a rope knotted round his chest and the other end attached to a bathing machine on the beach. Ever the practical man, he waded out waist-deep, then lathered himself with a cake of soap.

George Freeman (1865–80), the first of the county's really quick bowlers, was described as 'so fast that a man he hit in 1871 still bore the visible mark of the blow in 1917'. (Fred Trueman would give his eye teeth to carry that legend about with him.)

Great characters. Great cricketers. Great Yorkshiremen.

3
Two Captains

Of the thirteen 'gentlemen' who captained Yorkshire between 1883 and 1959 it is fair to say that there were a number of lightweights who would have found it difficult to get a place in the county side on their cricketing ability alone. There were also one or two whose achievements as leaders of the side were made more remarkable by the timing and circumstances of their appointment. In that context the name of Ronnie Burnet comes immediately to mind, and we shall look at his two years in office (1958–1959) in due course. Norman Yardley (1948–55) was arguably the best *player* to skipper the side in a period of around seventy years if one looks at individual ability in the context of the period in which he played, but his only success was in seeing Yorkshire share the 1949 championship with Middlesex. In his spell as England's captain, Yardley was unfortunate in coming up against the mighty Australian tourists of 1948 and the West Indian spin-twins, Ramadhin and Valentine, in 1950. The two most significant Yorkshire captains from the amateur ranks in the past hundred years have got to be Lord Hawke and Brian Sellers. Their common bond was an attitude which was quite feudal, and yet each manifested his feudalism in an entirely different way. Hawke was Victorian, Sellers a man of the twentieth century. Hawke's way was one of paternalism; Sellers could curse and converse in exactly the same language as his battle-hardened mercenaries but deep into the 1960s (when he was chairman and the game had been dramatically democratised) he saw nothing anachronistic in addressing senior players curtly by their surnames in the manner of a squire to his humbler tenants. In some ways Hawke was ahead of his time; Sellers grew out of his and didn't realise it.

Martin Bladen Hawke was a member of a Cornish family whose most distinguished ancestor was that Admiral Hawke who, on a dusky November evening in 1759, stormed under full sail past dangerous shoals to chase the French fleet into Quiberon Bay, taking six ships.

> Twas long past noon on a wild November day
> When Hawke came swooping from the west;
> He heard the breakers thundering in Quiberon Bay
> But he flew the flag for battle, line abreast.

Admiral Hawke was no pampered popinjay whose family bought a commission for him. He joined the navy as a twelve-year-old volunteer (!), rose to become an able seaman and after ten years reached the rank of third lieutenant. He married a Yorkshire heiress, Catherine Brooke, and 101 years after Quiberon Bay the descendant who was to captain Yorkshire CCC was born near Gainsborough, in Lincolnshire!

His father, the Rev. Edward Henry Julius Hawke, was a noted angler and a fine pistol shot from the back of a pony (*his* father, Martin Hawke, could hit a five-franc piece, tossed into the air, with one shot from his duelling pistol). The Rector of Willingham, however, was no cricketer. A broken leg which had been badly set ruled that out, but it did not prevent an intense love of the game which he passed on to his son, the second of ten children. When the parson inherited the barony he moved his family to Wighill Park, near Tadcaster, which is just about as close to the geographical centre of Yorkshire as one could find, and it was from there that young Martin went off to Eton where he shot his first rabbit and became a noted athlete of a pretty versatile nature (he won the mile, 440 yards and hurdles, and was second in the sprint and the steeplechase). In October 1881 he went up to Cambridge (Magdalene) and in his first cricket trial, against Lancashire at Old Trafford, was a member of the side bowled out for 31. His lasting memory of the game was not that modest total but of seeing his captain, G. B. Studd, *miss three catches off consecutive balls at cover point*. Verily the game was to change, if not in his life time.

Hawke had played for the Yorkshire Gentlemen during his holidays from Eton; now, at the end of his first year at Cambridge, he had his first game for the county against MCC at Scarborough.

His mentors were the Rev. E. S. Carter, a canon of York Minster, and M. J. Ellison, the county club's first treasurer and second president, who was, to young Hawke, 'the founder of modern Yorkshire county cricket'. He was no ascetic: indeed, at twenty-one he had been made a member of the Carlton Club by his father, where he could get 'a good chop for ninepence and a bottle of Perrier Jouet, '74, for seven shillings'. Hawke nevertheless developed a Spartan approach to life when he was involved in a game of cricket – as Bobby Peel was to find to his cost. He enjoyed a pipe of tobacco, but never when playing, and was aghast at what he saw as a complete dependence upon it by J. T. Brown, the opening partner of Long John Tunnicliffe: 'nothing could keep him from tobacco when he was off the field'. Hawke was convinced that Brown died of 'a smoker's heart' and insisted that, 'There is too much smoking amongst those who play in first-class cricket. It is not good for the eye and does not strengthen the nerves. I never smoke until cricket is done and never drink anything but water while playing in a match.'

Tom Emmett, a grizzled veteran of forty-one, was captain of Yorkshire when Hawke became regularly available for the side, and, knowing well enough who put the jam on his bread, promptly volunteered to give up the captaincy to the young honourable. Tom had been skipper for the previous four years, appointed by a Committee on terms graciously recorded in the minutes 'in the absence of a gentleman'. Hawke declined, for the time being, telling Emmett: 'Let me play under you for a season and pick up a few wrinkles.' By the following year (1883) he decided he had picked up enough wrinkles and accepted the captaincy. He was twenty-two years old, and the very first 'wrinkle' he had picked up was the realisation that a mid-Victorian professional found it difficult to establish and maintain any real authority in a dressing-room of paid players. The pro, Hawke reasoned, could be nagged at by his fellows and was always liable to be a butt for grumblers. It was a far-sighted view, especially when one looks at the England dressing-room in the first half of the 1980s! He saw, too, the weaknesses of the talent-money system which gave the pro a sovereign for fifty runs or six wickets. A professional captain, or one of his pals, was often allowed to go on bowling in the hope of a sixth wicket when he was plainly not shaping too well. Again, can we not see this in the present era when the prize is a world record rather than a sovereign?

Hawke introduced a system which was quite simply a form of benevolent dictatorship. He privately awarded marks to players who performed well, but not on a straightforward basis of scoring fifty or taking six wickets. A batsman got more marks for making his runs on a 'sticky' than on a plumb pitch; a bowler was rewarded correspondingly (or, rather, in reverse). Marks went to smart fielders who caught catches, saved runs or ran out batsmen. The financial basis was five shillings per mark, and when, at the end of the season, Hawke entertained all the players at Wighill Park the rewards were doled out in unmarked envelopes. The highest amount he ever paid out to an individual player was £52 10s. to George Hirst. Hawke insisted (and few people would argue with him) that only an amateur, remote and with a personal financial self-sufficiency, could enforce such a system. It was Hawke who instituted the award of county caps to players who made the grade, although he did admit to pinching the idea from Lancashire.

Hawke (the Hon. M. B. Hawke in his first four years of captaincy; he succeeded to the title in 1887) may perhaps be seen as a sort of nineteenth-century *condottiere*, marshalling and organising his forces into the most efficient unit possible. There is no doubt that he was fond of his men, watching over them with fatherly affection, but, like Victorian children, they most certainly had to do as they were told. My Lord was The Boss, and everyone knew it. It took Hawke ten years of captaincy to win his first championship title, but Yorkshire then went on to repeat the success in 1896, 1898, 1900, 1901, 1902, 1905 and 1908. In 1900 and 1908 they did not lose a single match of the twenty-eight played. In 1904, 1906 and 1907 they were runners-up and in 1903 and 1909 they came third – but those, in Yorkshire terms, were years of failure.

His lordship, as we have seen, was not a Yorkshireman by birth – the most notable of a couple of dozen who slipped through the screening process over 150 years – and even though the family home was in the broad acres, even though he undeniably did an enormous amount for Yorkshire cricket, it is difficult to believe that he really thought like a Yorkshireman. There have been a few, no doubt, who have enjoyed a good dinner at the Carlton Club, but for the most part we tend to regard the best parts of London as being St

Pancras and King's Cross stations – the first step on the way home. There cannot have been many who would echo Hawke's view on one point: 'To no one will I yield in my supreme affection for Lord's and MCC. To me, Lord's is the Mecca of cricket, the sanctuary of the greatest game in the world. MCC is the one club to which all lovers of the game look with respect and, as a rule, veneration.'

Personally, I detest the place. If the Yorkshireman who established the game's headquarters could have foreseen how time would stand still there, if he could have known that MCC's thinking and attitude would be no more advanced in 1987 than it was in 1787, I like to think he would have built his ground at Headingley.

Brian Sellers came from no aristocratic stock; the family background was in trade but it was sufficiently successful trade to allow him to play as an amateur. He joined a side, however, of cricketing aristocrats who had just won the County Championship outright for the seventeenth time and were to win it again in 1932 as he was being 'blooded'. The senior member of the side was no Tom Emmett anxious, as a matter of simple expediency, to ingratiate himself with the new leader but Herbert Sutcliffe, a figure far more patrician than the new captain himself. A man of lesser mettle than Sellers might have found the going too tough but The Crackerjack (as he came to be known) followed a good Yorkshire principle of starting as he meant to carry on. Forty years afterwards, in one of those long conversations with Herbert Sutcliffe which became so precious to me, he told me of his first encounter with Sellers as captain. It was at Lord's, a golden Saturday with the ground packed. Sellers took himself to the amateur dressing-room and in due course emerged through the amateur's gate to take the field. The professionals looked to Sutcliffe.

> He had made no contact with us before taking the field, so I considered the position for a moment and then decided to let him know that we did not feel his attitude to be the right one. I said to the others, 'Let's wait for a minute or two.' Sellers slowly walked to the middle until he stood there, with the great crowd filling the ground, quite alone. A few minutes went by and then I said, 'Right. I think he might have understood the point,' and we joined the captain. It must have been quite an unpleasant experience for him standing

out there on his own for what would seem a very long time,
I'm sure. Nothing was said. He never referred to the incident
and, to give him credit, he never did it again.

So Sellers's first attempt to assert himself as Yorkshire's captain
had failed. It could have led to open warfare between him and the
senior professional and there were, in fact, occasional slight brushes
between the two of them in the future. But above anything else both
of them realised that they were involved in something bigger than
themselves as individuals. No man was more important than Yorkshire cricket. They were never to be the closest of friends or team-
mates; each would irritate the other in the future, even when their
playing days were long since ended and they were Committee men
together. They were quite different personalities, but above all they
were Yorkshire cricketers and their mission in life was to work for
the greater glory of Yorkshire cricket. Sellers would ask for Sutcliffe's advice and not always take it, which annoyed Sutcliffe.
Sellers believed it right to draw upon the other's greater experience,
but felt there were occasions when he had to back his own
judgement.

The Crackerjack had come up through Bradford League cricket
as Sutcliffe had, but was not in the same street as a batsman –
scarcely in the same hemisphere, in fact. But he *could* bat and he
was a fighter; he was also a brilliant and fearless close-in fieldsman.
He was an expert on the Laws of the game and in due course made
himself into one of its best tacticians. By 1938, Bill Bowes reckoned,
he was 'unquestionably' the best captain in the world. Always he
was assailed by fears that his batting was not good enough to justify
his place in the side, but instead of dwelling on those fears he
worked hard to build on the positive aspects of his cricket, in
particular his fielding and his tactical leadership. In some respects
he *was* like Hawke. He liked to play the role of the martinet, for
instance, but he could take as well as dish out the sarcasm. In a
game against Gloucs, Sellers was chasing his fieldsmen about
between the overs in an effort to take the last wicket, and Bowes
annoyed him by striding merely with measured tread to his position.
'Get a move on,' he roared. Bowes, needled by his tone, riposted,
'I'm marching to the strains of Colonel Bogey. Do you know it?' It
was Bowes himself who took the last wicket and Sellers grinned at

him, 'Two good performances – that wicket and the Colonel Bogey remark.'

One cannot imagine a professional ever dreaming of metaphorically saying 'Bollocks' to Lord Hawke, even with Bowes's subtlety, and indeed there was no subtlety at all in a personal exchange I recall with Sellers. In my days as Northern cricket correspondent of the *Daily Mail* I had written something which displeased the then Cricket Chairman of the club and he then referred to me steadfastly as 'that shit who writes about Yorkshire cricket'. He went into hospital for an operation to a hip to relieve the arthritis which troubled him in his later years and returned to the fray, as it were, during a rain-affected match at Harrogate. He spotted me walking through the drizzle towards the pavilion, waved one of the sticks on which he was hobbling, and roared over the heads of startled (and very wet) spectators, 'I suppose you'll be sorry to see me around again.' 'No,' I replied, 'As one of them-there to another, welcome back.' He took this in, considered it, then bellowed a great laugh. We never had a cross exchange of words after that.

Whether he believed in his own ability or not, Brian Sellers averaged 23 in scoring just under 9,000 runs for Yorkshire, with four centuries and 204 against Cambridge University in 1934. But it was as a captain *per se* that he will be remembered. The strain of *making* something happen when nothing apparently was *going* to happen can be seen running through modern Yorkshire captaincy and emerging particularly in Brian Close. Sellers and Close were so much alike it seems incredible that Sellers was the man who got rid of Close in 1970 and in doing so plunged Yorkshire into its darkest period in more than a hundred years. But perhaps it was *because* they were so much alike that it happened. Sellers was no less autocratic in his chairmanship than in his captaincy. He raised captaincy, the tactical dictation of a game, to the point where it became an art in itself rather than a means to an end, and that was something we saw in an England captain during the regime of Mike Brearley – if not a Yorkshireman, at least the son of one. Under Sellers Yorkshire won the County Championship six years out of nine, and that's a good enough epitaph for anyone.

4
Preacher, Clown and Toper

Lord Hawke, like most amateur captains of his day, liked to have a good, solid, experienced shoulder to lean on at times, and that is how the position of 'senior professional' developed. His lordship's first aide was George Ulyett, and his second was an entirely different character from Happy Jack. Long John Tunnicliffe might be said to have established the tradition of Pudsey-born players within the county side which was to be followed by Sutcliffe, Hutton, Harry Halliday and Ray Illingworth, while Philip Sharpe lived within the borough for a time.

Tunnicliffe was the Sutcliffe of his day within the Yorkshire side. When Lord Hawke invited all the players to his home at the end of a season, Long John was the spokesman for the team. In a gathering of men who knew very well how to handle a pint, he was a prominent Wesleyan Methodist, a lay preacher, and it is clear that he enjoyed enormous respect amongst his fellows, just as Sutcliffe was to do later. Tunnicliffe was a big man in every way and there is one slight contradiction in his character – for a sober and responsible individual, he batted in a relatively carefree way and was, in fact, renowned as a big-hitter. His partnership with the Driffield man, J. T. Brown (that inveterate smoker), produced the record first-wicket score of 554 (against Derbyshire in 1898) which stood for thirty-four years, and they had another opening stand of 378 against Sussex in 1897. Brown died in his mid-thirties but Tunnicliffe lived to the age of eighty-one, leaving behind a legacy of more than 20,000 runs (twenty-two centuries), though he never played for England. The real mark he left on the game, however, was his 678 catches for Yorkshire, mostly at slip, which at least in statistical terms must stamp him as the greatest fieldsman of all time. In 1891–2 he went behind the stumps in six games and claimed sixteen victims – nine stumped and seven caught! Tunnicliffe's share of the partnership of 554 with Brown was 243 (J. T. scoring 300) and the circumstances were quite remarkable. On his way to Chesterfield the previous day he had been directed to what was described as 'a dirty inn' where he suspected that the bed was damp. Rather than risk sleeping in it, he sat on the edge of it all night and left in the morning before breakfast to catch the train which would get him to the game on time. No lunch was provided for the professionals in those days – they had to fend for themselves and all he could manage to get was a twopenny sandwich. It must have been the highest score ever made on a thoroughly empty stomach. I once mentioned this to one of Yorkshire's more renowned trenchermen, Geoff Cope, and he went white at the thought!

A Yorkshire team without a slow left-arm bowler would seem like an army without a general, a jockey without a horse, fish without chips. The line runs from Peate in 1879, through Peel, Rhodes, Kilner, Verity, Wardle, Wilson to the man appointed captain (amidst another domestic upheaval) in 1987, Phil Carrick. It is the most marvellous of cricket's dynasties, ranging through a series of fascinatingly different characters. Contrast, for instance, the bubbling Bobby Peel with the austere Hedley Verity; the grim concentration of Wilfred Rhodes with the bounding (and boundless) expectancy of Don Wilson. All, in their day, have produced great bowling, some of it greater than that produced by others; some of it by the exercise of special, painstakingly perfected skills, others with the help of cunning captaincy and the brilliance of close catchers. All have their place in Yorkshire's story, as do peripheral characters like Horace Fisher and Arthur Booth.

And it all began so improbably with a circus clown. Edmund Peate was born in Holbeck, one of the unloveliest of south Leeds districts, reared six or seven miles away at Yeadon and developed his natural cricketing talent in his spare time between shifts as a warp-twister in a local mill. When he felt his sporting career was not developing quickly enough he committed the sort of sin of which no Yorkshire cricketer since that time has been guilty (perhaps through lack of opportunity?): he joined a group of strolling players – eight acrobats, eight clowns and eight cricketers –

who somehow contrived to combine their various skills as an open-
air entertainment. It's just a bit difficult to picture, isn't it? Anyway,
the bizarre troupe known as Treloar's Clown Cricketers appear to
have been reasonably successful in the effete South but were then
ill-advised enough to put on a show in Sheffield. They were pelted
from the arena by a crowd throwing turf sods and Peate decided
that cricket had to be taken a little more seriously than that. He
took up professional cricket with Manningham (Bradford), was
recommended for a Yorkshire Colts trial and took ten wickets for
11 runs, followed by seven for 23 which brought him the compli-
ments of a Committeeman for 'giving the others a chance by not
trying in the second innings'.

Like so many others he started out by bowling as fast as he could
but after spending a winter in a shed practising a greater refinement
he emerged from six months of experiment as a spinner, announc-
ing: 'There is a length where no batsman can play and I have studied
to find it.' Either batsmen of the 1870s were less mobile than those
of twenty years later or Peate in his philosophy of bowling was
totally at variance with Hirst and Rhodes and those who followed.
At all events, it worked for Peate, so who is to quarrel with his
approach? Anyone who did would quickly be shot down by his
figures. Peate went to Australia on the 1881-2 tour and in his first
Test bowled 59 overs for 64 runs and one wicket; in his second he
bowled 52 overs for 53 runs and one wicket. He came home and
took 165 wickets for Yorkshire and then, at The Oval on 28 and 29
August, he bowled for England in what was to become the most
significant Test of all time. Peate took four for 33 in the first innings,
four for 40 in the second and was last man in when England,
needing just 85 to win, found themselves at 75 for nine. Charles
Studd, who was regarded as one of England's outstanding batsmen
of his day, had batted at no. 6 in the first innings and had gone in at
no. 10 in the second for the specific reason of coping with the sort
of crisis that had now developed. Amidst all the bally-hoo which
surrounded that game – and there was so much of it – I treasure as
much as anything I have ever encountered in my life a contemporary
report of what followed: 'The Yorkshireman made a hit for two,
foolishly tried to repeat it next ball and was clean bowled. When
remonstrated with for his foolhardiness in attempting to hit out,
Peate had the cool audacity to reply, "I am very sorry, gentlemen,

but the fact is I couldn't trust Mr Studd.'" Oh the joy of the perfect Yorkshireness of that response! There were six amateurs and five professionals in that England side and I find it utterly delightful to picture the scene – the former Treloar's clown, with deadpan expression, surrounded by an outraged band of 'coloured caps': W. G. Grace, A. P. Lucas, A. G. Steel, the Hon. A. Lyttleton, A. N. Hornby, and C. T. Studd. And Hornby, the captain, played for Lancashire! How Ted Peate must have treasured that moment for the rest of his life. And how must Yorkshiremen treasure it for ever.

It was, of course, the occasion which gave us – or rather Australia – the Ashes. After that defeat the famous notice appeared in the *Sporting Times*: 'In affectionate remembrance of English cricket which died at The Oval on August 29th, 1882. Deeply lamented by a large circle of sorrowing friends and acquaintances. RIP. NB. The body will be cremated and the ashes taken to Australia.'

Having horrified his peers by what they regarded as an act of irresponsible folly, Peate stuck to his guns when he returned home, confiding that, 'Ah were all reight missen but ah couldn't trust Mr Studd at t'other end.' In some ways I like to think that he really believed his story. It would fit with Peate's contention that he had discovered the perfect, unplayable length – a sort of bowler's Holy Grail. But common sense demands a verdict that Edmund Peate lost his head in a moment of crisis, was compelled to dream up an explanation, however implausible, and was stuck with it. It is entirely possible to see Fred Trueman in a later age taking exactly the same course, no matter how vehemently my friend would deny it!

Peate was undoubtedly a remarkable bowler who brought a new dimension of thought and skill to the art of bowling. His eight wickets for 5 runs against Surrey in 1883 is one of the great analyses of all time. Deteriorating eyesight gave him only eight seasons at the top and he had only just passed his forty-fourth birthday when he died. In statistical terms his epitaph is 819 wickets for Yorkshire at 12.55, but posterity will probably take the view that, far more importantly, he founded the greatest dynasty in the game, he refined bowling techniques, and through sheer Yorkshire bloody-mindedness he created the Ashes. Few have made a greater impact upon the history of the game – in such a short space of time and in so many ways. It is true that there had been left-arm bowlers before him, notably Emmett and Hodgson, and though we have seen that Tom Emmett in particular was a splendid cricketer and great character, in all other ways it has to be felt that the line begins with Peate.

Although a great bowler in his own right – and a character who was destined to achieve his own place in cricketing history – Bobby Peel has to be seen in the first instance as Ted Peate's understudy. Peate was a bare eleven months older but was three years ahead of Peel in playing seniority. He went with England to Australia in 1881–2; Peel had to wait until 1884–5. Peate *started* his career amongst the clowns; Peel *ended* his as something of a clown himself, at least in the culminating incident which ended his first-class career. Lord Hawke, who summarily sacked Peel in 1897, undoubtedly had the highest regard for his bowling ability but the paternal benevolence with which his lordship liked to regard his flock must have been stretched at times, notably in 1889 when Peel pressed his captain to put Kent in to bat at Maidstone. They suffered such a fearful drubbing that Hawke declared he would never again do anything except bat if he won the toss – whatever the state of the wicket – and he stuck resolutely to that decision for the remainder of his career.

Bobby's problem was a fondness for the bottle, and ultimately it brought about his downfall. Whether it influenced his judgement in giving Hawke advice which proved disastrous, we shall never know, just as it is not easy to discover the *exact* details of his last game. Yorkshire (like most counties in prim Victorian days) have always been rather coy about the match against Middlesex at Sheffield in 1897 and the most diligent search through available reference books does not disclose anything like a fully detailed account. Four versions, however, give the broadest hints about what was amiss. They don't unfortunately give us the full facts (which must have been hilarious, at least to those of us looking back nearly a century) but the implications are clear enough: (1) George Hirst urged Peel to go to bed rather than out on to the field; (2) 'after a bit too much to drink he spoke "out of turn" to his lordship'; (3) a newspaper report: 'Peel was obviously unable to do himself justice'; and (4) he muttered and shouted at Lord Hawke. Fred Trueman – with a gleeful chuckle – has come up with the story that Bobby actually set off from the stumps to bowl at the sight-screen! It's the version which makes better reading than any other and I'd love to believe it was true. The one fact that has been fully established is that his lordship dismissed Peel from the field, followed him for a consultation with the Committee, and Peel's services were instantly dispensed with.

Newspapers, which handled their cricket coverage in 1897 with rather more dignity than they do today, were nevertheless compelled to seek quotes from all sources. Peel's admissions were restricted to the story: 'Before I went to the ground I had two small gins with water. Nothing at luncheon.' Most of the sketchy evidence suggests that Peel under-estimated the amount he had drunk or else he had miscalculated the effect of those two small gins upon the volume of his previous night's supping. Since Lord Hawke knew Peel and his habits very well indeed it seems pretty obvious that to be dismissed from the field he had to be substantially more worse for wear than he had been in the past. George Hirst urged Peel to write and apologise for his lapse, but with characteristic stubbornness he refused. He was convinced that Yorkshire could not do without him and that the Committee would, in due course, have to say to him, 'Come back, Bobby Peel. All is forgiven.' He lived until he was eighty-four and Yorkshire never did. Like Johnny Wardle was to do sixty years later (when *he* was summarily dismissed, but certainly not for drunkenness), Peel turned to the Lancashire League for cricketing comfort and a great bowler was lost to the first-class game.

Bobby Peel came from Churwell, just south of Leeds, and two of the senior players – Tom Emmett and Ephraim Lockwood – immediately saw his potential when he joined the Yorkshire side in 1882. Accomplished left-arm bowler he might be, but there was more to Peel than that. 'We're going to make thee into a batsman,' he was told by Emmett and Lockwood. In the year before he was fired, Peel scored 210 in Yorkshire's huge 887 all out at Edgbaston – an exercise in overkill by Lord Hawke which resulted in a drawn match but which gave Yorkshire the county's highest score in 125 years of championship cricket. After Peate's enforced retirement Peel celebrated his installation as *the* Yorkshire slow left-armer by annihilating Notts at Sheffield with eight for 12 in the first innings, six for 21 in the second. Only 165 runs were scored in the whole game by both sides, but Yorkshire won by ten wickets. Peel's dismissal can only be seen as a tragedy and yet, in its context, it had to be done. That most fair-minded of men, George Hirst, felt it was necessary in the interests of team discipline and, taking the broad view, that seems right.

The pages of cricket history may be sprinkled with individual examples of men who have played memorable innings after a rattling good night out, but we have seen that Martin Bladen Hawke, who by no means shunned the good life, set himself high standards of self-denial while actually involved in the playing of a game and it was abundantly clear to his men that he demanded nothing less from them. Batting with a hangover may possibly escape attention if the results work out well, but bowling and fielding while currently and ostentatiously the worse for wear could never go undetected, and thus unpunished.

Ironically, Peel's departure saw Yorkshire win the championship in 1898, falter only in the final weeks of the 1899 season, then take the title in 1900, 1901 and 1902, but this was the age of Wilfred Rhodes. There were, of course, all kinds of contributory factors but it is impossible to resist a comparison, even if on the most superficial terms, with the decision to part company with Johnny Wardle after the 1958 season. Yorkshire won the championship in 1959 and 1960, were second in 1961 and won it again in 1962 and 1963. Wardle, like Peel, was the greatest bowler of his type and, like Peel, departed at the height of his powers.

5

The Triumvirate

It is difficult to imagine any cricketer of any county in any era being viewed with the same respect and affection as George Herbert Hirst, of Kirkheaton, Huddersfield. He played for Yorkshire for thirty years (1891 to 1921) and although he lived until he was eighty-two it is one of the great regrets of my life that I never met him. Never have I heard from those who did even a single syllable of criticism or complaint; indeed, never have I heard anyone speak of Hirst in anything but terms of near-reverence. He really must have been one of the *nicest* men ever to play cricket. Fred Trueman, who does not bestow character references lightly, has never spoken in anything but terms of the warmest sentiment of the 'wonderful old man' who gently and kindly encouraged him as a young tearaway fast bowler. Bill Bowes, Herbert Sutcliffe, Len Hutton, Brian Sellers have all in their time talked with something approaching awe of the generosity of the man who spent as many years going round the clubs of Yorkshire looking for young talent as he had done playing for the county. He never 'knocked'; he always encouraged. He was modest about his own achievements as a player – which were phenomenal. His approach to coaching was to build on natural ability, never seeking to dismantle a player and restore him as a new, mould-produced cricketer. (He had received little or no coaching himself and firmly believed that constant practice was the best way to improve individual ability.) He was primarily a left-arm in-swing bowler of medium pace who varied his attack with the slower ball, spun to turn away from the batsman. As he was also adept at pitching on a yorker length it all added up to a formidable armoury for a bowler in an age when batting technique was less sophisticated than it became a couple of generations later, especially as Hirst also contrived to get considerable 'nip' off most pitches. He liked to bowl into a wind which blew to him from the area of third man, arguing that movement in the air was more important to him than sheer pace through it.

In an age when it was regarded as a virtue in many circles to be able to pitch a ball at will on a handkerchief or a folded newspaper as evidence of perfect control of length, Hirst (like Rhodes in the following generation of bowlers) argued that there was no such thing as a 'perfect length' unless this was related to the batting technique of individual players. Hirst *thought* the game with as much shrewd-ness and concentration as Rhodes, but played his cricket with less intensity. He loved to tell against himself the story of a game against Derbyshire in which he got no wickets and no runs 'apart from a snick or two' before being bowled by a delivery which broke a stump in two. As he returned to the pavilion he mused quietly that all he needed now was to drop a catch and, sure enough, he put down 'a nice easy one'. From one of the opposition then came the suggestion that to have had a really good match he now needed to miss the last train home and have his pocket picked on the way. Rhodes would never have told a story like that against himself; nor would Macaulay, or Wardle, or Close or Illingworth. It would not have been considered a fit subject for humour.

Hirst's career record was 36,323 first-class runs at an average of 34.13 and 2,739 wickets at 18.72. He ranks fourth in the list of players who have scored 20,000 runs or more and taken more than 2,000 wickets, but he did the seasonal double (1,000 runs, 100 wickets) on fourteen occasions, far more than any of the three names above him in that list (W. E. Astill, T. E. Bailey and W. G. Grace), and only Wilfred Rhodes achieved it more times. He is the only man to have taken more than 200 wickets in a season (208) while scoring more than 2,000 runs (2,385), and when one considers what this all-round career cost him in terms of physical effort, those years of patrolling the league grounds – talent-spotting and coaching – become all the more remarkable. He was pained by a left knee injury for twenty years of his playing life and he played for more than half his career with a damaged rib-muscle. Looking back on that 'double double' season of 1906 he was to recall: 'The physical strain was too much for one man in one season. By the time August

came round I was terrified I would not get through a day's play. My
legs were like iron, with the muscles seized up, and I was thankful
when each day's play finished.' And then we see the real Hirst: 'It
might seem fine to have a record like that but in the physical sense
it just wasn't worth it. *But it was my duty.*' Can anyone conceive a
player of the 1980s with an attitude like that?

Huddersfield's contribution to Yorkshire CCC in the nineteenth
century was immense. They sent three men to what we might call
Yorkshire's first official county match against Surrey at The Oval in
1863, and through the 1870s and 1880s the England side was rarely
without at least one man from the town or its surrounding villages.
Yet from all the county cricketers Huddersfield produced – nearly
fifty by the turn of the century – three names have always been
grouped together: Rhodes, Hirst and Schofield Haigh.

To this day they are referred to in hushed tones as The Triumvirate. Their careers overlapped (Hirst, 1891–1921; Haigh, 1895–1913;
and Rhodes, 1898–1930) and they all wrote their own names in
Yorkshire cricket history. Hirst and Haigh were particularly
chummy. They played practical jokes on each other in a way which
must have seemed like a form of blasphemy to the third member of
the trio, immersed as he always was in the very serious business of
playing cricket. At Northallerton, Haigh told the gateman that Hirst
was a hanger-on who had been following him about and making a
nuisance of himself. 'Don't let him into the ground,' was his
instruction. 'He'll try to tell you he's a player but take no notice.'
Hirst had to enlist the aid of officialdom before he could get in to
play for Yorkshire. He got his own back at Chesterfield later in the
season by spinning a similar yarn to the burliest waiter he could find
in the luncheon tent. Haigh, who was injured and therefore not in
whites, was turfed out by the scruff of his neck. Towards the end of
their careers they arrived for a game in Bath and were asked if they
were the umpires. 'Yes,' they chorused and marched with due
dignity into the ground. Today, of course, when every player has
been seen on television regularly, even the most unobservant
gateman would scarcely make a mistake of that kind, but in the
reign of King Edward VII it was perhaps forgivable. All the same, I
like to think it was the game in which Hirst scored 111 and 117 not
out against Somerset, and to conjure up a picture of the gateman's
face as the runs were scored.

Haigh was a splendid fast bowler who, like so many of his contemporaries, developed his batting as his career progressed. He took 1,916 wickets for the county at an average of 15.42 and had four centuries in his 11,099 runs. He played eleven times for England and topped the first-class bowling averages in 1902, 1905, 1908 and 1909. Huddersfield is understandably very proud indeed of The Triumvirate.

Whenever the conversation in the 'Test Match Special' commentary box turns to all-rounders – and it frequently does in this age of Botham, Hadlee, Kapil Dev and Imran Khan – my eyes usually meet those of Freddie Trueman and we exchange a quiet, knowing smile. Invariably it happens when Trevor Bailey is talking; invariably he intercepts the glance and stops: 'I know . . . there are two people here thinking about Wilfred Rhodes – and undoubtedly he was a very great all-round cricketer – but . . .'

But? There is no 'but' about it. Never has there been a bowler-batsman (or batsman-bowler) who has ever got near the record of the grand old man from Kirkheaton, Huddersfield, whose figures will almost certainly never be equalled. He played top-class cricket for thirty-two years, and who is ever going to do that in the late twentieth century? – except, perhaps, Brian Close, and his chance of touching Rhodes's records has gone, even though he has already played first-class cricket for longer.

He scored 39,802 runs in his first-class career and took 4,188 wickets. He hit 1,000 runs in a season twenty-one times and took 100 wickets twenty-three times. He batted no. 11 for England and he opened for his country. In 1911–12 he and Hobbs put on 323 for the first wicket in Melbourne, and in 1903 he and R. E. Foster put on 130 for the tenth wicket in Sydney; both are still records in England–Australia Tests. He did the double sixteen times, twice more than George Hirst. He also did the same double (1,000 runs and 100 wickets) in Tests v. Australia. In 1900 he took 261 wickets in a season, the highest number by a Yorkshireman. He was anything but a colourful character yet he inspired some of the finest prose in the literature of cricket. Jim Kilburn, of the *Yorkshire Post*: 'Every over by Rhodes was a creation of beauty. There was no crudity, no self-consciousness, no striving after effect. Rhodes bowled always with the maturity of the practised husbandman scything corn, all economy of effort and patience and unbroken rhythm. He might have bowled unsuccessfully, but he never bowled badly.' During the 1926 Roses match at Old Trafford, Neville Cardus wrote this of Rhodes in the course of a match report for the *Manchester Guardian*:

> There was another sight well worth our while at Old Trafford – Rhodes bowling his beautifully-curved flight. The man's action is just as always it has been these many years, easy and masterful. History hangs all about him – the legendary Rhodes. Men who are playing with him in this match were not born when he first came to us, the greatest of our slow bowlers – and only a youth with an innocent, unrazored face.
>
> He was England's last man in, then, and he won a match for his country, with Hirst, by one wicket. Whereupon he sighed for new worlds to conquer; with every batsman, even Victor Trumper, in his thrall he turned from bowling and took up batsmanship. He went in first with Hobbs and over the seas, on the scorched earth of Australia, he was the helpmate of Hobbs in the greatest first-wicket stand ever accomplished for England. Rhodes and Hobbs in partnership on the world's other side, cutting and driving the day long and letting the crowd see, time after time, 'the run-stealers flicker to and fro'. And there is this same Rhodes with us yet, top of the English bowling averages. His performance in this game on a flawless wicket, in torrid heat, out of a total of 509 for nine – seven wickets for 116 in 42 overs – why, the man has surely taken hold of Time and thrust him, scythe and all, behind him. This Rhodes who saw Grace and Shrewsbury plain is without end. His face is dyed with the strain of a thousand days in the sun; he is the image of the 'Old Soldier' as he waits to bowl, tossing the ball from hand to hand, fingering it with the intimacy of one of whom the touch of round leather is nature's own touch. If he does not play for England at the Oval next week then our Selection Committee is lacking the sense that knows greatness.

Isn't that absolutely marvellous? Selectors, since time immemorial, have been given advice from all quarters but surely never with such felicity of phraseology which imparts its own thundering impact? Frankly, it brings tears to my eyes to read Cardus in that mood – and he was rarely in any other. Can we ever hope to see writing of that quality again? But then can we ever hope to see cricket of the quality to merit it? Away with cynicism and back to our story. The Selectors took heed and brought back Rhodes for that Final Test at The Oval – at the age of forty-eight! He returned figures of 25-15-35-2 and 20-9-44-4 and scored 28 and 14. England won.

In 1965 Brian Close married his wife, Vivienne, in her local church at Ottery St Mary, Devon, and in making arrangements to travel down for the ceremony I remembered that Wilfred Rhodes, eighty-seven years old, now lived with his daughter and son-in-law at Canford Cliff, Bournemouth, which I reckoned was about an hour-and-a-half's drive away. It seemed too good an opportunity to miss because I had always been fascinated by the statistics of the Rhodes career, by the character of the man as it had been handed down to us. I had seen him at Scarborough Festivals, blind for many years, sitting *listening* to the game with vital intensity and following its course, it was said, by the sound made when bat made contact with ball. Marvellous stories were told of the detail which he demanded about the placing of a bowler's field to enable him to 'picture' the whole scene. My friend Freddie Trueman had a fund of stories about the old man on these occasions which he told in awe-struck tones. Frankly, and perhaps heretically, I found it difficult to credit some of them and I badly wanted to talk to Wilfred Rhodes myself for professional reasons. He spanned the whole golden age of cricket; he had bowled at Grace and he had bowled at Bradman. His record was phenomenal and I felt it was vital to have some of his memories of the game on tape; it would be a unique record of cricket as recalled by a man whose record was itself unique.

So I wrote to his daughter to ask if the great man would agree to my interviewing him on the Sunday morning after the Close nuptials and to my immense delight a reply came saying that I would be welcome if I called about 10.30 a.m. Wilfred at first categorically refused to discuss anything at all, insisting lugubriously that he 'were not talking to a box'. A dozen times I tried to get him talking but each time I switched on the recorder as he got into his stride he stopped, with the same terse reproach: he was not talking 'to a box'. It was all very much like those American Indians who refused to be pictured by early pioneer photographers lest their spirit be trapped in the camera! The Rhodes voice was not going to be captured in an old 'Emmy' tape-recorder. His daughter gently reproached the old man that Mr Mosey had come a long way to see him and he *had* agreed to talk to his visitor. He changed tack. He looked sightlessly across the room and said, 'Well, what does ta knaw abaht cricket then? Tell me.' It was roughly the equivalent of an aspiring young singer, auditioning before the greatest maestro, being asked to sing the whole Winterreise cycle, unaccompanied. But I tried. I talked about my childhood memories of Sutcliffe and Hutton, of the current Yorkshire team and how I thought it had achieved four championship titles and a runners-up position between 1959 and 1963, I talked about Close and Trueman and Illingworth and after ten gabbled minutes Wilfred Rhodes interrupted: 'Well, tha seems to know summat abaht it. What's tha want to talk to me abaht.' No greater compliment has ever been paid to a mere observer of the game.

Prompted gently from time to time, the greatest all-rounder of all time then talked for nearly an hour – about Grace and about Bradman, about Lord Hawke, about bowling with the most delicate subtleties of flight, about placing his field, about walking down from his hill-top home in Huddersfield to go to Headingley for the first time. It was the sheerest magic. I took the tape back to my office in Manchester, edited it and sent it to London to be placed in the BBC Archives, the most precious recording stored there as far as I was concerned. When Wilfred Rhodes died on 8 July 1973 he was ninety-five years old and BBC Archives could find no trace of the tape. A unique piece of cricket history was lost for ever.

He learned to bowl in a barn, a solitary figure working for hour after hour with an old ball on which he chalked stripes so he could observe how the ball performed through the air or with various grips employed on it. When the space in the barn was required by a farmer (who might have changed the course of cricket history) he moved his practice-wicket out into a meadow where a path ran across the field. Using just five or six yards of the path (he only needed a space to *pitch* the ball), he cut the grass with a scythe and partially levelled it with a stone roller he had borrowed and trundled up to his practice ground. There he perfected the art which Cardus was to admire and generations of batsmen were to respect. He never actually played on a cricket *ground* until he was fifteen years old. Above all, Rhodes was a master of flight, deceiving countless players of other counties and countries through the air. No one ever fully mastered him in a long and wonderful career. At seventeen he believed in himself sufficiently to apply for a professional post at Barnsley, where he was considered too young so took himself off to Scotland and played as a pro with Galasheils.

He described himself, even at seventeen, as an all-rounder, and would probably not have got the job had he claimed otherwise. He bowled as fast as he could, mixing in the occasional spinner, not yet confident enough to try out variations of flight except on occasions when he found himself dominating the opposition and fully in control of the situation. At nineteen he had a trial with Warwickshire, who then decided that for financial reasons they could not offer him a contract. One shudders at the thought that he might well have been lost to Yorkshire because he had decided that cricket was an infinitely better way of earning a living than on the land or in a mill. In 1897 came the summary dismissal of Peel, and Yorkshire were in need of a left-arm bowler. Mercifully, before he had found employment elsewhere, Wilfred Rhodes was called up by Yorkshire after showing what he could do in the Headingley nets in April 1898.

His first game was at Scarborough, as his last was to be thirty-two years later. He was fifty-two years old when he had Bradman dropped, first ball, by R. E. S. Wyatt, who was subsequently to be an England captain. Rhodes, who never had the highest regard for amateurs in any form, laconically recalled the incident some years later when asked about bowling at Bradman, 'I'd 'ave 'ad him but t'fielder were too slow.' He had started his life as an all-rounder and was keen to carry on as such, but Lord Hawke wanted his specialist talent as a left-arm bowler, now more slow than fast. He instructed the young man from Kirkheaton, 'Now, Wilfred, you are not to get more than twenty runs,' surely one of the strangest orders ever given by a captain to one of his players. His lordship feared that over-indulgence with the bat would diminish skill with the ball but Rhodes, in a low key, rebelled, once going so far as to tell his lordship, 'Ah, 'ope some day Ah'll be picked for England for me batting.' He was, he was.

He studied every aspect of the game in minute detail. Apart from his technical skill – and, in relative terms, there can have been none greater – he was a brilliant analyst of conditions. He always seemed to know exactly the right moment for him to bowl and he was meticulous to the most minute degree in the placing of his fieldsmen. He was in many ways a bit of a loner but he never withheld advice from young bowlers when he felt he could help them for the good of the team. That was one of his cardinal virtues: despite his enormous individual ability he was a team-man in the context of winning for Yorkshire. That was what mattered more than anything else.

Notwithstanding Rhodes's tremendous achievements, he was not a man around whom legends were easily built. The grimness and intensity of his devotion to cricketing duty formed his trade mark; epigrams in the Tom Emmett and George Ulyett idiom were utterly foreign to Wilfred. Those who knew him well, or even fleetingly, find it difficult to find many laughs in his life story. Indeed, there were not even many smiles. Cricket was a very serious business indeed to Wilfred Rhodes. So it was to Emmott Robinson, but there is something in the very nature of Robinson's seriousness which invariably brings a smile to most faces. It was not so with Rhodes. Folklore tried to build up one romantic legend around him – and failed. At The Oval in 1902 Rhodes went in last to join George Hirst with 15 runs still needed to win the final Test of the series and together they brought off the first-ever one-wicket victory by England over Australia. For years I had treasured the story of Hirst telling young Rhodes not to worry: 'We'll get 'em in singles.' It was a lovely story because that is what the two great all-rounders proceeded to do. But at my 1965 meeting with Rhodes – naturally enough I wanted to know about that conversation and the partnership which followed – he summarily dismissed it: 'It were nivver said. Nowt like that. I don't remember owt being said at all. We just got on wi' it.'

Almost any other great player of almost any generation would have loved to be associated with a romantic little legend like that. Most would have fostered and probably embellished it. Not Wilfred Rhodes. He was essentially a practical man.

6

Archetypal Yorkies

If I were ever invited to nominate one man as the archetypal Yorkshire cricketer, covering all the ages of the county's history, it would have to be Emmott Robinson. Now this might require some explanation, given the rich cavalcade of personalities in something like 150 years, and it is difficult to find a completely satisfactory one. On the whole it is simply a *feeling* that Emmott's character was made up of more of our native characteristics than any other player's. He ate, drank, lived and breathed Yorkshire cricket and at night he can have dreamed of little else. Like everyone else, he hated to lose and he would never have settled easily in his bed if he thought that one single thing had been left undone during the day in the quest for victory.

He firmly believed that a cricketer should learn something new about the game and about all opposition, every day of his life. He urged young players to keep a notebook and jot down each item of newly acquired knowledge before retiring for the night. Beside some of the Corinthian figures of amateur cricket in the pre-war years he was an incongruous figure. Indeed, beside the immaculate Herbert Sutcliffe he looked like someone who had strayed in from a quite different sporting arena. He was small, slight and bandy-legged; he walked about the field with head down, not in despair – *never* in despair because he believed in his Yorkshire cricket more passion-ately than Napoleon loved his guards – but always deep in thought. He knew everything there was to know about every cricketer who played in his age. He knew about weather conditions, turf and umpires as well as about batsmen and bowlers. For a wedding present he gave young Bill Bowes a barometer: 'I've brought you a weather-glass, Bill. It's same make as mine an' tha wants to look at it night an' morning. It's nice to know when there's a sticky wicket in t'offing.' There was no jest in his words; cricket was not a matter for jest. His motto was, 'Never take a risk if tha can win wi'out one', and if Raymond Illingworth in a later generation had adopted a motto it would undoubtedly have been that. They were so much alike, those two. Rarely if ever did either of them smile during a game. Robinson was 'always nattering' according to his team-mates; Illingworth would certainly have been always nattering to himself, watching every move in a game like a hawk, approving of some, greeting others with a metaphorical shake of the head.

Emmott Robinson came from Keighley, my own home town, and for more than fifty years the story has been handed down at Lawkholme Lane of the time when he was nearing his half-century in a Bradford League game which was going to be won comfortably. Just before the winning score was reached, and just before Emmott reached 50, the crowd began to stream away, happy in the double knowledge that (a) the home team had victory in the bag and (b) they could save themselves a copper or two in collection money. Emmott halted the game and almost ran to the boundary fence nearest the exit, flinging his arms wide in supplication: 'Nay, not yet, not yet. Gi' me a chance to get me fifty.' Alas, the crowd heeded him not. We are nothing if not practical people in Keighley.

He was thirty-five years old when he first played county cricket, so he brought to it much of the fierce competitiveness of the great Bradford League in twelve years at the top. He was the sort of character Cardus loved, and he wrote of the wiry little man that he carried the new ball from one bowler to the next in hands 'cupped together like a chalice'. Once again the greatest cricket writer had found the *mot juste*: Robinson regarded the new ball as the most precious object in a game of cricket and the sight of its being accidentally spilled while the shine was still there was enough to make him swoon. Indeed, twenty years after his retirement I sat with him at a game where the 'cherry' was bowled back to the stumps by a long-leg fieldsman, bouncing twice on the way. Each time it hit the ground the little man shuddered convulsively; it was as though a knife had been thrust between his ribs.

Although he came so late to the first-class game he scored nearly 10,000 runs and took 892 wickets; even so, there are those who

remember him more for his fielding in all the kamikaze positions –
short leg, silly-mid-off, silly-mid-on – in which he was the forerun-
ner of Brian Close. To a kindly disposed young gentleman in a
'Varsity match who was concerned at a possible injury to the
crouching figure only two yards away, he growled: 'Thee get on wi'
thi laikin'. I'll tak care o' missen.' Emmott certainly didn't play his
cricket for fun.

He became one of the great characters of his day as much for the
sheer intensity with which he played cricket as for anything else.
Paradoxically, when he went on to the first-class umpires' list his
attitude was very much more relaxed. Never was this better
exemplified than at Trent Bridge in 1938 when just about every
batsman in the First Test got a century: Bradman, McCabe, Brown,
Paynter, Compton, Hutton and Barnett. Stan McCabe's 232 is rated
as one of the greatest innings in Test history, of course, but Charlie
Barnett nearly turned the records upside down by reaching 98 at
lunch on the first day. When he completed the hundred off the first
ball of the afternoon old Emmott Robinson so far forgot the
traditional impartiality of the umpire as to shake Barnett warmly by
the hand! He took up umpiring again after the Second World War –
when he was sixty-four years old – and when he died one day after
his eight-sixth birthday the game had lost one of its most unforgettable figures. He never played for England but if it came to a choice
of the most perfectly cast Yorkshire cricketer ever to wear the white
rose badge, mine would be Emmott Robinson. In that unlikely,
slightly scruffy figure, were embodied so many of our most typical
and cherished characteristics: the thought, preparation and concentration of Rhodes, Verity, Sutcliffe; the intensity of Macaulay and
Trueman; the lovable, off-the-field personality of Hirst, Leyland,
Tony Nicholson; the fearlessness in the field of Mitchell, Sellers and
Close; the unswerving belief in the specialness of Yorkshire cricket.
And what could be closer to Yorkshire hearts than that burning
desire to look after our brass than that touching scene at Keighley
when he saw his collection melting away with the departing crowd?

We have seen that Bedale, as a small rural community, played a
significant part in early Yorkshire cricket history. It is time now to
look at the role of Wombwell, a small urban community which has
a quite unique connection with the county club: *three* members of

the same family in Yorkshire colours. In some ways this is a more sentimental than statistically dramatic connection because one of the three, Roy Kilner, was one of the best-loved men ever to play the game and his personality and character place him clearly in the George Ulyett/Maurice Leyland line of succession. But let's start at the beginning with the help of research carried out by three members of the Wombwell Cricket Lovers' Society, an organisation which despite modest origins has contrived to get itself known all over the cricketing world.

As the Industrial Revolution killed off the cottage industry of the home weavers around the Huddersfield area they were forced to search for employment elsewhere and one of them, Seth Kilner, went to Wombwell where the village was dominated by two coal-mines, Wombwell Main and Mitchell Main. He got a job at Mitchell Main and, on the strength of his cricket back home in Lascelles Hall, was quickly involved in the game in Wombwell. There he became friendly with a talented local batsman, Irving Washington, and married Irving's sister, Mary Alice. They brought up seven sons and four daughters and the family in one way and another were to exercise a remarkable influence upon cricket in that particular area for the next hundred years.

Irving Washington played for Yorkshire Colts when he was seventeen and made his début for the full county side in 1900. Like so many distinguished players were to do in the future, he started with a duck. It was not until 1902 that he got a regular first-team spot, a miserably wet summer when only players of high technical skill on sticky wickets could hope to score well. Washington, a left-hander, was one of these and was widely tipped to become one of the outstanding batsmen of his age. Tragically, a series of colds led to tuberculosis and he never played for Yorkshire again. His first-class cricket career ended before his twenty-third birthday, but he had made his mark. Contemporary writers singled out his innings against the 1902 Australians as that of 'the one batsman who could fathom the vicious off-spin of Hugh Trumble'. At a time when batting and spin-bowling were becoming more technically accomplished with each new season, Washington was recognised as one of the outstanding bad-wicket players of his day – and that is a title which has rarely left Yorkshire. Herbert Sutcliffe, Len Hutton and

Geoffrey Boycott in turn were to become recognised masters in this field.

Washington's two nephews, Roy and Norman Kilner, both became noted county cricketers – Roy for Yorkshire and England, Norman for Yorkshire and Warwickshire. Roy was the second son of Seth Kilner and Mary Alice Washington and, like his father and uncle, played his first cricket on the Mitchell Main colliery ground. When he was only fourteen he played alongside both of them and as a stroke-making left-hander he soon became noticed by Yorkshire. His first innings for the Colts passed without any effort required by the scorers, and his early games for the First XI were undistinguished. At Trent Bridge in 1912 he registered a duck in his first innings, but a brilliant 83 not out in the second was the major factor in Yorkshire's win. As he had taken four for 66 in the Notts first innings with his left-arm slows the county were looking at yet another all-rounder of outstanding promise. When all the county's front-line bowling was available, however, there was rarely any call for Roy's bowling and he had to establish himself as a front-line batsman in order to compete regular for a place in the senior side. He had managed to do this and could look forward to a long career as an established first-teamer – with the retirement of George Hirst, David Denton and Schofield Haigh – when the First World War broke out. Along with his friend Major Booth (Major was his Yorkshire team-mate's first name, not a rank, and that must have caused a few fun and games in the Army), Roy joined the West Yorkshire Regiment. In 1916, Booth was killed in the same action which saw Kilner wounded. He was subsequently wounded again and went right through the war before returning to play for Yorkshire in 1919. By now, Wilfred Rhodes had led the county bowling for nearly twenty years and, looking round for a successor, he thought Roy Kilner could be groomed for the role. So he spent a whole winter practising the art which had become a little rusty from disuse and reached his bowling peak in the 1922, 1923 and 1924 seasons.

He played twice against South Africa in 1924 and went on Arthur Gilligan's tour to Australia in '24–5, where he found himself playing primarily as a bowler while batting at no. 8 or 9 – an experience shared by the later all-rounder Ray Illingworth in *his* England days. For Yorkshire, Roy Kilner scored 13,014 runs at nearly 30 and took

858 wickets at 17.33 before he died, tragically young, from enteric fever contracted while coaching in India. He was just thirty-seven.

What singles out Roy Kilner in this portrait gallery of some of the county's finest players is his universal popularity with just about everyone in the game. It is a reputation which few of his countrymen have been able to achieve. Everyone who knew the man has either spoken or written about him in the most affectionate terms, and his generous and outgoing nature undoubtedly made him one of the best-loved cricketers ever to play the game. When Tony Wood-house, Roy Wilkinson and Jack Sokell were compiling their booklet *Cricketers of Wombwell*, they asked Arthur Gilligan for an appreciation of Roy. He wrote:

> I shall remember him as a great team-man; he never played for himself but always put his side first. He had the most charming personality, was never at a loss for a word and he succeeded in leaving a host of friends wherever he went in Australia. Roy was a dedicated Yorkshireman and one of the great cricketers which the White Rose county has produced ever since the game started. I shall always remember him as one of the greats but above all as a great gentleman and friend.

Not many Yorkshire tourists have earned a tribute as generous as that from an England captain, and a Sussex man at that! Was Roy, then, perhaps a little out of character in this company of tough, grim and often dour individuals? Certainly not if one bears in mind that it includes, also, men like Happy Jack Ulyett, George Hirst, Maurice Leyland. It is necessary only to look at the intensity he brought to his cricket – his batting and bowling partnerships with Rhodes, his epic stands with Sutcliffe and his bowling alliance in Australia with Woolley – to realise that. Kilner may have loved his game (and his fellow man) but he didn't just play it for fun.

His funeral service at Wombwell Parish Church brought a crowd to the mining village which has been estimated at not less than 100,000 and possibly as large as 150,000. They stood shoulder-to-shoulder in the streets. Two years later the touring Australians travelled from Bradford to lay a wreath on his grave. The local council have designated a 'Roy Kilner Road' in the village. The love and respect of one's fellows may perhaps be deemed a better epitaph than all the records in the book.

The fourth son of Seth Kilner and Mary Alice was Norman Kilner, and I had watched him play for four or five of my schoolboy years before I learned that he was a Yorkshireman. Perhaps I would not have hated him so much if I had known that earlier! My childhood memories of Yorkshire *v.* Warwickshire are marked by the alliterative partnership of Croom and Kilner always doing well, and thus they were marked down as enemies. I have never been quite sure how I would have felt about it if I had known that Norman was one of us. He was, of course, from 1919 to 1923 but I wasn't even born then.

Like his brother, he served in the First World War and, like Roy, he was wounded. Again like Roy, he had to fight hard to establish himself as a Yorkshire player but there the resemblance ends, because although he played sixty-nine times the games were spread over five seasons and he could never really regard himself as an established member of the side. Norman was a right-handed batsman with none of the natural elegance of his left-handed brother, and he never had any formal coaching. But by diligence and sheer persistence he developed his own technique, which involved hitting particularly hard on the on-side of the field, and in 1924 he moved to Warwickshire, perhaps one of the earliest examples of the modern brain-drain which was to see Yorkshire in the 1930s, and particularly after the war, furnish almost every other first-class county with one or more players. He started at Edgbaston as a middle-order batsman and his first experience of playing against his native county was a salutary one. Warwickshire were bowled out on a drying wicket for 162 and 65, with Rhodes taking nine for 59 in the match and brother Roy nine for 80. He was to get his own back on a number of occasions after that, as I recall. He was moved up the order to become a sound opener who could be very difficult indeed to shift. He reached 1,000 runs in a season twelve times, retiring to become a first-class umpire in 1938 and then to coach at Edgbaston.

Wombwell, through the Kilner–Washington family connection initially, has become an honourable name in first-class cricket. Its cricket society pursues an almost obsessive search for more and even better county players and has developed through its winter coaching classes a steady flow of players who, if not Wombwell born, owe a great deal to the society based in the heart of the South Yorkshire coalfield: Martyn Moxon, Arnie Sidebottom and Ian Swallow (Yorks), Graham Stevenson (Yorks and Northants), Tim Boon (Leics), Mark Beardshall (Derbys), Peter Hepworth (Leics) It's a quite remarkable record, but then Wombwell has a remarkable cricket society, of which we can see more in the later pages of this book.

Yorkshire's teams in the period between the world wars could probably have taken on any side ever seen in this country. In general terms, there were *two* major elevens in this period – that of the 1920s and that of the 1930s. A few names overlapped, like Percy Holmes, Edgar Oldroyd and George Macaulay who all played in the thirties, but in real terms they were men of the twenties. The exception would have to be Sutcliffe, who was certainly a major force in the twenties but remained a dominant batsman and personality right up to the start of the Second World War.

In 1919 Yorkshire won the county championship, and their worst position in the next twenty-one seasons was sixth in 1934. Apart from that year, and 1920 and 1928, when they finished fourth, they were never out of the top three, but since second and third always represented failure let us not dwell too long upon the details. The facts are that those marvellous men of 1919 to 1939 achieved championship positions in this sequence: 1919, 1st; 1920, 4th; 1921, 3rd; 1922, 1st; 1923, 1st; 1924, 1st; 1925, 1st; 1926, 2nd; 1927, 3rd; 1928, 4th; 1929, 2nd; 1930, 3rd; 1931, 1st; 1932, 1st; 1933, 1st; 1934, 6th; 1935, 1st; 1936, 3rd; 1937, 1st; 1938, 1st; 1939, 1st.

Now let's look at Yorkshire's contribution to England Test teams in that period. On the 1920–1 tour to Australia: Wilfred Rhodes, Abe Waddington, Arthur Dolphin, Evelyn Wilson. At home to Australia, 1921: Rhodes and Percy Holmes. In South Africa, 1922–3: George Macaulay. At home to South Africa, 1924: Macaulay, Herbert Sutcliffe, Roy Kilner. In Australia, 1924–5: Sutcliffe, Kilner. At home to Australia, 1926: Sutcliffe, Kilner, Macaulay, Rhodes. In South Africa, 1927–8: Holmes, Sutcliffe, R. T. Stanyforth. At home to West Indies, 1928: Sutcliffe, Maurice Leyland. In Australia, 1928–9: Sutcliffe, Leyland. At home to South Africa, 1929: Sutcliffe, Leyland. In West Indies, 1929–30: Rhodes. At home to Australia, 1930: Sutcliffe, Leyland. In South Africa, 1930–1: Leyland. At home to New Zealand, 1931: Sutcliffe, Hedley

Verity. At home to India, 1932: Holmes, Sutcliffe, Bill Bowes. In Australia, 1932–3: Sutcliffe, Leyland, Bowes, Verity. In New Zealand, 1932–3: Sutcliffe, Bowes, Verity. At home to West Indies, 1933: Sutcliffe, Leyland, Verity, Macaulay. In India, 1933–4: Arthur Mitchell, Verity. At home to Australia, 1934: Sutcliffe, Leyland, Verity, Bowes. In West Indies, 1934–5: Leyland. At home to South Africa, 1935: Sutcliffe, Leyland, Verity, Wilf Barber, Bowes, Mitchell. At home to India, 1936: Mitchell, Leyland, Verity. In Australia, 1936–7: Leyland, Verity. At home to New Zealand, 1937: Len Hutton, Verity. At home to Australia, 1938: Hutton, Verity, Bowes, Leyland, Arthur Wood. In South Africa, 1938–9: Paul Gibb, Norman Yardley, Verity, Hutton. At home to West Indies, 1939: Hutton, Wood, Verity, Bowes. It may well be right that a strong England needs a strong Yorkshire.

Now let's look at some of these men of the twenties and thirties. Edgar Oldroyd provided many valuable lessons in technique, especially on difficult pitches, for a young Len Hutton. The two opened together for Pudsey when Oldroyd had retired from Yorkshire (15,876 runs at 34.66) and Hutton was beginning to make his name. Oldroyd's reputation probably rests on his ability as a stonewaller, though they might not agree at Pudsey, where he could certainly play his shots. In the first-class game, however, he was a more obdurate type in the recollection of those who played alongside him. He was a careful man in every way: careful at the crease, careful on the field (he hated the more dangerous positions on the field), careful with his money. What could be more Yorkshire than that?

George Macaulay, alas, I never saw play. At least, I do not recall seeing him play and everyone, from Wilfred Rhodes to Bill Bowes, has assured me that no matter how immature I might have been at the time, I would assuredly have remembered. He was the most belligerent of bowlers. Starting life as a quickie, he cut down his pace over the years and 'did more with it'. Often, in newspapers and reference books, you will find references to his bowling off-spin in partnership with Verity's slow left-arm but then a glance at other bowling analyses will reveal him as an opening bowler. But legend has it that no matter *what* he was bowling his most burning desire at any moment of any day was to get batsmen out. As Cardus wrote in the *Manchester Guardian* after a memorable White Rose victory at

Old Trafford: 'Give me eleven Macaulays and you can have the others, Bradman and all.' There can be no doubt that George Gibson Macaulay, from Thirsk, really hated batsmen in a way which even the volatile F. S. Trueman would have found difficult to emulate. The records bristle with phrases like 'Macaulay looked daggers at the batsman who had dared to hit him for four', '. . . screamed his appeal to high heavens', '. . . shouted for lbw when the ball plainly struck the batsman in the small of the back'.

He had a biting wit which could be on a relatively lofty plane or could plumb the depths, as on the occasion when the Yorkshire side, *en route* from Lord's to Glamorgan, waited for their coach on the train to be uncoupled and shunted on to their connecting train in the West Country. George urgently needed to use the toilet facilities but dutifully held off as long as possible in deference to the 'not while standing in the station' notice. The delay lengthened to a point where he could stand it no longer. As he returned to the team coach he was confronted by a wheel-tapper, much aggrieved and brandishing a badly soiled hand: 'The stationmaster won't have this, you know.' Macaulay's patience had been tried enough for one day. His reply was snarled venomously: 'Well tell him to share it out amongst t'porters then.' An uncompromising man, G. G. Macaulay, but a fine cricketer and great competitor: 1,773 wickets for York-shire at 17.08, 5,759 runs and an unrecorded number of catches, so many of them brilliant, in close-to-the-wicket positions. He rates no fewer than forty entries under 'Exceptional bits of bowling' in the Yorkshire handbook, most of them involving hauls of six, seven and eight wickets for ridiculously small concessions of runs.

Arthur ('Ticker') Mitchell first played for Yorkshire in 1922, but in my mind he has always been a man of the thirties because I saw so much of him from my schoolboy seat and it is as a fieldsman rather than a batsman that he comes to mind, although he scored 18,034 runs (37.64) for the county and played six times for England. Good though it was to see Sutcliffe, Hutton, Leyland and the rest stroking the ball around Headingley or Park Avenue, it was when Yorkshire were in the field that my soul rejoiced. They were like tigers savaging their prey. There must have been big partnerships by at least some of the 1930s opposition but my mind has patrioti-cally refused to retain any memory of them. What I do recall most clearly was the constant expectation of a wicket, through every moment of the day, and it was of course the near-certainty of this which made Yorkshire the force they were. Always in the foreground of those memories is a scoreline 'caught Mitchell, bowled Verity'. It happened on 160 occasions and Verity, remember, only played from 1930 to 1939. My eternal picture of Verity bowling includes four or five crouching accomplices round the bat: Mitchell, Sellers, various combinations of Cyril Turner, Ellis Robinson and Herbert Sutcliffe, with Arthur Wood behind the stumps. Mitchell's anticipation was as important as his sticky fingers; it was almost uncanny and it enabled him to make the difficult chance look straightforward. 'Ticker' had no time for show, for ostentation of any kind. I love Bill Bowes's story of the time when Ellis Robinson brought off a spectacular catch with his finger-tips after a full-length dive and Mitchell growled: 'Gerrup. Thar't makin' an exhibition o' thissen.' Dour was the word for Arthur Mitchell. Dour and grim. He rarely smiled and couldn't understand those who did.

Arthur Wood, as bubbly and irrepressible as 'Ticker' was taciturn, had the ability to blow bubbles without artificial aid, simply by pursing his lips, and delighted to float them across in the direction of Mitchell standing at short gulley or slip. Thirty years afterwards, telling me the story, Woodie cackled with delight at the memory of Mitchell's fury, as much at the simple frivolity of the act as the distraction it provided for a waiting catcher. No, Arthur Mitchell above all others, did not play cricket for fun. In the postwar years, as Yorkshire's batting coach, he terrified generations of schoolboys attending the Headingley nets – amongst them my younger brother – in the hope of being noticed and singled out as Yorkshire players of the future. Few went home rejoicing that they had been noted by the coach to any significant degree. The Rhodesian verdict on Verity, 'He'll do,' was the ultimate in lavishness any prospect could expect from Arthur Mitchell. Yet who is going to question the accuracy of his judgement considering the players who came through the ranks in the 1950s and 1960s? Arthur Mitchell was as Yorkshire as Ilkley Moor – perhaps not baht 'at but with a cap bearing the white rose pulled down over the right eye.

Wilf Barber may perhaps be seen as the ancestor of Doug Padgett in the excellence of his batting technique. Somehow he seemed to me to accumulate his runs by stealth rather than flamboyance, and more than once in the thirties I found myself startled by applause

for a Barber 50 when he had, apparently, only just got off the mark.
In the field, he was more often than not Yorkshire's odd man out
and specialised on the deep square-leg boundary, where he waited
patiently for a batsman to mistime a hook from Bowes's bouncer.
He played Bradford League cricket after retirement and coached at
Ashville College, Harrogate.

7
Sutcliffe and Leyland

One of the greatest delights of my life has been that cricketers who were my heroes, worshipped from afar in my schooldays, afterwards became my friends. It never occurred to me – not in my wildest flight of fancy, and there are many when one is young – that I would ever be able to meet Len Hutton and Herbert Sutcliffe, let alone play golf with them or spend hours in conversation. Yet that is how it turned out and I am forever grateful. The first time I saw Herbert Sutcliffe bat was at Bradford Park Avenue on a sticky dog. If I had known the word 'imperious' at that time it would have come immediately to mind; if I had known what batting was like on a drying Park Avenue wicket my admiration would have been even more profound. He was not a tall man but somehow he radiated authority. It was if all others on the field were of lesser significance, extras on a stage on which he was a star of the first magnitude. Not only his batsmanship but his very presence demanded respect. From the moment he took his bat to the wicket, Herbert Sutcliffe was *in charge*. If dismissal should by chance occur it could only be due to some strange quirk of fate, because in all truth it seemed unlikely that it could be brought about by man. I went home and told my father of the miracle I had seen involving 'Mr Sutcliffe', and that was how I thought of him for the rest of his life. In all our conversations through the sixties and seventies I never once addressed him as anything but 'Mr Sutcliffe'. It was unthinkable to contemplate anything else because in my mind I *thought* of him as 'Mr Sutcliffe'. Once, at the funeral of Bright Heyhirst (that great character of a masseur to the Yorkshire team) he was asked by a *Yorkshire Post* reporter at the church door for his name – to be

included in the list of mourners recorded in the paper. The earth
stopped for a moment. Mr S. looked the reporter slowly up and
down and we waited for the explosion. Then he turned to a
companion, said simply, 'Tell this young man who I am,' and
stalked majestically into the church.

Mr Sutcliffe was one of the greatest products of that wondrous
nursery of Yorkshire cricketers, the town of Pudsey, although he
was not in fact born there. The family moved from Nidderdale into
the industrial West Riding when he was very young and, like his
direct cricketing descendant Len Hutton, he followed a family
connection with the St Lawrence Club. His father was a medium
pace bowler of great accuracy. He was fourteen and a half when he
first played for the senior side there, batting at no. 6, describing
himself later as 'a terrified little figure in white shorts'. With great
respect I doubted that when he told me the story and he smiled,
quietly pleased. He batted for forty-five minutes and scored just one
run, but was highly delighted that he was not out when the innings
closed. He was soon being coached at the Headingley nets, shortly
after that was picked for the Colts and was 'disappointed' not to be
given a first-team trial before the Great War of 1914–18. He joined
the Army and was fortunate enough to find himself posted to York
where, as Cpl Sutcliffe of the Sherwood Foresters (and he didn't
like *that* overmuch), he gave himself unofficial leave on Saturday
afternoon, cycled twenty miles to the tram terminus at Killingbeck
(then on the eastern outskirts of Leeds; it has long since been
engulfed by the spread of suburbia) and then rattled across the city
to play for St Lawrence under an assumed name. As it was to do
during the Second World War, the Bradford League attracted many
of the greatest names in the game and young Corporal Sutcliffe
found himself competing with men like Jack Hobbs and Frank
Woolley. Predictably, he won a commission before the war ended
and had just taken up a professional contract to play for Allerton
Bywater, in the Yorkshire Council, when he was called up again,
this time by Yorkshire. His first game was against Gloucs; he made
11 runs and afterwards could remember nothing of the innings.
(Years later I once asked him if he remembered an Indian bowler
named Nissar. Mr Sutcliffe looked blank, then replied, 'No. Should
I?' In India's first official Test match played at Lord's in 1932,
Nissar bowled him for 3 and his Yorkshire and England partner

Percy Holmes for 5. Typically, he had been dismissed from the Sutcliffe mind.)

His opening partnership with Holmes was legendary. They were entirely contrasting individuals – Holmes, a part of that great Huddersfield dynasty of batsmen but very much a working-man type of cricketer; Sutcliffe, from an equally great tradition in Pudsey but an aristocrat in character. They met on a Leeds tram and one cannot help feelng that if the Pudsey man had been the senior (he was seven years younger than Holmes) the meeting would have taken place in a Rolls-Royce. They were both on the way to Headingley and an improbable friendship developed. When their cricketing days were over they rarely if ever met socially but always exchanged birthday and Christmas cards. In between, they created cricket history.

At Leyton, in 1932, Sutcliffe and Holmes opened the batting against Essex with the whole team smarting from a narrow escape in the previous match with Kent. Needing only 67 to win the game, the last five men in the batting order had changed into 'mufti' and were making their way out of the ground when they paused to see Sutcliffe, Holmes, Leyland, Mitchell and Barber skittled in an unprecedented collapse and there was much scurrying back to the dressing-room and pulling on of whites over street clothes before the win was accomplished. Yorkshire dignity had been severely affronted. On to Leyton: Holmes was suffering badly from lumbago and far from optimistic about his chances of staying long at the wicket, but it was one of those days when things went absolutely right out in the middle. With the total at 4, Holmes got a thin edge to a ball from Maurice Nichols and the catch was dropped behind the wicket. At the end of the day, Yorkshire had scored 423 for no wicket.

By the next morning the press had descended upon the ground in force along with film cameramen, a huge crowd of supporters and a mountain of telegrams urging the first-wicket pair on to the record 554 scored by their illustrious Yorkshire predecessors, Brown and Tunnicliffe, thirty-four years earlier. One man had chased down from Hull overnight (which couldn't have been easy in 1932) to see history made, but his optimism was not shared by the not-out partnership. Holmes's lumbago was worse and he was in acute discomfort; his partner, with aching muscles and a lack of sleep, said he wouldn't give twopence for their chances of reaching 555. First there was a new ball to be faced and with that threat seen off the pair gradually took the score up to 551. It was Herbert Sutcliffe who hit the four to pass the record, aimed a most uncharacteristic slog at the next ball and dragged it into his stumps. Brian Sellers declared at ten minutes to one: Yorkshire 555 for one; Sutcliffe 313, Holmes 224 not out. And as they walked slowly back to the pavilion through crowds of wildly cheering spectators, the scoreboard tottered back to 554! Billy Ringrose, the Yorkshire scorer, had one run fewer in his book than his Essex colleague and, a stickler for accuracy, Billy argued that while it might be hard luck on the batsmen (he didn't think of the historians) 'fair's fair and reight's reight'. Not unnaturally, there was a certain degree of pandemonium in all parts of the ground, not least the Yorkshire dressing-room where Herbert Sutcliffe was outraged. If he had known the declaration was coming he wouldn't have given away his wicket so lightly and if he had known there was the slightest doubt about the record after labouring so long, well . . .

Recalling that moment even more than forty years afterwards, I have known Mr Sutcliffe's voice rise in a high-pitched crescendo of horror. Billy Ringrose was adamant in the face of all the tumult and shouting; the score according to his book was 554 for one. The details were checked minutely, right through both books, and finally it was established that the Essex scorer had recorded a no ball which Ringrose had missed. But no one was going to shake a Yorkshireman from his conviction without some pretty substantial evidence, even if it meant that two compatriots were to be deprived of their place in history. There has long been a tendency to regard that discovery of the missing no ball in Yorkshire's scorebook with a cynical smile, but Billy Ringrose would not accept it until the fact had been checked with the umpire who called it *and* the bowler had been questioned. Only then was peace restored. Nowadays that 555 ranks behind one of 561 for the first-wicket record, but that was scored by two chaps named Waheed Mirza and Mansoor Akhtar for a team called Karachi Whites against Quetta some forty-four years later, when cricket was a different game. Who is going to compare that with Sutcliffe and Holmes in the English county championship? Certainly no Yorkshireman.

That was the last big partnership by the Yorkshire pair because a leg injury restricted Holmes's mobility and after one more season he

retired. He had scored sixty centuries for Yorkshire, so many of
them in partnership with Sutcliffe that some of the details, at least,
demand to be recorded. After that 555 opening stand come 347 *v.*
Hampshire (1920), 323 *v.* Lancs (1923), 309 *v.* Warwicks (1931),
290 *v.* Middlesex (1928), 274 *v.* Somerset (1927), 274 *v.* Gloucs
(1921), 272 *v.* Leics (1925), 268 *v.* Essex (1928), 265 *v.* Surrey
(1926), 253 *v.* Lancs (1919), 241 *v.* Surrey (1929), 235 *v.* Glamorgan
(1930), 227 *v.* Leics (1928), 221 *v.* Glamorgan (1925), 210 *v.* Notts
(1928), 200 *v.* Oxford University (1930). We won't bother with
mere century partnerships! Together they topped the hundred mark
sixty-nine times for Yorkshire, which is three more than Sandham
and Hobbs for Surrey, and that brings us logically to Herbert
Sutcliffe's Test association with the one and only Jack Hobbs.

While he rated Don Bradman as the best batsman he ever saw on
good wickets he placed him second to Hobbs on all wickets. Sutcliffe
had an immense admiration for Hobbs's technique on rain-affected
pitches and felt their most enjoyable and 'thrilling' partnerships
were those played on 'stickies'. His outstanding memory in this
respect was of the Third Test in Melbourne on the 1928–9 tour. In
what was probably the first cricket book by a professional cricketer –
certainly the first by a Yorkshire pro – he recalled:

> We wanted 323 to win and we started on a wicket (after
> overnight rain) which was the worst I had known. It was so
> bad, in fact, that before we went out for the tricky 25 minutes
> before lunch we were told by everyone (good judges as well)
> that England would do well to score 90 runs on it. For two
> hours after lunch the wicket was a nightmare. Some balls rose
> above my head. Twice Hobbs was struck a glancing blow on
> the side of the face. Even a good length ball at which one
> would ordinarily play forward, would stand up almost
> straight. There were balls that had to be played because they
> threatened the sticks and there were balls that had to be left
> alone because the batsman, who was relieved when he got his
> bat out of the way of them, knew that three-quarters of the
> Australian XI circled him. The decision to play or not to play
> had to be made generally after a ball pitched – no one could
> tell what it was going to do until it had hit turf which had so
> much help for the spinning ball. Runs did not matter. It was

simply a matter of staying there as long as we could in the
hope that when the wicket eased there would be an
opportunity for some run-getting. It all came right in the end.
The victory we secured gave us the Ashes for we had won the
previous Tests at Brisbane and Sydney but I carried on my
body for many a day afterwards the marks of the ball which
did such fearsome tricks on the rain-ruined Melbourne
wicket.

'It all came right' indeed! What Herbert Sutcliffe did not write
was that he scored 135 out of 332 for seven on the worst wicket he
had ever seen, and that for long afterwards Australians swore it was
the greatest innings they had ever seen (by a Pom, of course!).
Privately, Mr Sutcliffe rated it his best innings but only when
pressed; he didn't write that about himself. He often, however,
looked with a critical eye at what others wrote. He was more than a
little piqued to read that Hobbs had 'nursed' him through the early
part of an innings on another gluepot at The Oval against the 1926
Australians. He and Hobbs put on 172 for the first wicket (Hobbs
100, Sutcliffe 161) in a Test which saw Wilfred Rhodes recalled by
England at the age of forty-eight. He was downright annoyed by
Neville Cardus's claim (more lyrical than factual) that 'Sutcliffe
could play and miss at six balls in an over yet lean nonchalantly on
his bat at the end of it with the air of a man who has hit each one
for four'.

'I *never* played and missed at six balls in any over I ever faced,' he
snapped when I once dared to put the point to him. 'It was naughty
of Neville to say that.' Which would have delighted Cardus if he
had lived to hear the remark.

In the Second World War Herbert Sutcliffe was commissioned
again – anything else would have been unthinkable! – and one of
Captain Sutcliffe's earliest duties was to arrange for uniforms big
enough to go round the frames of Privates W. E. Bowes and H.
Verity when they joined up in November 1939. They knew instinc-
tively that he would succeed where their quartermaster had failed.
Sutcliffe was in every way a meticulous man, as neat and methodical
in his care for his cricket gear as he was in analysing the bowling of
the opposition, whoever it was. He had quite superb self-discipline
and it made him intolerant of lack of discipline in others, whatever

the context. His handwriting, correspondingly, was tidy and orderly in the extreme; his conversation clipped and precise, his choice of words impeccable. If I dared to think he had a fault I perhaps felt that he was just a little short on humour – until Charlie Brett, proprietor of the fish-and-chip shop close to Headingley and dear to the hearts of cricketers, pressmen and commentators, told me a story about him:

> He used to park his Rolls-Royce outside with his two damn great dogs in the back and come in for an order which never varied – haddock and chips with just a sprinkling of vinegar and salt and two fish, wrapped separately with no seasoning. One day I asked him about this order and he told me, 'I drive up the road towards Otley and stop outside the Parkway (a large residential hotel). The dogs have a fish apiece and I eat the haddock and chips and sit looking at the Parkway, wishing they could serve food as good as this.

So he certainly *had* a sense of humour, but for Herbert Sutcliffe it would always be the quiet smile rather than the deep belly-laugh of, say, Arthur Wood, so long his wicket-keeping colleague in the Yorkshire side. He was a marvellous raconteur of stories of great cricketing occasions, his narrative clear and precise with never a word wasted. In my forties and fifties I sat listening to him with the fascination of a fourteen or fifteen-year-old boy, at his home in Ilkley and later in Addingham, or (later still) in the nursing homes where he spent his final years. In his eighties his mind was razor-sharp and his tongue could have the same cutting-edge, too. He was fond of a gin-and-mixed (Vermouth), which was not in liberal supply in a nursing home so it became necessary to use orange juice as a mix. Then the staff began to insist that, for one reason or another, a glass or two of Gordons was not good for him. It then became necessary to smuggle the stuff past a Praetorian guard of nurses, sisters and matrons, who became as expert at spotting the gin-smugglers as customs officers are at detecting those with more than their allowance of duty-frees. Unfortunately, I quickly went to the top of their black-list. In November 1977 I called to see Mr Sutcliffe at Glusburn, near Keighley, with a bottle secreted in a holdall and covered by a tape-recorder. The staff headed me off before I could even start up the steps to his room, searched out the

gin and confiscated it. In the utmost state of dread I tapped on the
door, went in and met the peremptory demand I knew awaited me:
'Have you brought the gin?' Silently, I looked at the carpet; there
was nothing to say. Mr S. sat bolt upright in his chair, 'You've let
those bloody awful creatures take it, haven't you?' My hang-dog
expression said it all. I then stood like a schoolboy on the mat before
his headmaster (or how schoolboys *used* to stand on such occasions)
while the great man gave me the most comprehensive dressing-down
of my life. After ten minutes' fluent denunciation of the thieving
staff (and of my ineptitude as a smuggler) he stopped abruptly,
nodded me to a chair and normal service was resumed, as they say.
We chatted for half an hour and as I left Mr Sutcliffe said, 'So you
are off to Pakistan and New Zealand next week. When you get back
I shall want a report on every ball bowled and every stroke played,
though there won't be many of those, I'm sure, with *that* fellow
playing' (a reference to Geoff Boycott, whom he cordially detested).
Those were the last words my hero spoke to me. Three months
later, with a considerable degree of emotion, I recorded an obituary
tribute to him from the commentary box in Karachi. A very great
Yorkshireman died on 22 January 1978, aged eighty-four.

In his first-class career he scored 50,138 runs at an average of
56.1, with 149 centuries. In fifty-four Tests for England he scored
4,555 (average 60.73) with sixteen hundreds, and remember that
most of those Tests were against great Australian sides. He scored
two separate hundreds in a Test match twice, four hundreds in a
series twice, three hundreds in consecutive Test innings. Not once,
from his début in 1919 up to the outbreak of the Second World
War, did he fail to make at least 1,000 first-class runs in a season
and six times he topped 2,000. He could have been Yorkshire's first
professional captain in the twentieth century but declined the
honour – *why* was the one thing he would never tell me.

He was a great admirer of Lord Hawke and the Corinthian
approach to cricket. Any act on the field which smacked of poor
sportsmanship was anathema to him, and while pointing to the way
Hawke raised the status of the professional he never mentioned that
he himself did more than anyone else in that respect by personal
example. There were many in the 1920s and 1930s who felt that
Herbert Sutcliffe was playing on the wrong side in the Gentlemen
v. Players match.

His son, William Herbert Hobbs Sutcliffe, became a Yorkshire player in 1948 and captained the side in 1956 and 1957. Sadly, he suffered because he was his father's son. There is an appalling Yorkshire fixation in damning as sub-standard any boy whose father was a great player. Bill Sutcliffe knew he was not as good as his father and he knew that he never would be. Lightning simply does not strike twice to that extent. But he was a damn good cricketer who might have become better but for the millstone of his parentage. He, too, played in a side of great players, but the team of the 1950s somehow never had the spirit of togetherness which his father had known before the war. The post-war years had evolved a different type of individual. There were strong personalities in Yorkshire's side who made life difficult for Sutcliffe Minor as a captain, and when he ceased to enjoy his cricket he got out of it. Bill was too genial and easy-going to stomach a life which, for four months every summer, was a constant battle with warring factions within his own ranks. Nevertheless, he was Yorkshire cricketer enough to take a place on the county Committee and make his contribution from that quarter. But the words, 'Ay, lad, tha's all reight but tha'll nivver be as good as the faither' must still haunt him. Why do we do it?

As a human being – if not, technically, as a cricketer – Maurice Leyland simply had to be the reincarnation of George Herbert Hirst. He was a short, roly-poly figure; he was genial and good-natured, with a pleasant sense of humour; he was kind, generous and everybody loved him. Just as Hirst had done, he spent so many of his later years giving everything he had to give to Yorkshire cricket. He coached, he scoured the county for young players of promise, he encouraged them. Long before I met him, he appeared as a sort of favourite uncle to me. It was an impression he created without conscious effort and even without personal acquaintance. Every time I watched him play I thought of him as somehow out of place amidst the naked aggression of Macaulay, the brilliantined imperturbability of Herbert Sutcliffe, the regal dignity of Hedley Verity, the saturnine intensity of Arthur Mitchell. And yet he was so much a part of the Yorkshire team that it was unthinkable that they could ever take the field without him. I thought of him with genuine *affection*. At the age of eleven, I went camping with fellow choirboys from St John's Church, in Keighley, to the Crimple Valley, just outside Harrogate. On the second evening I walked into town, asked for directions to the home of Maurice Leyland and stood for something like an hour outside his house, simply looking at it, picturing the man who lived there and recalling days in the sun when I had watched him. It never occurred to me for one moment to knock on the door and ask if he was at home. It was only thirty years later (when I told him of the incident) that I realised he would have been 'reight pleased to see me'.

His cricket in some ways belied his sunny character. He was the most determined of batsmen, and one of the most hard-hitting, but he could be grimly watchful and stonewall with the best of them. I rather think that it was after his death (on New Year's Day, 1967) that the discovery was made of the correct spelling of his name as 'Morris'. And I suspect that the discovery was made by that great watchdog of journalistic fact, Dick Williamson of the *Telegraph and Argus*, Bradford. But 'Maurice' it had been throughout his playing career and his coaching days; that is how we all knew him and he never corrected the impression, so I feel it only right now to keep so personal a memory in the way it had always existed: 'Maurice' it is, in this book.

He made a modest start to his first-class career but ended by averaging 41.03 runs for Yorkshire and 46.06 for England, for whom he very rarely failed. He was a deep fieldsman who never looked built for the role, with short legs and a well-rounded figure, but he had a fine 'arm' and a great determination to save every run he could. He bowled the Chinaman, the left-armer's wrong 'un, and bowled it remarkably well. Playing alongside Rhodes, Kilner and then Verity, his opportunities for regular employment as a bowler did not occur very often and it seems to me, casting around in boyhood memories, that whenever Leyland was called into the attack it formed the subject of special comment in the *Yorkshire Post*, the *Leeds Mercury* or the *Telegraph and Argus*. He took 409 wickets for the county; as a breaker of long partnerships – which were regarded as a sort of blasphemy by Yorkshire bowlers – he was invaluable, and then almost invariably it was time to bring back the front-line bowlers.

He was a great believer in taking a long look at opposition bowling before mounting any sort of attack – a characteristic we see, too, in Herbert Sutcliffe – and it was a policy he urged upon young players.

But he was by nature a generous batsman and was always willing to take on bowlers of world renown if the going was tough for less experienced partners. Once, in a moment of crisis against Grimmett and O'Reilly, the truly great Australians, he told his captain: 'Let me get in. If I can't hit 'em, I'll stop 'em.' And like most generous men, he was modest in the extreme. After hitting 211 not out against Lancashire at Headingley in 1930, with Bill Bowes keeping vigil at the other end (6 not out – one of his more distinguished knocks!), Maurice dismissed the congratulations of the dressing-room thus: 'Nay, tell Bill, not me. Ah'm expected to get runs. He made it possible.'

Like Hutton, he was out without scoring in his first Test innings, but he made a hundred the first time he played against Australia – 137 and 53 not out at Melbourne in 1929 in a match which England lost! – and he scored another century on his *last* appearance against the Aussies. Much as he had done with Rhodes in 1926, Neville Cardus jogged the collective elbow of the Selectors during the Old Trafford Roses match of August, 1938: 'When Nutter came on for Pollard at the Manchester end Leyland struck his first ball for four and, having done so, stood entirely still and watched the perspective. In the same over he pulled to the on and drove to the off, both fours also. If Leyland is not good enough to play for England, who amongst living cricketers is?'

After missing the first four Tests of the series, Leyland was recalled at The Oval, just nineteen days after Cardus's piece appeared in the *Manchester Guardian*. He went in at no. 3 with England 29 for one and left at 411 for two – run out for 187.

Maurice scored sixty-two centuries for Yorkshire. He was capped in 1922 and scored more than 1,000 runs in every season up to the Second World War. For England, he played forty-one times and had nine centuries in his 2,764 runs. Those figures are a fit enough epitaph for any man, but statistics are not what Maurice Leyland was about. I do not know anyone who heard him utter a spiteful or malicious remark about another player and never have I heard one uttered about him. His whimsical humour is enshrined in a hundred Yorkshire anecdotes and the one I like as well as any is about his partnership with R. W. V. Robins at Melbourne in 1937. England were 698 runs adrift when they started their second innings and they had reached 195 for six when Robins joined Leyland. He was 'on a pair', so jumpy in the extreme. He got off the mark with a scampered single and then proceeded to call for ones and twos in a sort of frenzy. After just getting home in response to a particularly hazardous call, Maurice drew his partner's attention to the scoreboard and gently admonished him: 'Steady on, Robbie. I don't think we shall get 'em all tonight.' The pro to the amateur! But Robins enjoyed the remark. It was difficult not to enjoy everything about Maurice Leyland.

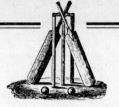

8
Sir Leonard Hutton

Len Hutton was born at a time when the most appalling carnage of the First World War was taking place on the Somme, and yet there was a complete inevitability about his becoming a cricketer. From his cradle the sound of bat on ball was clearly audible in the unique village of Fulneck, no more than five miles from the middle of Leeds, yet with a character all of its own. It was established as a mission of the Moravian Church, which in turn originated in the Austro-Hungarian Empire. The first Moravian place of worship was built in 1746; the houses on the hillside around it were let to tenants who embraced that particular branch of Protestantism and its famous school soon followed. The Sunday School – like virtually every other in the West Riding of Yorkshire – produced its own cricket team and the Hutton home was within a six-hit of the ground. Len's father was a cricketer; his great-uncles were cricketers; his three elder brothers were cricketers. As a very small boy he habitually carried a ball in his pocket in the hope that someone would suggest an impromptu game. And, like many a Yorkshire youngster before and since, his first competitive game came when the Sunday School side (one mid-week evening) found themselves a man short and the young Hutton, bearing a bat which came up to his chest, marched out at no. 11 through outfield grass, resplendent with buttercups and daisies, brushing around his knees.

At eleven, Len and five of his contemporaries were allowed to join the neighbouring and famous Bradford League club, Pudsey St Lawrence, as junior members, and this meant farewell to overgrown outfields where cattle grazed during the week. In one corner of the Pudsey ground they staged their own Test cricket, rushing home from school to savage a sandwich, gulp down a cup of tea and hurry away to the club. The exclusive club of eleven-year-olds could not mount a full-scale match of their own, so they evolved the simplest of all systems: each batted in turn until he was out. Young Hutton, starting on one glorious Monday evening, was still there with the bat in his hand at close of play on Friday! After that, his innings of thirteen hours twenty minutes at The Oval in 1938 presented fewer problems than it might have done to batsmen who hadn't done their groundwork so proficiently.

Leonard was twelve when his batting down in the furthest reaches of the ground began to be noticed by the St Lawrence Committee. He was given a chance to play for the club's Second Eleven and to his utter disgust the Saltaire fast bowler switched to slow deliveries when the slim, pale youngster came in to bat at no. 8. Years later he was to think that he ought to have been grateful for the consideration of an adult, but all he could think in the summer of 1928 was that in the company of men he was being treated as a child. He made the bowler regret his generosity . . . At fourteen he was promoted to Pudsey's first team and in January, 1930, came a letter which every Yorkshire schoolboy of the day dreamed of getting – a letter bearing the imprint of Yorkshire County Cricket Club. It asked for details of the Hutton average during the previous season. Trembling with a hope he scarcely dared allow himself, young Leonard filled in the form: batting average–34.5; bowling–11 wickets at 14 runs each. Two weeks later came a second letter: 'The Yorkshire CCC will be pleased if you can attend practices at the Headingley ground.' And in February Len trudged through the slush and snow to the start of a wonderful cricketing life. Five years earlier his father had prophesied that Len would make the best cricketer in a marvellously talented family. How right he was.

At Headingley he came under the wing of George Herbert Hirst. Fifteen minutes' batting in the indoor shed earned Hutton the comment: 'Well played. Try to improve on that.' From George Hirst to any Yorkshire schooboy that was the ultimate in approval. The coach had already decided he had got a winner. He confided in Bill Bowes, then Yorkshire's opening bowler and a man who was destined to become a coach and mentor enjoying the same sort of respect: 'I've got a good lad. Come and have a look at him.' The first batting lesson Hutton learned at the Yorkshire nets was how to apply more left hand than right in playing a quick ball down the leg side – in short, to keep the ball down.

At seventeen Leonard Hutton played his first game for Yorkshire II and was out without scoring in his only innings. His second match was in the Rosebuds fixture at Bradford Park Avenue, and again he failed to trouble the scorers. As the start of the cricketing career he had decided upon when he was barely fourteen it was disastrous, but to hear Len talking of that 1933 season is to know at once that while he felt disappointment he felt nothing remotely approaching despair. He has never been a man to exhibit extremes of emotion and it is entirely possible to visualise him working things out. His philosophy was based on avoiding mistakes, of cutting out unnecessarily risky strokes, but at the same time he was determined that whatever he accomplished should be done with style – the direct result of watching so much of Herbert Sutcliffe, without doubt. But the care with which he fashioned an innings was to bring criticism from time to time: 'Hutton batted under the impression that it was a four-day, not a two-day match'; '. . . putting the efforts of any self-respecting tortoise in the shade, he took three-quarters of an hour to reach double figures.' Yet there was a kindliness in 1930s journalism which one does not find quite so readily fifty years later. Cricket writers had more space to spread themselves, to write reasoned and responsible appreciations of all aspects of a game. And there was a generosity in dressing-rooms, too, towards young players despite the fact that they had to be seen as potential challengers for regular first-team places.

In that first summer of second-team cricket he faced S. F. Barnes, then sixty-two years old and still capable of bowling like the master-craftsman of all time that he has, for so long, been considered. He played against Cyril Washbrook, who was to become his partner in what was one of England's best opening pairings of all time, perhaps the second-best after Hobbs and Sutcliffe. Despite those two ducks, Hutton's first eight innings in the Colts produced 453 runs (three not-outs) for an average of 90. People were beginning to talk about a first-team appearance; the dreams were beginning to come true, the dreams he had dreamed three years earlier when he watched Don Bradman hit 300 in a day at Headingley.

Hutton was not a naturally gregarious and outgoing youngster but nor was he introspective and withdrawn in a dressing-room. He

had a severely practical approach to his burgeoning life as a
cricketer. Just as he had worked conscientiously to learn his trade
as a carpenter on leaving school, the fact that his natural gifts as a
sportsman seemed likely to give him the chance to join the élitism
of the Yorkshire CCC was not a matter to be taken for granted. To
Hutton it was another trade, one to be pursued assiduously in search
of greater skills. There were lessons to be learned in every match he
played; there were more lessons as the opposition became more
distinguished. When he was not batting he *watched* batsmen,
searching for some subtlety of technique which might help his own
game. When he was not watching batsmen he observed bowlers
closely, seeking out their secrets. And when there were neither
batsmen nor bowlers to study he practised fielding, the running
pick-up, the throw to the wicket-keeper which must be judged to
the last inch. He was equally meticulous in looking after his
cricketing gear. In his days as a league cricketer, Friday evenings
were given over to making sure that boots and pads were cleaned to
a pristine whiteness. His kit had not come to him easily; he saved
up until he could buy his own after reading that Jack Hobbs used
only his own personal equipment. And so, looking back to his teens
from his seventies, there is no pretentiousness – only a great
earnestness – in the recollection: 'I found real happiness in keeping
my gear in condition.' When he became a regular first-class player
he watched almost with anguish as these duties were taken over by
the dressing-room attendant, but once the season was over and he
was in possession once more he returned to the loving care of the
tools of his trade with that same 'real happiness'. Nothing had come
easily to him and that youthful evaluation of his personal tackle and
'togs' was something which governed, in a way, his thinking about
cricket throughout his career. He weighed up soberly, and applied
his own sense of values to, every aspect of the game.

Leonard's first-team opportunity had to wait until 1934 and he
was to be 'blooded' in the opening fixture at Cambridge University.
He batted at no. 5 and, with the memory of those two second-team
'blodgers' very much in his mind, he was painfully anxious to get
off the mark. He played the second ball he received towards cover
and set off for the run which would mean his first-class career was
off the mark. At the other end stood the rotund figure of Maurice
Leyland who, unfortunately for the seventeen-year-old Hutton, did

not even contemplate the possibility of a run. He knew that J. G. W. Davies, the cover point fieldsman, was one of the quickest in the land. Hutton was run out by two yards and another duck was chalked up. It was no great comfort to him when Leyland came back to the dressing-room, sought him out and twinkled, 'Never mind. You've started at t'bottom,' but young Leonard still remembered it years later as an indication of the kindly encouragement he got from his peers in the Yorkshire side of 1934. He needed it after the first innings at Cambridge where the card read Sutcliffe, 152; Mitchell, 61; Barber, 103; Leyland, 51; Hutton 0; Turner, 33; Sellers, 52 not out . . . As Yorkshire won by ten wickets there was no time to put things right in that game and Hutton chafed as twelfth man in the second game of the season against MCC at Lord's.

It seemed a lifetime before he returned to action at Oxford University, and this time he scored his first runs in senior cricket – just 5 of them. Rather to his surprise he was given the job of opening the second innings – and with his hero, Herbert Sutcliffe – and at close of play Leonard had not yet scored in Yorkshire's 20 for no wicket. The following morning he made a not-out half century before Sellers declared, and fifty years later Hutton remembered 'that Friday morning, rich in bird-song and sparkling light'. It is memories like that, surely, which give cricket its unique place in sport? A couple of weeks later Leonard played his first championship game at Edgbaston (where Maurice Leyland's father was the groundsman) and got another 50, but three games later he had his first close-up glimpse of the great Frank Woolley, then forty-five years old. Now here it is possible to pause for a moment and consider the respect that players of fifty years ago had for each other. There is respect today, true enough, but relatively little of it because modern players do not seem capable of the humility which marked even the greatest of those of the 1930s. Fourteen years after seeing Woolley at Headingley, Hutton was asked about his impressions of the Kent left-hander. He replied: 'He batted as gloriously, I was told, as he had ever done in a quarter of a century. To have watched him, close up instead of from the ringside, I count a privilege.'

The impressions might have been those of the starry-eyed seventeen-year-old, but they were translated into words by a mature cricketer of thirty-one, a man who was firmly established as the greatest opening batsmen in the world with a record innings of 364 long behind him. The truly great player has always been able, and ready, to identify greatness in others. Hutton had learned one of the most important lessons of the game very early in his career. Perhaps he didn't even have to learn it; one likes to think that it came to him quite naturally.

He has always been more than generous in his recollections of the way senior players helped and encouraged him as a teenager, apart, perhaps, from a grimly smiling opinion that Herbert Sutcliffe was one of the best counters of the balls in an over he ever met (a claim which Herbert, in turn, made in relation to Jack Hobbs and one which most junior partners have made since the game began). On his first appearance at Lord's Hutton was involved in a run-out with Wilf Barber: 'I played a ball to short leg and set off for a run. Wilf responded, although with his greater experience he must have realised the run was impossible. He could have sent me back, but he didn't. We crossed and he was run out. I firmly believe he sacrificed his wicket to save mine.' Barber had been an established player for eight years; Hutton was seventeen and in his first season. Leonard never forgot the incident, or Barber's smiling reassurance when he saw the senior man in the dressing-room afterwards: 'You've nowt to worry about.' Such generosity became rarer in later Yorkshire teams; so did appreciation of that sort of attitude.

It is interesting, too, to look at a great Yorkshire team's attitude to the cricketing press fifty years before such relationships became tarnished to the point of open hostility. The distinguished veteran journalist A. W. Pullin died during the 1934 season and the Yorkshire team members, the subject of so much of his writing, were genuinely distressed. The young Hutton already felt he owed something to the man whose pseudonym was 'Old Ebor' for his encouragement, and years later he was to recall 'how significant in the game are writers of "Old Ebor's" standing; what would we have done without them as men who love the game so much they want everyone else to enjoy it?'.

Hutton finished his first season in senior cricket with 863 runs from twenty-six completed innings and an average of 74.5 from his seven Second XI games. In 1935 he might be said to have slipped back a little because he played nineteen innings for only 425, but there are two ways of explaining this. The first was that although he had been a robust youngster, free from most of the debilitating illnesses which affected so many West Riding children in the thirties, he experienced a lot of trouble after a blow on the nose from a ball which had rebounded from the Lancashire wicket-keeper's gloves while batting in the 1934 Roses Match. An operation did not entirely clear up certain breathing problems and in the game at Edgbaston in the following season Leonard suddenly found his legs giving way and he collapsed on the pitch shortly after running a four, followed by a three. His doctor ordered a complete rest. However, before this he had completed his maiden first-class hundred – 196 in that loveliest of settings, New Road, Worcester – and had taken the opportunity to have a close look at the two greatest batsmen in the world, Bradman and Hammond. The second reason for a thin season in '35 was that his opportunities to bat, never mind open the batting, were directly related to the number of players Yorkshire had to contribute to the Test side. At one time or another Sutcliffe, Mitchell, Verity, Leyland, Barber and Bowes were all called up by England, but it was still not easy for an uncapped player to find regular employment in the First XI. Hutton found, as so many other talented young men had found before him and many more were to learn in the future, that the first lesson to be learned as an aspiring Yorkshire cricketer was patience. Indeed, after his first century, completed on 26 July at Worcester, he did not play in any of the next six matches. Nevertheless, there were two significant factors in that score of 196, as I see it.

Up to that point, Hutton's reputation as a batsman centred upon the more durable aspects. His philosophy was based quite simply on waiting for the right ball to hit and not, under any circumstances, taking any chances against anything that pitched outside the off stump and lifted. In short, Hutton set out to eliminate the possibil-ities of error just as Geoffrey Boycott was to do in a later era, and (in his England captaincy) Raymond Illingworth too. It was a method which contrasted with that of his brilliant England contem-porary, Denis Compton, though it has to be remembered that 'Compo', as a no. 4, stroke-playing batsman, could enjoy adopting a different technique from that of an opener.

Where Hutton's style took a different course from that of Boycott was that once he had established a dominance over the opposition,

Leonard would then systematically take the bowling to pieces, to the obvious benefit of all the batsmen who followed him. Hutton based his batting on how he felt, not on how the scoreboard read. And thus we see him at Worcester on 25 July 1934 still a fledgeling, still a long way from being capped, still a long way short of his first century – completing the first day's play with nine scoring strokes which read: 6, 6, 4, 4, 4, 4, 1, 3, 4. He felt good. In fact years later he recalled, 'I was seeing the ball as I had seldom seen it before.' And so he played the bowling on its merits and if the reputation for dourness was not finally dispelled in that last half-hour, the young Hutton was at last seen in a new (and, as things turned out, a more realistic) light. The following day he added another 121 runs; a new star was born. But how did Len Hutton feel about it? Dissatisfied. On 196 he shaped to hit a boundary which would have given him the double hundred and was bowled by a yorker from Reg Perks. He was furious with himself. *He* had made the mistake. The 196, in that moment, meant nothing beside the fact that he had given away his wicket by playing a shot which passed the initiative to the bowler. And perhaps it was there that a major part of his batting philosophy began: 'I never felt completely satisfied with an innings. No matter how good it looked to others, I always felt I could have done better. I always felt that the best innings was still to come.'

In the cricketing summer of 1936 I was eleven years old. A trip by bus or train to Headingley or Park Avenue plus the admission price to the ground to see a county match was far beyond the means of my parents. Two years earlier I had been taken to see Don Bradman play at Headingley by a friend of my father who sang with him in a choir and I was hooked on cricket for the rest of my life. There might possibly have been an odd visit to watch Yorkshire after that – I cannot be sure – but my cricketing heroes were now the members of the local sides for which my uncle, Arthur Ruddock, played in Keighley where the West Bradford League was made up of teams representing, for the most part, Sunday Schools. I watched Cross Roads and Ingrow and Knowle Park and hero-worshipped men called Edwin Greenwood (he was a handsome man with brilliantined hair like Herbert Sutcliffe), and Charlie Scruton, Herbert Stott, George Lathwell, Raymond Simpson and Jim Chadwick.

Hutton and Sutcliffe, Leyland and Mitchell, Verity and Bowes were simply names in newspapers. I read about them in the *Daily Herald* (for some reason which I never quite understood my father, who voted Conservative all his life, insisted on taking the *Herald* because it was 'the working man's newspaper') or in more detail if I was able to find a discarded copy of the *Bradford Telegraph and Argus* on a bus. They were heroes, true, but heroes of such Olympian stature that never in my wildest dreams did I foresee the possibility of observing them at close quarters. There was no television to bring these paladins into our homes and make every feature or physical characteristic familiar to us. Not too many homes had a radio set on which to hear Howard Marshall's commentaries. The Huttons and Sutcliffes were so remote they might have been creatures from another planet. But through the newspapers I knew everything it was possible to know about them.

Then I won a scholarship to Keighley Boys' Grammar School, the only conceivable way any boy like me could contemplate a future which did not involve as a matter of sheer inevitability going into t'mill when his schooldays were over. My reward, in the immediate context, was twofold: my parents broke their life-long, sacred principle of having nothing to do with hire-purchase by buying me a Hercules Safety Model bicycle for four-and-sixpence down and two years of sixpence-a-week instalments, and my maternal grandmother gave me half-a-crown from her ten shillings-a-week old age pension. Permission to ride my bike twenty miles to Headingley was prised with difficulty from my parents, sandwiches were packed and at 8 a.m. – I could wait no longer and no one knew how long it would take the frail legs of a sickly child to pedal their way to Leeds – I set off. The steep hill up Kirkstall Lane nearly finished my adventure before it had begun and the stern reminder over the gate, 'No money refunded in the event of no play being possible', caused my heart to lurch with sickening uncertainty, but there was no turning back now. I paid my money and took my seat amongst the multitudes on the western (Kirkstall) side of the ground. Hutton scored a hundred, Sutcliffe scored a hundred, Leyland scored a hundred and I was their slave for life. Alf Gover bowled at a speed which terrified me and Hutton, Sutcliffe and Leyland smote him to all corners of the ground. I wished for nothing more than to be able to go on watching it for ever.

At close of play, unable to tear myself away from any of it, I positioned myself behind the pavilion and watched my Ulysses and my Achilles emerge. As long as I live I shall believe that Hutton's eyes for one moment rested on me; the adoration there positively willed him to look at me. Years later I pleaded with Leonard to acknowledge the moment as one he remembered but, alas, men of his stature have no need to dwell on such fantasies. Within a week I was back for more, this time at Park Avenue, ever my favourite ground, where I saw Harold Larwood bowl for the first time but, more importantly, where the Yorkshire Committee met and awarded a county cap to Leonard Hutton. He was twenty years and eighteen days old, the youngest player to be capped since George Hirst and possibly even younger than the great all-rounder – records were imprecise at that time.

Hutton started 1937 with 161 in the traditional opening fixture against MCC at Lord's and felt an increasing maturity in his batting. His favourite stroke was the cover drive, and it is certainly the shot for which he will be remembered. A score of judges I have consulted from time to time, notably Cyril Washbrook who opened so many England innings with him, have been unanimous in the view that Len's expertise with one of the best-looking strokes in the repertoire was due to his beautiful balance as a batsman. He had, of course, an ideal build for classical stroke-making – not too tall or too short, a fairly slight figure with a splendid sense of timing. My childhood memories are of Hutton, perfectly poised on the front foot, driving through the covers or, with immaculate timing, cutting the ball to third man so late that the wicket-keeper's gloves must have been in the act of closing around the ball. Obviously this must be an idealistic memory of Hutton's career as a whole because in 1937 (in the course of a Roses match at Old Trafford of stupefying dullness) Cardus wrote in the *Manchester Guardian*: 'Hutton has something of Sutcliffe's method but so far he is just a technician (who will shortly play for England).'

Perhaps it was that which caused the Selectors to take the hint as Leonard was chosen to open for the North *v*. South in the first Test trial, then in the second – The Rest *v*. MCC (the side in Australia during the previous winter). In the first of these he scored 102 and 15 and in the second, 18 and 50. He reached 1,000 runs by early June and on the Sunday morning when the Test team was due to be

announced he could not bear the suspense of waiting. He went out
for a walk, asking his mother to write down the names of the team
when she heard them on the radio.

On his return, mother duly informed son that his name was on
the list and he commented, 'That's grand.' 'Aye,' she responded,
'it's grand.' It was a characteristically low-key reaction to news
which filled both of them with all-transcending delight. Leonard
was twenty-one years and four days old. The Test series was against
a New Zealand side of modest pretension; he went into it with a
first-class average for the season so far of 80.53 from thirteen
completed innings and he was bowled by Jack Cowie, o in an
England total of 424. Nearly forty-two years later I was commentating on the Third Test between New Zealand and Pakistan in
Auckland when I saw a young man called John Reid (no relation to
the former New Zealand captain) get nought in his first Test innings
and said, 'He can console himself in the knowledge that this has
happened to great batsmen like Len Hutton.' John's mother left a
message for me in the Auckland club offices thanking me for a
sympathetic comment. That was generous of *her* and, bless her, she
couldn't have known just how sincere my remark was, based as it
was on the knowledge of how Leonard felt at Lord's on 26 June
1937: 'I had not slept a wink the previous night. I had lain with
shut eyes picturing the crowds packing the ground and expecting a
century from me. Jim Parks had made all the thirteen runs scored
when I was beaten by a ball which kept low as I played forward.'
But is it possible that any captain has bettered the remark of his
captain, Walter Robins, as the crestfallen young man made his way
sadly back to the dressing-room? 'For goodness sake,' said Robins,
'don't do that against Australia next year.' In one simple phrase he
acknowledged the failure and gave the youngster the most enormous
vote of confidence for his future. I think I have always admired that
more than any remark from any captain.

Hutton set out to convince the Selectors that they had not been
wrong to pick him. He hit 125, his seventh century of the season,
against Essex, 67 against Surrey, 59 not out *v.* Middlesex and
another hundred against the tourists. He was retained for the Second
Test and hit exactly 100 at Old Trafford. Now we see one of those
marvellous little touches of superstition which thread their way
through cricket at all levels. On reaching three figures, Leonard

asked for the England cap which had been resting in the umpire's pocket so far. He was immediately caught out!

England was a joyful place for young Len Hutton in that summer of 1937. True, a man called Adolf Hitler was making threatening noises on the Continent and in Africa the Italians were embarking on a new colonialism. But at home the land was gay with bunting for the Coronation of King George VI and war seemed unthinkable. Hutton had topped 2,000 runs, played in three Tests for England and in Scarborough had met the young woman who was to become his wife – Dorothy Dennis, sister of one of his Yorkshire Second XI colleagues. His confidence was brimming, his technique improving with every innings. His playing of leg-spin bowling brought praise from C. B. Fry and one can see the foundations being laid for his subsequent reputation of being the best bad-wicket player in the world, a title which Geoff Boycott was to inherit.

Happily, Hutton's superstitions did not extend to the figure 13 (in fact few cricketers have ever worried about it) and when he started 1938 with two scores of 13 against MCC at Lord's he felt no more concern than he would have about any other low total, and immediately put things right with 141 at The Parks followed by 93 not out at Ilford. He went into the Test side against the Australians automatically and scored exactly 100 once again on a Trent Bridge pitch he recalls as one of 'heavenly perfection'. Denis Compton, at twenty years and nineteen days, joined Hutton in the record books as a century-maker in their respective first Tests against Australia; Charlie Barnett missed by a whisker hitting a century before lunch (only to complete the ton from the first ball afterwards!), Eddie Paynter hit 206 not out, Stan McCabe 232 in Australia's first innings, Bill Brown 133 and Don Bradman 144 not out in their second. It was to be a summer of runs . . .

After the Second Test had been drawn and the Third (at Old Trafford, of course) washed out without a ball being bowled, Hutton missed the Fourth, at Headingley, because of a fractured finger. Australia won that one, which meant that the series depended upon the final match which was to be played to a finish at The Oval – the timeless Test. Five Yorkshiremen were in the side: Hutton, Leyland, Bowes, Verity and Arthur Wood, the wicket-keeper. The crowds started gathering soon after midnight and when the gates opened at 9 a.m. The first influx saw 4,500 pass through the turnstiles.

Now, with no television and not much radio cricket there was tremendous dependence upon newspapers for our knowledge of cricket. Players acquired a mystique which a modern youngster will be quite incapable of understanding. It was entirely possible to fail completely to recognise a famous player in his off-the-field dress, no matter how intently we studied newspaper photographs. Cigarette cards were a better bet; most of the leading tobacco companies issued small cards in every packet which covered a multitude of subjects, and while we might not have known much in the 1930s about the damage to health caused by smoking, those companies certainly added to the store of human knowledge of just about everything from wild flowers to Test cricketers. John Player issued a set of these in 1938 and included the Australian tour party, so we knew a certain amount about some of the lesser mortals in the side. *Everyone* knew everything about Bradman, of course, and after Trent Bridge we knew a great deal about Stan McCabe, too. 'The best Test innings I have ever seen,' was the description of R. E. S. Wyatt, a former England captain.

Always the legends grew best by word of mouth, certainly amongst young schoolboys. Somebody's uncle knew a man whose brother-in-law had emigrated to Australia and sent back blood-curdling stories of the fate in store for English batsmen when Ernie McCormick reached England. The bodyline tour of 1932–3 was not so far in the past and echoes of it rang around every Test ground whenever fast bowling was mentioned. We knew that the Aussies thirsted for revenge, and in 1938 McCormick was the man who was going to extract it. So, knowing nothing of featherbed wickets, we felt a sense of anti-climax when the bogeyman returned figures of one for 108 at Trent Bridge. Four for 104 seemed a little more threatening at Lord's (and certainly he *looked* fast on those flickering, speeded-up, black and white newsreels in the cinema) and from time to time he cut loose around the counties. But Headingley favoured the spinners and it was the great O'Reilly, with eccentric assistance from Fleetwood-Smith, who did the damage there. So it would have to be at The Oval that McCormick let loose his thunderbolts. Anti-climax again. He was injured and did not play at all.

It is still impossible to look at the card for that game on 20, 22, 23 and 24 August 1938 without a sense of wonderment (did it all really happen in just four days?) and yet, if you take out Hutton's miraculous innings it has to add up to anti-climax itself. Without McCormick, Australia were forced to open their attack with the medium pace of Waite and the very-occasional-indeed bowling of McCabe. Bradman and Fingleton were unable to bat in either innings because of injury, Bradman's a flaked fracture of the ankle after he had pressed himself into service as Australia's seventh bowler – someone had to relieve the exhausted Fleetwood-Smith (87 overs), O'Reilly (85) and Waite (72), while even the makeshift McCabe and the even more makeshift Barnes bowled 39 apiece.

Yet Hutton's 364 has to be seen in context. Men have batted longer (Hanif Mohammad in a Pakistani first-class match in 1958-9) and scored more runs in a Test innings (Gary Sobers *v.* Pakistan at Kingston in 1957-8), but in 1938 no one had visualised anything like that. Hammond's 336 not out in 1933 had been made in New Zealand and in 1938 terms it did not rank anywhere near Bradman's 334 against England at Headingley eight years earlier. That was *the* landmark in Test cricket. And Bradman was seen as very much a man apart, a run-making machine who was a phenomenon. No Englishman, however patriotic, not even a Yorkshireman, thought anyone on this side of the world capable of making such scores in a Test against Australia. Hutton went out with Bill Edrich as his partner at 11.30 on the morning of Saturday, 20 August. At 29, Edrich was lbw to O'Reilly for 12 and Maurice Leyland (in what was to be his last Test) joined Hutton. To this day Hutton remembers only one exchange between himself and a batting partner in the whole of his career. He remembers that Leyland said to him, 'Keep it up, young Leonard.'

They both kept it up, the two Yorkshiremen. They scored at 60 runs an hour with Bradman racking his brains for a way to take a wicket and Hutton beginning to worry because the finger (broken a month earlier) was beginning to swell and become painful. At close of play England were 347 for one wicket and Hutton generously acknowledges that Leyland had taken the bulk of the strike from O'Reilly, at that time probably the most dangerous bowler in the world with his mixture of quickish, fizzing spinners. Hutton spent Sunday lying on the beach at Bognor Regis and returned to a massive stack of congratulatory letters and telegrams for himself and his partner.

At ten minutes past one on Monday, the total at 411, Leyland was run out as the pair tried to take a second run because of a misfield by Hassett at long off. Is it perhaps to that incident that we owe the modern maxim: never run for a misfield? Hammond, the captain, replaced Leyland and at a quarter to four was lbw to Fleetwood-Smith for 59 – 546 for three. Hammond had impressed upon his whole side that this was a *timeless* Test and that they should play accordingly, so Hutton refocused his concentration, especially when O'Reilly was bowling: 'I place him as the most interesting bowler I ever faced. Every ball he sent down needed watching; he changed his pace with genius and he always attacked. He put everything into every ball that he had it in him to give.' (Small wonder, then, that as a cricket journalist in the post-war years O'Reilly has had little time for some of Australia's bowlers, particularly in the seventies and eighties.)

Astonishingly, the innings as a whole now faltered. Paynter came and went for a duck, Compton for one – 555 for five – but now came Joe Hardstaff, as handsome a stroke-player as he was a man. Hutton, in the meantime, had overtaken R. E. Foster's 287 against Australia and the country had virtually stopped work as everyone sought information on what was happening at The Oval. At close of play on the second day of his greatest Test, Hutton was 300 not out. It was during that Monday evening that other things began to creep into his mind. He had talked to Bradman during the season about the time, eight years earlier, he had watched that masterly batsmanship at Headingley and had dreamed of somehow, some time, playing at that level of cricket. He would have been something less than human if he had not, now, begun to think of the 334 target the great man had set. Only another 35 needed to break that record . . . He hardly slept that night. His legs ached and he felt stiff in every limb. In that dim, never-never land somewhere between sleeping and waking he saw himself hitting a gentle full toss straight down mid-off's throat. And then he saw a scoreboard showing that he had made 335 so that, like Shakespeare's Caliban 'when I waked, I cried to dream again'.

With defensive field-placings Hutton scored 10 in the first half-hour, another 10 in the second. At 328, Bradman positioned himself at silly-mid-off, gazing straight at him from three yards. O'Reilly bowled with immaculate line and length as he had done throughout the previous two days, but Hutton's concentration was now absolute. He reasoned that by the very nature of his bowling, Fleetwood-Smith (now operating from the Vauxhall end) would be bound to deliver a loose one sooner or later. So he waited and waited, inching his way to 331. At a quarter to one the left-armer dropped one short; Hutton cut, giving it all he had got in those tiring and aching wrists, and stepped into the pages of history. Not merely The Oval, but the whole of Britain was in uproar. Bradman was the first to congratulate Leonard and I seem to conjure up from childhood memories the picture of an exhausted Bill O'Reilly, somewhere near the boundary, falling on to his back for a brief rest. Lunch came and went and at half-past two Hutton wearily lofted a ball from O'Reilly to Lindsay Hassett at cover point. He had been batting for thirteen hours, twenty minutes, and had scored 364 runs (35 boundaries). Cricket would never be the same again, and neither would life for young Leonard Hutton from Pudsey. One of the 1,500 telegrams which were delivered to The Oval expressed the hope that he would do the same in the second innings. It came, of course, from a fellow Yorkshireman. Hutton's departure meant that Arthur Wood now had to start his first Test innings and, with a glance at a scoreboard now reading 770 for six wickets, he unsmilingly announced that he was just the man for a crisis.

That evening Pudsey Parish Church bells rang out a peal of 364 chimes and the mayor, an old friend of the Hutton family, sent Leonard a telegram which read: 'Twenty-six thousand Pudsey people are filled with pride at your magnificent achievement. The joybells are ringing.' A thirteen-year-old schoolboy wept at the pure magic of it all; nearly fifty years later I cannot think of the occasion without getting a huge lump in my throat.

What could a young player look forward to after that? There has to be a great temptation to feel that Leonard Hutton's career had perhaps 'peaked' too early and all that followed was bound to seem of lesser significance, but that, of course, would be totally wrong. It is more logical to speculate on what might have been achieved if the Second World War had not taken away six years of his sporting life, as it did with so many great players of all games.

Hutton had already savoured the pleasures of an overseas tour –

with Yorkshire to the West Indies in the winter of 1935–6 – and three years later he became a fully fledged MCC tourist in South Africa. Both excursions whetted his appetite for seeing more of the world; there is no doubt that young Hutton got the taste on those two tours. But by the time the 1939 domestic season dawned, the storm-clouds were gathering over Europe. Hitler was now very much more than a funny little chap with an odd moustache; he was a threat to the whole world and especially to a Britain where, with the economy at last beginning to make a sluggish progress after the First World War and the General Strike, we basked in a sunny complacency – but only if we pretended that Hitler's Germany would go away. Miss Dorothy Dennis had, in the close season, become Mrs Leonard Hutton and life looked pretty good to the young couple. It looked even better when, in the Whitsuntide Roses match, Yorkshire made their highest total against Lancashire for fifty-two years – 528 for eight declared – to win by an innings and 43 runs. But even the majestic prose of Neville Cardus was beginning to take on the idiom of European affairs as he described the event: 'the policy of appeasement, as I feared, had no effect on Yorkshire', 'a Siegfried Line was built by Sutcliffe and Mitchell'. By the time Yorkshire completed the double at Headingley, thanks largely to a not-out 105 by Hutton, Mr Chamberlain's declaration of war on Germany was but twenty-six days away. The match was finished in a thunderstorm, with the sky as black as night. Perhaps sensing that the lights were going out on cricket all over the world, the players stayed on the field and the spectators stayed in their seats. They grabbed mackintoshes and put up umbrellas; those without either sought shelter under copies of newspapers, one of them perhaps the *Yorkshire Evening Post* in which John Bapty described the Hutton hundred as one 'which would never be forgotten by those fortunate enough to see it'. Pools on the pitch turned to lakes as the game finished. It was as though everyone sensed that this was the end of an era.

The Germans were already bombing Warsaw when Yorkshire beat Sussex at Hove; the Scarborough Festival had been cancelled; the team came home in a hired charabanc to avoid possible disruption of rail traffic, driving through towns where evacuee children were already congregating and lights were blacked out. Very soon Len Hutton, hero of The Oval, hero of every Yorkshire schoolboy, was Sgt Hutton, L., of the Army Physical Training Corps. On the final day of his passing-out test from a Commando course he fell with his full weight on the left forearm, breaking the radius and dislocating the base of the ulna. It was a devastating injury for any professional sportsman. For one who, the world hoped, had still a great deal of distinguished cricket to play, it was horrifying. Month after month Leonard lay in hospital – in York, in Wakefield, in Leeds. When manipulation did not improve the condition of his arm, an operation was carried out. Three inches of bone was taken from his right leg and grafted into his left arm; that didn't work. The bone-graft was discarded and another carried out using bone from his *left* leg. While he waited for the results of this operation the Army decided that Sgt Hutton was no further use to them and he was given a medical discharge. Finally, after something like eighteen months of hospitals and operations, he looked at the arm which had been in plaster three times: it was shrivelled to the size of a boy's. Now it is especially important to view this period of Hutton's life not in the context of a war which was going on all over the world outside his hospital walls, but as the prelude to the cricketing life which was to follow. It was in that crook of that pathetically wasted arm that he held his first son, Richard, who was also to play for Yorkshire and England.

Leonard was able to get *some* cricket during the war as the Bradford League carried on a competition which was a tremendous morale-booster not only to players but to the sport-starved public who watched in their thousands. In his first game for Pudsey St Lawrence, away to Bankfoot, he got a duck! In the late summer of 1945, the war over in Europe if not yet in the Far East, England played a series of 'Victory' Tests against Australia, represented largely by servicemen, at Lord's (twice), Old Trafford and Bramall Lane, Sheffield. Hutton, with his left arm shorter and frailer than his right, averaged 42 in nine innings and had his first glimpse of K. R. Miller. A new era was dawning.

It was not the Yorkshire he had known which resumed County Championship cricket in 1946. Hedley Verity had been lost on the beaches of Sicily, a noble figure in every way, and others had suffered in one way or another from the rigours of five and a half years of war. Despite his years in a prisoner-of-war camp, Bill Bowes still contrived seventh place in the national bowling averages, but plainly his seasons were now going to be numbered. Maurice Leyland, Wilf Barber, Arthur Wood and Cyril Turner announced their retirement and Arthur Booth, who had finally claimed a regular place in the Yorkshire side at the age of forty-three, led the first-class averages with his left-arm slow bowling before being forced out of the game by rheumatism one year later.

Hutton went on the tour to Australia in 1946–7 with a side which was not really good enough and returned prematurely because of illness. There was a comfortable togetherness between England and Australia, no doubt because it was so soon after a war which had brought the people of both countries so close to each other, and he came back with happy memories of Australia despite the disappointments of a series in which three Tests were lost and the other two drawn. He made friends through his batting and on the golf course, having developed a passion for the game in his early days with Yorkshire. At the end of the 1947 season he prepared for a rest that he felt he needed and which the county most certainly wanted him to have. But by February of that winter he was called upon to answer an SOS to fly out to the West Indies. Following a slightly arrogant (but possibly justified) tradition of sending out virtually a 'B' side to the Windies, MCC found themselves stricken by injury and in danger of being outplayed. Leonard, with no practice for six months beyond a quick knock in the Headingley indoor shed, joined them for the last two Tests, too late to do anything beyond personally scoring 171 runs, but both matches were lost. He never forgot that . . .

In 1948 Leonard scored 1,565 runs for Yorkshire with an average of 92.05, but weightier matters concerned the visit of the greatest touring side I have ever seen. The West Indies of 1967, 1980 and 1984 became ever more formidable, but cricket had taken on a different complexion by this time. A non-stop barrage of intimidatory fast bowling, six hours a day, bore little relation to a game some of us (in our quaint, old-fashioned way) had grown to love as an exhibition of grace and charm and athleticism as well as a contest of finely honed skills.

Don Bradman, on his last tour of England, brought not one but two bogeymen to open his attack – Ray Lindwall, the epitome of lithe, panther-like balance and speed, and Keith Miller, the playboy of cricket endowed with so many gifts. He was just as likely to bowl

a lightning delivery from five yards as from twenty-five; he was
entirely likely to send down a leg-break out of the back of his hand
with the shine still brilliant on the new ball. As a batsman, he had
all the strokes in the book to be played, at his whim, with delicacy
and timing or with clubbed belligerence. He was an entertainer of
the highest quality and had an off-the-field personality to match his
cricket. To back up his own batting, Bradman had the masterly
talents of Sid Barnes, Bill Brown, Lindsay Hassett, Arthur Morris,
Sam Loxton and a young man who stroked the ball around with the
incomparable elegance of the classic left-hander, Neil Harvey, seen
scoring a century in his first Test match in the never-to-be-forgotten
game in late July at Headingley. As support for Lindwall and Miller,
Bradman could call upon the swerve and bounce of Bill Johnston,
the nagging line and length of Ernie Toshack, and the off-spin of
Ian Johnson. It was a marvellous side completed by the dazzling
wicket-keeping of Don Tallon, whose catch to dismiss Hutton at
The Oval is still to my mind the greatest catch behind the stumps I
have ever seen in a Test.

England, steadily rebuilding, had Hutton and Washbrook followed by Compton and Edrich, who, during the previous summer,
had forged a partnership which will linger for ever in thousands of
memories. They were backed up, in one Test or another, by Jack
Crapp of Gloucs, Tom Dollery of Warwickshire, Alan Watkins of
Glamorgan and the spritely young wicket-keeper from Kent, Godfrey Evans. The bowling, if not quite so incisive on paper, had
considerable variety, with Alec Bedser, Dick Pollard, Jim Laker,
Doug Wright, Ken Cranston, Eric Hollies, Jack Young and (once)
Alec Coxon of Yorkshire being called up by the Selectors during
that series. The summer was all about a truly marvellous Australian
side which won four and drew one of the five Tests, but this book is
not about Australia so let us record that in his first three innings of
the series the immortal Bradman departed, 'caught Hutton bowled
Bedser' on each occasion, while the Aussies reserved the final
humiliation for The Oval, where they themselves had suffered so
grievously ten years earlier. I remember going into a London pub
for a pie and a pint at lunchtime on the first day of the game with
an early edition of the *Star*. The front page lead snarled at me:
'Edrich, Dewes and Compton go for 17.'

That spelled disaster for England only in relative terms; our Len was still there. With a muttered prayer for him to stay there I cancelled my more pressing arrangements for that day and hurried to The Oval, where I was able to talk my way through the locked gates with the help of a press card and a pack of lies in time to see the end of the innings: England all out 52. The last man to go was Leonard Hutton of Pudsey – brilliantly, superbly, magnificently caught by Tallon flying to his left – for 30 of that total. Later in the day I saw The Don walk slowly to the wicket through an avenue of applauding England players and a sentimentally cheering crowd to be out second ball to Eric Hollies. At the age of twenty-three, not for the first time and not for the last, I watched cricket through a blur of tears. It was impossible for me to stay to see Hutton make the top score of 64 in the second innings as well, but if in my whole life it had been possible to see only one day's cricket, that would have been enough! Lindwall six for 20 . . . Hutton . . . Bradman.

Leonard went back to South Africa the following winter, scoring two more centuries and an aggregate of 577 runs (63.3), and started 1949 by taking 101 off a New Zealand attack headed by Jack Cowie. In the third Test of the series he was joined by a fellow-Yorkshire-man, born just across the Aire Valley from Fulneck eighteen years and 149 days earlier – Brian Close, who was out for a duck in his first Test innings. In 1950, as England grappled with the complexity of the West Indian spin twins, Ramadhin and Valentine, Hutton carried his bat for 202 (out of 344) at The Oval. In the winter of 1950–1 he gave one of the most masterly displays of bad-wicket batting ever seen to make 62 not out in a total of 122 on a sticky dog at the Brisbane 'Gabba. At Adelaide, on the same tour, he again carried his bat through a complete Test innings, making 156 not out in a score of 272, but England lost four Tests out of five and Hutton made a little promise to himself. In 1951 he went into the record books once again – this time an unsolicited entry – when he was given out, obstructing the field, for preventing Russell Endean from completing a catch from a top edge which was, in fact, in danger of dropping on to the stumps. In 1952 he was made England's first-ever professional captain, hit two centuries and averaged 79 in leading his country to three big wins and a rain-ruined draw. In his first Test as captain he took under his wing a tempestuous young fast bowler named Freddie Trueman and saw an Indian scoreboard which read, '0 for four wickets'.

Greater triumphs lay ahead. After four drawn Tests against Australia in 1953, Hutton led England to victory in the final game, inevitably, I suppose, at The Oval and so England at last regained the Ashes after they had been in Australia's possession for a record period of a few days under nineteen years. It was a magnificent rubber for Alec Bedser, who took thirty-nine wickets; Hutton averaged well over 50 with the bat. The following winter he took a side to the West Indies, where excitement was at a fever pitch. It was not an easy tour in any way because, apart from the fervour of the crowds who at last were beginning to see their players as a real force in world cricket, he had to open the innings without a recognised partner, and in the first two Tests England were comprehensively beaten. Handling the side did not come easily to him, for in many ways Leonard was an austere and at times a remote captain. Blood might be thicker than water but he did not find the fiery young Trueman easy to handle. Hutton adopted methods which might have been seen as necessarily ruthless in dealing with what he saw as the excesses of the fast bowler who was dropped for the Second Test which began on his twenty-second birthday. From that tour, and some events which followed, Trueman brought back a lasting bitterness against his captain, yet – paradoxically in just about anyone except a Yorkshireman – has always cherished an admiration for Hutton the batsman which borders on the idolatrous. To discuss Hutton's handling of him on that tour and to realise the depths of Fred's resentment, then in the next minute to hear F.S.T.'s boundless regard for 'the greatest batsman I have ever seen' is a remarkable experience. After England had won the Third Test (with the not inconsiderable help of 169 from the skipper) and the Fourth had been drawn they squared the rubber in Jamaica, where Hutton made the first double century by an England captain in an overseas Test, and Johnny Wardle, at no. 8, hit 66 – 271 by a brace of Yorkies in a total of 414. But let us not forget that great all-rounder Trevor Bailey, nominally an amateur player but with the resolution of the finest-tempered professional steel, who took seven for 34 in the West Indies innings and then went out to open the batting with Hutton.

What was there left for Hutton to accomplish? Nothing less than to go to Australia and retain the Ashes, a feat which he accomplished in an uncompromisingly professional manner.

Trueman was omitted from the touring party, an omission which is seared on Fred's soul, but Hutton (recognising the success of Lindwall and Miller, backed up by Bill Johnston) had Frank Tyson, who in his prime moments was the fastest bowler in the world, to partner Brian Statham. And for back-up there was Bailey, Bedser (who, in fact, played in only one of the five Tests) and the marvellous Bob Appleyard who had been 'discovered' by Yorkshire when he was a mature twenty-six years old. The slow left-arm bowling of Wardle was used very sparingly indeed until the final, rain-affected Test, and by that time the series was won. Hutton had decided that on quick, bouncy Australian wickets pace would be his most potent weapon, and he justified the policy in spite of a horrifying first match in which he put Australia in to bat in Brisbane and saw them declare at 601 for eight; the match was lost by an innings and 154. No spinner at all figured in that England side, and though Hutton compromised by including Wardle for the remaining four he bowled no more than thirty-four overs in all at Sydney, Melbourne and Adelaide. It was by no means a bodyline revival but Tyson's bowling in Melbourne in particular has always been regarded by the members of his side as the fastest they have ever seen. It was only twenty-two years since Jardine had caused the whole of Australia to rise in fury, and the Aussies have good memories. Hutton, who was held in the highest regard in that country as a batsman, won no laurels as a Test captain. But he was not there to court popularity. As he saw it his job was to retain the Ashes against a very good side playing in conditions they knew well; he chose the weapons he regarded as his most potent and used them to the fullest extent. England won the Second, Third and Fourth Tests, their first Ashes victory there since the bodyline tour. Leonard went on to New Zealand to superintend the dismissal of the opposition in Auckland for 26 – the lowest total in Test history – and to make the top score of 53 in what was to be his last innings for his country.

Hutton was chosen as captain for the series in 1955 against South Africa but, plagued by back trouble which was to haunt him for the rest of his life, he withdrew before the Tests began and then, right at the very top, he retired from first-class cricket altogether. That was absolutely right; in reflecting that it would have broken my heart to see Leonard being dismissed by bowlers of modest ability I feel pretty sure that that is a general Yorkshire view.

The war gave him less than fifteen full seasons in first-class cricket, yet he scored 40,140 runs, held 400 catches and (let us not forget that he always rather fancied himself as a leg-break bowler) he took 173 wickets. In seventy-nine Tests he had 6,971 runs at an average of 56.67 and held 57 catches. Outstandingly his best season with the bat was 1949, when he totalled, 3,429 runs. Nine times he topped 2,000 runs in a season and he hit 11 double-centuries. As England's captain he won a series against Australia at home and away, and in the West Indies his side achieved a two-all drawn rubber. In 1956 his services to cricket were recognised by the conferring of a knighthood. The frail youngster from Pudsey had come a long way.

He started his batting life with a reputation for dourness, and to some extent this was re-bestowed when, after the war, he had to adjust his technique after the operations on his left arm. But most certainly it is not as a dour batsman that I remember him, and I am sure that is true of most Yorkshire folk. We have all seen him take opposing attacks completely to pieces; indeed, an innings at Trent Bridge in 1950 springs immediately to mind, and that is merely a random thought prompted by writing about his batting. The sight of the ball racing through the covers, all along the grass, remains most admirers' lasting memory of Leonard Hutton as a batsman – the stroke executed with perfect timing which imparted effortless grace. As a captain of his country he was tough, shrewd and entirely ruthless. In 1954–5 he went one better than Jardine in putting a battery of fast bowlers to the best possible effect; he provided us with the first noticeably recorded instance of slowing down the over rate. It has to be remembered that Hutton was brought up in an era when Australia were very much the ancient enemy and other Tests were a reasonably interesting way of whiling away the years between Australian series. To Hutton, Australia *had* to be beaten. If he could get the right forces to wage the right sort of campaign then he knew it could be done. From his first moment as a little boy he had observed other players closely, seeking always to improve his game. In his maturity the knowledge was used as an offensive weapon, and it is one which Close and Illingworth in particular used to great advantage when they in turn became county and England captains. Know the enemy. If Hutton had been made captain of Yorkshire I have little doubt that Surrey would not have enjoyed their remarkable success in the county championship through the 1950s, but Yorkshire were not ready to take the revolutionary step which England had already taken. It is ironical that amidst our age-old clamour about the 'old school tie' complex at Lord's continually militating against Yorkshiremen, the sages of St John's Wood were light-years ahead of the White Rose Committee in their thinking. Right up to 1959 Yorkshire remained resolutely feudal in its approach to that part of its policy-making.

Hutton succeeded as a captain because, as Richie Benaud has said, he was a winner. He thought like a winner; he approached every innings, no matter how difficult the conditions or adverse the circumstances, like a winner; he operated like a winner because he was a winner. Yet somehow this harsh and uncompromising captain is revered in Yorkshire simply as a batsman. When two or three are gathered together – most of us greybeards by this time – it is not of the man who slew the Australians as a captain that we think. It is of the young man who put them to the sword at The Oval in 1938. It is a strange, sentimental attachment to a man who was anything but sentimental in *his* approach to cricket. In a county which regards itself as special, Len Hutton was very, *very* special.

One of the most impossible tasks in cricket is to follow a famous father and nowhere is it more difficult than in Yorkshire where we absolutely delight in the unfavourable comparison, the calculated put-down. Once, in a pub right outside Pudsey Town Hall (and you can't get much more Yorkshire than that) I listened in squirming embarrassment as the landlord told Richard Hutton: 'Tha might be all reight, lad, but tha'll never be as good as thi faither.' In that curious way that we have, the man would feel that in knocking the son he was paying an extra compliment to the father; there would be no thought that anyone could be offended by the gratuitously offered opinion. Richard, at an early cricketing age, learned to expect the approach and to understand it. He gave himself an even more difficult target by setting out to be a top-class all-rounder and achieved it at Test level.

Additionally, he had to cope with the disadvantage of joining the Yorkshire side in 1962 with a background of public school and university cricket. It was not the background of *many* players who joined the side and he was the first to join in the new age when there were no amateurs and professionals – just 'players', all of whom qualified for payment. His first meeting with Geoffrey Boycott, when both were still uncapped, brought a sardonic comment about the quality of cricket he (Hutton) had been used to playing up to that point – and that was one relationship which was doomed from the start. Richard cultivated what seemed to be a rather remote sort of personality within the Yorkshire side. It was rooted in humour, and most people understood that. Brian Sellers, El Supremo of Yorkshire cricket at the time, probably didn't. When Richard went into the First XI for the first time at Old Trafford the chairman told the captain, Vic Wilson: 'Keep an eye on him. He's so dreamy that if you put him on the boundary he's liable to wander off into the crowd.' Hutton loved to encourage the unwary to take this view of him. Once, during a game at Clacton-on-Sea, a group of us who usually spent our off-duty moments together, were taken to Butlin's Holiday Camp by Frank Clough, a redcoat-turned-newspaperman, and invited to taste the delights of Wednesday night in the Crazy Horse Saloon. We found a large room of pseudo-Western décor packed with a heaving mass of humanity with just one area of space. In it, half a dozen Glaswegians were hard at work knocking seven bells out of each other with a variety of weapons. Hutton, towering four or five inches above the next-tallest in our group, surveyed the scene for a moment and then, with an exaggerated drawl, inquired: 'I say, Clough. You don't mean to tell me people come to places like this to *enjoy* themselves?' It was the sort of remark which, if it had been offered in the context of a comedy film, would have caused an immediate hush to fall over the whole company before it turned its collective wrath upon us. In real life, mercifully, it went unheard in the general bedlam of that night in the Crazy Horse Saloon.

Hutton had (and has) a splendid wit, the driest possible sense of humour and a superficially relaxed approach to life which, in fact, cloaked a very positive attitude on the cricket field. None of these were characteristics which were readily understood by Geoffrey Boycott, and throughout their twelve years together in the same Yorkshire side they rarely if ever reached any point of mutual agreement. Richard scored just under 5,000 runs for the county and took 468 wickets at 21.91. He was also a good slip catcher and he played in five Tests for England against India and Pakistan. Was his career overshadowed by that of his famous father? I think not. Richard achieved enough, certainly, to make his mark in his own right and to distract attention from the enormous problems he faced as the son of Sir Leonard Hutton. But this distraction does not alter the fact that they did exist.

In a very moving Foreword to Sir Leonard's book *Fifty Years in Cricket* (Stanley Paul and Co., 1984) Richard writes:

> During my childhood I discovered most about my father through the back page of the daily newspaper; quietly leaving my bed in the early morning I waited patiently by the letter-box for its arrival. I learned to read by picking out my father's name and his score from the scoresheet. Often they were in the headlines, which made it easier. Eventually I moved on to the match reports and thence to taking cricket books to my bed. By then, I was devouring every word written about my father; he had become greater than God. To be sure of seeing him when I wanted to I had to go to the cricket ground. For hours I would sit enthralled as I compiled his score in my own scorebook, anguishing over every ball in the fear that the apparent frailty of his play (which I failed to recognise as artistry) would let him down. How little I knew and I wonder if he had any idea of the torture I suffered.
>
> At the age of ten I disgraced myself, my mother and my school in public on that awful day at Headingley when Lindwall bowled him out second ball. It was made worse by the fact that, as far as my young eye could judge, there was an easy single off the first ball. Before too long, however, I was bathing in the reflected glory of the Ashes and then the successful defence in Australia. After his retirement there seemed to be little left to follow. Instead, the nature of his influence shifted and my adolescence met the hand of paternal discipline as if the returning hero felt the need to make up for lost time.
>
> To put the varied careers of my father and myself into perspective, I suppose I could say my bad days were as numerous as his good days and my good ones about as infrequent as his bad.

That is unnecessarily modest. The question mark which hangs
over him as far as I am concerned is: would he have been the right
choice to take over as captain of Yorkshire when Brian Close was
dismissed in 1970? As events turned out, he certainly could not
have brought about a more melancholy state of affairs than the
regime of Boycott produced. He was certainly worth his place in the
team simply as a player; he got on well with other members of the
side, and yet his background and his own personality equipped him
to stand, at times when it was necessary, aloof from his personal
friendships within the team and to take a long, objective view at the
progress of a game. Above all in his favour was his attitude to
captaincy: 'An essential part is the ability to make *other* people play
to the best of their ability and beyond it. I think all the successful
captains of sides which have not been outstanding sides have had
that ability.'

It is very much worth considering that another Hutton might well
have played a major part in changing the course of Yorkshire cricket
history. That Richard achieved as much as he did is in itself a
remarkable tribute to his character. In turn it placed a totally
intolerable burden upon his younger brother, John, who was a
notable fast bowler from his schooldays onwards. Coping with the
reputation of a world-famous father was load enough; having a
distinguished cricketing brother as well just had to be too much. He
turned away from first-class cricket and who can blame him?

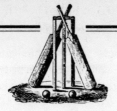

9
Verity and Bowes

We shall never know just how great Hedley Verity would have become if it had not been for the war. He was given to us for just ten first-class seasons in which he wrought miracles of slow left-arm bowling. He died on the last day of July 1943, in a German prison hospital in Italy from wounds received nearly a fortnight previously while leading B Company of the First Battalion, the Green Howards, in an attack on the Catania Plain, in Sicily. He was a gallant soldier, a great gentleman and probably the most successful bowler of his type the game has ever seen.

Throughout the history of cricket we have come to speak of many pairs of bowlers in the same breath: Lindwall and Miller, Laker and Lock, Ramadhin and Valentine, Trueman and Statham, Lillee and Thomson, Hall and Griffith. But all these pairings have been of a similar type – either quickies or spinners. The first pair ever to come to my schoolboy notice were quite, quite different: Verity and Bowes – slow left arm and fast-medium right arm. To this day I still think of them operating together because they were, together, the most formidable force in the game in their hey-day, which covered the most impressionable years of my cricket-watching. Of course, we all at some time in our lives think we have discovered something entirely original and I nurtured the thought for years that I alone thought of Verity and Bowes as one and indivisible as an attacking combination. So it was something of a shock to find that Bill himself thought about the two of them in much the same way, and certainly their bowling figures – individually and in tandem – bear this out.

I knew that they were great friends; that much I had learned from many conversations with Bill, who I came to know well after the war, and I knew, too, how deeply distressed Bill was by Hedley's death *in* the war. At the same time I learned much from his friend about the tall, stately figure I had seen demolish so many sides at Headingley and Park Avenue, and whose autograph I had at last added to my collection after he had taken seven Leicestershire wickets for 18 at Bradford in 1938. I treasured it like a priceless jewel, showing it to school chums but refusing to allow it out of my hands lest in some way it was defiled.

It was in 1932 that the name first meant anything to me. I was seven years old and I remember quite clearly the excitement in my home when my father opened his copy of the *Leeds Mercury* (we were not yet into the *Daily Herald*) and, before I had time to ask to see the latest chapter in the life of Alfie Apple and Bertie Banana (with which I liked to start my day), there came a sharp intake of breath. 'Good Lord – Verity, ten for ten.' There was no television to bring this news to us the previous evening; the morning paper brought our first tidings of events in the outside world. And while there were political crises and international conferences aplenty in 1932 the most important item of news in Yorkshire that day was undoubtedly that Nottinghamshire had been beaten at Headingley and that Verity had taken all ten wickets for only ten runs including a hat-trick – and very nearly two of them. He had, in fact, taken all ten against Warwickshire the previous season but somehow that had escaped notice in my household, or perhaps I just hadn't been there when excitement reigned. But from that Wednesday morning in 1932 when the news reached my home I spent the next three months in a fruitless, futile and distinctly uncomfortable quest for the ability to bowl with the wrong arm.

Verity seemed, somehow, an unlikely professional cricketer to me, though it must be borne in mind that my impressions were formed as a small boy watching him from afar. He was tall and he had a dignity, a stateliness which made me think of my headmaster at school. I could more easily imagine him delivering a stern lecture to an errant pupil (schoolmasters used to do that!) than plotting the downfall of a great batsman. His height, of course, was a great asset to his art (for artistry his bowling undoubtedly was) because it enabled him to get bounce and this, allied to a masterly command of line and length, made him unplayable on wickets which responded to his spin. The records show that in those ten brief seasons he took 1,558 wickets for Yorkshire at 13.71. He took all ten in an innings twice, nine wickets seven times, eight thirteen times and seven thirty-four times. In forty Tests he took 144 wickets, 30 catches and averaged nearly 21 with the bat, too. In every full season he played he took 100 wickets or more and he rates thirty-three entries in the Yorkshire records under 'exceptional bits of bowling'.

Hedley Verity was born close to the Headingley ground where later he was to achieve cricketing immortality, and he was only five when the family home was moved to Rawdon, a few miles up the hill towards the watershed between the valleys of Aire and Wharfe. Later it was to become Brian Close territory and not far away was the birthplace of Bryan Stott, who opened the batting for Yorkshire in the late fifties and sixties. In fact both were taught in their early schooldays by Hedley Verity's sister. Hedley himself saw his first county match when he was eight, and after playing in school cricket he joined Rawdon's Second XI, as Close was to do around thirty years later; he was still in his mid-teens when he announced to his parents that his one ambition was to play professional cricket for Yorkshire. Mercifully for the game and for the county his parents were not unsympathetic, though naturally cautious, and they made sure the boy's formal education was not neglected. They in turn were fortunate in that Hedley, despite a consuming desire to play cricket and a preoccupation wtih physical fitness, was a compulsive learner with an encyclopaedia as one of his prize possessions.

At sixteen he was playing for Rawdon's first team, and this was no mean feat because in this pre-television age, when making one's own entertainment was very much a necessity, cricketers at league level tended to play to ripe old ages, and breaking into the ranks was far from easy for youngsters. The colourful Bobby Peel was one of his mentors at the Headingley nets when, in company with literally scores of promising youngsters, he was called up for trials. He was a tall boy and there was an air of puzzlement in many circles that he was not trying to develop as a fast bowler, but Hedley preferred to bowl at a pace just below medium and to use his head. From his earliest days he had *thought* about his bowling and he was at this time a most accomplished batsman as well. He moved from Rawdon to Horsforth Hall Park (both clubs these days in the Airedale and Wharfedale League), where he spent three years, and

it was primarily as a batsman that he found himself selected for a
number of Yorkshire Colts matches. But breaking through to a first-
team place, much less being offered a professional contract, was
difficult in the extreme and ironically Verity had to cross the border
into Lancashire to find his first paid post in the game.

For every place in the Yorkshire side there were a dozen or more
players of great talent waiting to be considered, and while Verity
had not abandoned his ambition of playing for the county he had
nevertheless stated his intention of making his career in cricket and
it was necessary to begin to make some money as well as extend his
experience. In 1927 he joined Accrington, in the Lancashire League,
as professional, recommended warmly by George Hirst. He was, at
that time, less a spin bowler than a medium-pacer who could swing
the ball both ways and his batting was something more than sound,
yet it was with the ball that he first made his mark in the Lancashire
League. He did not have a good first season, and although Accrington offered him a contract for 1928 he moved instead to Middleton
in the Central Lancashire League, where the clubs are grouped
rather closely around north-west Manchester.

He lodged in the home of John Kay, then a Middleton player
who was later to become cricket correspondent of the *Manchester
Evening News* and subsequently a member of the Lancashire County
Committee. John Kay, and his brother Edwin, have done much for
cricket in Lancashire. They and their parents did much to make
young Verity feel part of the family and his professional engagement
at Middleton was a happy one. It was here that he changed to spin
bowling in preparation for the retirement in Yorkshire of the great
Rhodes. It is an enormous tribute to the Middleton club that his
decision was accepted when they had hired him as a medium-paced
swing bowler-batsman and there must have been some mixed
feelings at Old Trafford during the next decade when Verity was
creating all kinds of havoc in the Roses matches. But in 1928 and
1929 there was still no call from his native county and Verity in fact
had a trial for Warwickshire. Fortunately for Yorkshire, he was
asked to bowl on a bone-hard, plumb wicket at Edgbaston and
consequently did not make much impression on the Committee.
They, too, were to learn their mistake in a very short time. (In fact,
one way and another, Warwickshire missed out badly with a number

of Yorkshiremen.) In 1930 he was offered a better contract by another Lancashire League club (East Lancs), agonised over it for a couple of weeks and finally turned it down. Within weeks the call finally came from Yorkshire and in twelve games he took 64 wickets at 12.42. Hedley Verity had arrived.

He was by now twenty-five, an age when a slow left-arm bowler has yet to see his best years, but at the same time a fairly venerable age to be starting a first-class career. Always a serious and studious youngster, he had now spent nearly ten years learning as much as he could about the game while still acknowledging that there was much more to assimilate. Now, he felt, was his chance to do so. His start was inauspicious – three for 96 in a friendly against Sussex at Huddersfield, but, much more to the point, he had had forty-six overs in which to start learning about the first-class game. And no matter how gifted a player, the jump from league cricket to county matches is an enormous one. There will always be men whose immense natural talent will project them into the county side and they will succeed, but for many more it is a long, hard apprenticeship. Which was it to be for Hedley Verity?

Bill Bowes, a little further along this road than the man with whom he was to have such a close and warm friendship, was at that time just a little more concerned with his own future as *he* competed with other candidates for the right to open Yorkshire's attack, men like Frank Dennis and Charlie Hall. He was just about in the depths of despair when he was awarded his county cap. Verity rejoined the party touring the west in time for the heavens to open, and rain seemed to continue for weeks, but in the intervals between the showers he found a rain-affected wicket to his liking in Glamorgan and took nine wickets for 60 runs – and so far few people outside Rawdon, Horsforth, Accrington and Middleton had heard of him! Verity followed this with five for 18 (Gloucs), five for 32 (Derbyshire), seven for 26 and six for 57 (Hampshire). The rain which provided soft wickets to dismay Bill Bowes – and give Yorkshire six successive drawn games – was a godsend to the new spinner. There was now no doubt who was to be the latest in line of descent from Edmund Peate, Bobby Peel, Wilfred Rhodes and Roy Kilner. He had started in the most spectacular way possible to fight off the challenge of three claimants for Rhodes's throne – Arthur Booth, Horace Fisher and Stan Douglas. He topped both Yorkshire's averages and the first-class list in his first half-season of county cricket. It was a performance which brought a typically monosyllabic accolade from the retiring Rhodes: 'He'll do.' In Yorkshire terms, never was there more lavish praise.

Verity was still uncapped when, in the following season (1931) he took all ten Warwickshire wickets at Headingley. It was his fourteenth first-class match and amidst the plaudits his immediate reaction was to offer half the credit to George Macaulay who at the other end had bowled fourteen very tight overs, never relenting in his search for a wicket, even when his partner had taken the first nine. 'Let him earn it,' grunted the taciturn Mac as he tried with all his might to take the tenth before Verity. Nothing could have been more characteristic of the man. Nor could anything have been more typical of Hedley Verity than his dive at short leg, badly skinning his right arm, in an attempt to take a catch off Macaulay. By mid-season he had represented Players versus the Gentlemen and at the end of July he wore England colours for the first time. He was a spectator for most of the first two days as Herbert Sutcliffe scored 117, Duleepsinhji 109 and Walter Hammond 100 not out, and then, as England beat New Zealand by an innings and 26 runs on a wicket which now favoured the quicker bowlers, he had two for 52 and two for 33. He was a spectator for the whole of his second Test (the third of that series against New Zealand) because at Old Trafford rain prevented any play on the first two days and in the time that remained England batted and scored 224 for three (another century for Sutcliffe). But it was not all glory. Just a week after his ten wickets against Warwicks, Hedley was taken completely to the cleaners at Park Avenue by Frank Woolley on a sticky dog. With the sort of inverted compliment that really could only occur in cricket, Woolley had decided that the tall left armer was a good bowler and so he would take the responsibility of dealing with him. As for the thoughtful Verity, he took away a good deal to ponder and analyse with regard to bowling to a class left-hand batsman. Clearly he had not mastered that particular problem by the first Roses match of the following season, when Eddie Paynter took 152 off the Yorkshire bowling.

His county cap came in June 1931, around a year after his first appearance in the senior side and only after the Committee's elbow had been jogged, so to speak, by the *Leeds Mercury*: 'Are we going to have him bowling for England before he has been granted recognition by his county?' County beat country by a matter of weeks; eighteen years later that was to be reversed in the case of Brian Close. Verity and Bowes, bracketed together in exalted company for perhaps the first time, were both among *Wisden*'s Five Cricketers of the Year in 1931. They celebrated by taking 66 per cent of the wickets claimed by Yorkshire bowlers in 1932, and both were selected to tour Australia the following winter. It was the bodyline series and Verity's role as a bowler was very much a low-key one; as a batsman, however, he averaged 28.5 and he took the wicket of Bradman in what I am pretty sure was their first encounter.

After a 1933 home season in which Hedley claimed another 153 county championship wickets for Yorkshire he went to India with Douglas Jardine's side (Jardine now one of his strongest admirers) and in Madras he had a first-innings haul of seven for 49. In 1934, a magic summer of cricket saw Australia win the First Test by 238 runs at Trent Bridge and England the Second, at Lord's, by an innings and 38 runs. Throughout that enchanted summer we saw great cricketers playing great cricket. At Sydney Cricket Ground, in the winter of 1986–7 I sat in the Brewongle Stand with an Australian supporter of my age group and recalled that year with more than usual nostalgia. Although Australia won that particular Test of January 1987, my new-found friend agreed that the team was beyond all doubt the worst ever to represent Australia. That of 1934 must have been very nearly the best – Bradman at his very peak, Woodfull, McCabe, Chipperfield, Darling, O'Reilly, Grimmett, Wall. At Lord's, in helpful conditions, Verity goaded Bradman into one of his rare desperation shots. He took fifteen wickets in the match for 104 runs, 14 of them on the third day and 6 of those in the last hour. At a strangely sunny Old Trafford the match was drawn after a remarkable first over from Gubby Allen in which he bowled three wides and four no-balls. At Headingley, Bradman followed his 334 of the previous tour with 304 and again the match was drawn. At The Oval he hit 244 and Australia won the match (and the Ashes) by a massive 562 runs.

That was the only full season in which Verity did not take at least 100 championship wickets for Yorkshire, but in all first-class matches he reached three figures, nevertheless. He loved to bowl at

Bradman, despite taking some stick at times because Verity loved a
challenge and The Don presented the greatest challenge of all. Again,
I think of the man as a schoolmaster because he seemed to approach
bowling at the master – and indeed at any top-class player – as a
mathematical problem which had to be solved: present an opportunity
for runs on the on-side and try to make him play against the spin;
move slip a little wider to try to induce the feeling that the ball was
turning a little more than it actually was (or least make the batsman
wonder why he had done it). Verity was always *thinking* with, in the
Yorkshire team of the thirties, the alliance of his captain and a close
cordon of hungry catchers, notably Arthur Mitchell. Even in the eyes
of a schoolboy with only the most elementary knowledge of what was
happening in the middle, he produced hours of cricketing magic. Jim
Kilburn, I think, summed him up magnificently thus:

> In Verity's cricketing philosophy the easy triumph was not
> the most satisfying. To dismiss a modest side on a turning
> pitch was to him no more than the routine of a bank cashier
> completing a single balance. It was professional obligation.
> Failure, or unnecessary delay, would have been professional
> weakness. Verity's idea of cricketing heaven was to bowl
> against Australia – with Bradman, of course – not when
> conditions left batsmen helpless but when one factor offered
> the bowler opportunity. A small, rough patch on the pitch, an
> encouraging breeze, a time element, something first of all to
> be discerned, then exploited, with success or failure always
> delicately balanced, gave Verity his greatest cricketing
> inspiration and joy. He wanted a challenge for his bowling
> mind as well as his fingers. There were times in county
> cricket when he appeared to be deliberately making the game
> harder for himself by insisting on achievement in a
> predetermined manner; when he seemed to spend three overs
> preparing an lbw snare against a batsman who, unharrassed,
> would probably have mishit into the covers anyway.

That says it all exactly. Even to a youngster it was patent that
traps were being laid for the batsman and sometimes it was equally
obvious that the batsman was aware of it. Why is that in pre-war
days there was time to observe these things, incidents and sequences
which gave an extra dimension to the cricket and to our pleasure? Is
it that a plethora of one-day competitions, of overs-restrictions in

the three-day games, have combined to give cricket, once the most leisurely of games, an air of indecent haste? I would have hated to see Hedley Verity playing in one-day cricket as much as he would have hated it himself. But if he had been called upon to play it for Yorkshire and England you may be absolutely sure that he would have worked out the way to play it most efficiently. His art might have been wasted but his science would have embellished the game.

The Yorkshire handbook shows us that he took 199 wickets in 1935, 185 in 1936, 185 in 1937, 137 in 1938 and 189 in 1939. In their ten seasons together, Verity and Bowes together accounted for more than 50 per cent of the wickets taken by Yorkshire in the county championship. What no record book can show is the extent of the mutual respect and the depth of the personal friendship which developed between these two bowlers with totally contrasting styles but one common factor: a conviction that bowling was a cerebral matter and not a mere physical one.

Their last game together was at Hove, in September 1939, a match Yorkshire had to win to take their seventh title in ten years (they were third in two of the other years and sixth in the remaining one). It was a match played under the shadow of war clouds; the Scarborough Festival had been cancelled and newspaper headlines were about Germany, not Yorkshire. Verity, even more thoughtful than usual, polished off the second Sussex innings by taking seven wickets for 9 runs in eight overs and as he left the ground he mused, 'I wonder if I shall ever play here again.' Travelling north together for the last time, the greatest of our county sides dined together in Leicester, and Bowes and Verity sat long into the night discussing the future. In October 1939 they went together to the recruiting office in Bradford and joined a searchlight battery. When they were offered commissions, to Bill's chagrin his suspect knee prevented his accompanying his friend into an infantry regiment. Before Bill was gazetted in the Royal Artillery he had just one chance to throw a salute to Captain Verity. They never saw each other again.

Hedley died as he had lived – doing his best for his team, in this case his company of the Green Howards who had been charged with taking a heavily defended farmhouse. How many more wickets would he have taken for Yorkshire? That is one of the things I thought about when I heard the news, now serving in the RAF, as I went for a long, sad walk in the Herefordshire countryside. A memorial match was staged for Hedley Verity in Roundhay Park, Leeds, in 1944. I could not be there but the girl who was later to become my wife cycled there with a group of school friends from Tadcaster. When she told me this, years afterwards, somehow I felt very glad.

Perhaps batsmen develop their ambitions earlier than bowlers. Certainly Herbert Sutcliffe and Len Hutton were in no doubt during their childhood about where their future lay. Bill Bowes, however, cannot recall giving it a thought when he was very young; nor was there any family tradition of cricket for him to follow. But as a teenager in the 1920s, the age of Rhodes and Sutcliffe, Macaulay and Kilner, Dolphin and Robinson, he could scarcely help being involved with the spirit of Yorkshire cricket. Perhaps his first conscious experience of the intensity of it all came when he was at West Leeds High School, the family having moved from Elland (where he was born) when he was five or six years old. In a school match Bill's side were bowled out for 33 by their deadly rivals of Saltaire and the headmaster Clifford Darling, ordered a week's detention for the whole team to attend cricket lectures! The boys' immediate answer was to dismiss Saltaire for 3. Young Bowes took four wickets without conceding a run and his captain, Frank Cooper, returned six for 1. Mr Darling, the most passionate of cricketing aficionados, had little alternative to cancelling the punishment but – and I find this almost more endearingly Yorkist than almost any other incident in this book – he gave the wicket-keeper an almighty rocket for allowing two byes! Even in a moment of triumph the head found cause for complaint about an imperfection and it allowed him the last word.

Once out of school, where he was awarded his colours after doing the hat-trick, Bill, to the dismay of his mother whose most earnest wish was to see him train for the teaching profession, joined the staff of an estate agent, still with no clear idea where his future lay and certainly with no plans for a career in cricket. The game was still merely a pleasant way of spending his leisure hours, and his first club provided no great incentive to look any further ahead. This was a Sunday School side in Armley, one of the less salubrious suburbs of Leeds, where finances were so tight that a £5 annual fee from a local farmer for grazing rights for his cattle saved the club money for a mower and made the difference between profit and loss in the annual accounts. The bovine grass-croppers left their mark in other ways, notably on the flannels of anyone chasing a ball into the outfield.

Bill Bowes's cricket career took a step forward by sheer accident. He remembers the day – Easter Monday, 1926 – when he was cycling past a field where a group of men were having net practice and stopped to watch. A ball was hit to the edge, where Bill fielded it and was invited to 'tak 'is coit off' and provide an extra bowler. He recalls being hit for six 'just about every' ball, but Bill was always a modest man so there is no reason to believe he was anything but a modest youth of eighteen. His performance in the nets resulted in a request for his name and address; three days later a card arrived from Kirkstall Educational Cricket Club to inform him he had been picked to play for the second team against Leeds City Gas Works the following Saturday.

Young Bowes was a big lad for his age, which meant that his estate agent employers entrusted him with duties which would normally have been left to an older man – trying to collect rent arrears from defaulters, or 'slow payers' – but he did a good deal of other work as well. He worked on Saturday morning as a matter of course, lunched on a bar of chocolate, turned out for Kirkstall Educational II with no particular feeling of excitement beyond a quiet sense of pleasure simply to be playing cricket in a more formal atmosphere than that of his Sunday School side, and took six wickets for 5 runs, including the hat-trick. This earned him a collection of modest dimensions and brought him the earnest advice: 'Tha wants to wait until ther's more fowk 'ere before tha does that.' Nevertheless, there was enough in the cap which had been taken around the spectators to pay Bill's subscription to his new club, to buy pies and 'pop' for his team-mates and to take a shilling home. This affluence was due largely to the fact that one spectator had put half-a-crown in the collection, an enormous contribution in those days of economic depression which was felt as keenly in the industrial West Riding as anywhere in the country. The philanthropist was a man called John Kaye, who was to have a great influence on young Bowes's life.

The following week Bill played in the Kirkstall Educational first team, took five wickets for 9 runs and was established in the senior

XI of a club he had stumbled upon, almost literally, by accident. He was a bowler of no great subtlety at that time. He was a six-footer, with good shoulders, and simply bowled as fast as he could while maintaining the best possible length, but gradually he began to develop a ball which cut back from the off. As his height and strength gave him natural 'bounce', and League wickets were sometimes less than perfect, he developed rapidly into a formidable bowler. Long before his twentieth birthday he had had a dozen offers of professional work with other clubs. Then came the offer of a trial with Warwickshire, but before he could take that up a neighbour showed him a report in the *Daily Mail* which said that MCC planned to increase its ground staff and invited applications. In January 1928 he went to Lord's for a trial. His experience: one season in the Leeds League and a winter of bowling snowballs at telegraph poles, or stones when there was no snow; of bowling a rubber ball down the central aisle of the sale-room at his estate agent's; of bowling imaginary balls at imaginary batsmen in Armley Park. Bill was never a man (or a boy) to show wild enthusiasm but the bug had, by now, definitely bitten him.

A major part of his Lord's trial consisted of bowling at 'Plum' Warner, who afterwards recalled with a grimace that Bowes 'was a bowler with the habit of grinding a batsman's knuckles against the bat handle'. He was offered an engagement for a season at £5 a week, which might not allow him to live in luxury in London but which in Leeds would seem a princely wage in 1928. Bill wrote back to say he would go for £6 a week! He was accepted. In the meantime the possibilities of this young man had finally come to Yorkshire's notice. It seems incredible that a player of promise, and particularly a fast bowler, could have been asked for a trial by Warwickshire before his own county had begun to take interest but that's how the Bowes career began. Now he was asked to see the Yorkshire secretary, Frederick Toone, who quietly advised him to accept the offer from Lord's rather than Edgbaston. In that way he would still be qualified for Yorkshire – if he made the grade. They weren't daft: 'I want you to go to Lord's, Bowes. Not only is it best for you, but Yorkshire will be able to play you if you turn out right.' It was, in fact, a marvellous deal for Yorkshire. Someone else could have the responsibility of schooling this young man, and paying him too. His native county would reap the benefit and it wouldn't have cost them a penny. There would be a few warm smiles and a certain rubbing of hands when the Yorkshire Committee next met.

I wonder how many people can ever remember seeing Bill Bowes wearing a cricket cap, either for Yorkshire or England. He was a distinctive figure, partly because he was taller than most of his contemporaries and partly because he wore spectacles. Somehow it seemed all wrong to my schoolboy eyes to see a fast bowler (who automatically spelled 'menace') wearing glasses, which to me denoted a quiet and studious nature. It was, of course, an association of ideas involving one's own school contemporaries but when I first saw Bill bowling, in the thirties, it just seemed all wrong. By modern standards he was *not* fast, but he was fast enough to command the respect of pre-war batsmen and, like Les Jackson of Derbyshire in a later era, one of his greatest assets was the ability to get lift on all but the most unresponsive of wickets and, as Sir Pelham Warner had discovered earlier, to trap the fingers against the bat handle. But about his cap . . .

He arrived at Lord's to start his apprenticeship with his school cap as the only form of cricketing headwear. It perched precariously on top of a mass of curly brown hair and the reaction of his new colleagues at Headquarters was predictable – to a man they hooted with laughter. The sole Yorkshireman in that happy band of pilgrims was furious, and there and then swore a solemn oath never to wear any other cap throughout his career. He may have been a quiet man but he was certainly not without a natural, native streak of stubbornness and I have no doubt he would have kept to that impulsive decision if the other young professionals had not 'borrowed' his school cap to use as a duster. He was livid, but he kept the promise he had made to himself. His Yorkshire, and later his England, caps were allowed to rest for one fleeting token moment on his head after being awarded and then put carefully away.

One of the men who must influenced Bill's development as a bowler at Lord's was, somewhat ironically, that fine Lancastrian Walter Brearley, who urged him to work on the ball that moved away towards the slips. Brearley it was who cut down the young fast bowler's run to ten yards and would have liked to make it a mere eight; in his later years as a Yorkshire bowling coach Bowes rarely had much sympathy with extravagant approaches to the bowling crease. His first three-day game was against Wales; he was not impressed with life at the top (not knowing that the game rated as a first-class fixture) but took five wickets for 69 runs. Then he was picked to play for MCC against Cambridge University, and this seemed to Bill more like a 'business' game. Just before tea on the second day his figures stood at one wicket for 70 as he started a new spell. With the fourth, fifth and sixth deliveries of his next over he bowled T. C. Longfield, had N. G. Wykes lbw and then bowled M. J. C. Allom. He finished with six for 89 and had thus performed the hat-trick for West Leeds High School, Kirkstall Educational second team and now MCC. The Marylebone Cricket Club promptly offered a second season's engagement, still on trial at the same modest sum, but the lanky young Yorkshireman was having none of that. He asked for top money, like the seasoned professionals on the Lord's ration-strength, or else he was going back to his estate agent's office in Leeds to await, perhaps, the call from Yorkshire. 'What?' he was asked. 'Do you rate yourself as good as Patsy Hendren then?' 'Not as a batsman,' Bowes replied stolidly, 'but how about comparing me with the bowlers here?' He got the engagement – on top money.

But people had begun to sit up and take notice in Yorkshire, too, especially after the hat-trick against Cambridge, and in particular that generous contributor to his Kirkstall collection, John Kaye, who had talked to Lord Hawke about Bill. As a result, during that close season, he was summoned – Yorkshire's equivalent of a Royal command – by the President. 'Now, Bowes,' he asked, 'do you want to play for Yorkshire?' 'Of course, my lord.' One did not utter heresy to Lord Hawke. Hawke then arranged for him to see a lawyer on the basis that his contract with MCC was invalid because Bowes was still under twenty-one and thus a minor. However, the well-known British compromise was reached without recourse to litigation and he could now play for Yorkshire when he was not required by MCC, but if he *was* required, even to play *against* Yorkshire, MCC had first call on his services. One way and another, Bill Bowes had arrived, not via the channels which brought together so many of the men who were to be his team-mates, but he was there none the less: there with Wilfred Rhodes and George Macaulay, with Emmott Robinson and Maurice Leyland, with Edgar Oldroyd and Arthur Mitchell and Wilf Barber, Percy Holmes and Herbert Sutcliffe. He was with the Immortals.

Like everyone who saw him play, from the gifted professional observer like Neville Cardus to the humblest practitioner in the opposition ranks, Bowes was immediately in awe of the massive cricketing intellect of Wilfred Rhodes. In his first game, at Oxford, he listened to Rhodes's pronouncement on the state of the pitch (before play began) and then found it totally accurate in every particular. In his second, at Leyton, he was instructed by Rhodes to 'go back a bit', at mid-off and did so. 'Too far,' remonstrated Wilfred. 'Come in a bit.' Bowes went in. 'Now a bit to your right . . . not too far, now. Come back a bit. Now, in a yard . . . nay, nay, nay.' And that grim campaigner of (at that time) twenty-seven seasons walked across to the tall youngster and scratched a cross in the turf with his spikes: 'Now that's it. Stand thee theer.' Three balls later the batsman drove the ball straight to him. It was hit so hard that Bill, never the most agile of fieldsmen, would not have got near it if he had been a foot either side of the mark. He held the catch and looked in wonderment at the master bowler whose geometrical precision had wrought this miracle. Rhodes explained simply, 'You see, lad, always go wheer th'art put.'

Bowes never forgot that lesson. Indeed, he digested it and used it to his advantage as all great bowlers have done. No wickets ever gave him more pleasure than those in which he 'thought out' the batsman as opposed to those achieved simply by his bounce or pace off the pitch. Probably the greatest triumph of all was his dismissal of Bradman for a duck at Melbourne on 30 December 1932, as we shall see. First, however, he had another lesson to learn. In that first season with Yorkshire, bowling at Edgbaston on a shirt-front of a wicket, he was vastly encouraged by the vocal support of the two senior opening bowlers, George Macaulay and Emmott Robinson, who were more than generous with their encouragement: 'Well bowled, lad. Keep it up, Bill.' He bowled and bowled and in the hotel that evening he looked for the first time at the bowling analyses. He had delivered 45 overs while Macaulay had bowled 29 and Robinson 24. Putting two and two together, he now remembered that the approval of the other two had always been directed towards him as he happened to be passing the skipper (William Worsley). The captain had fallen for it; the raw recruit had done extra duty and the two old soldiers were not nearly as footsore as they might have been!

There were times in that first season when Bill was assailed by a great deal of self-doubt. He was competing for a regular place in the side with Frank Dennis and Sandy Jacques, and he was convinced he would never win the fight. His lack of agility in the field did not help quell those fears either, and he never forgot how the Bramall Lane crowd gave him hell for misfields in a game against the 1929 touring South Africans. It was his first game for Yorkshire in the county, but there was no sentimental allowance made for blemishes in the field. But two seasons on trial at Lord's had been enough to convince MCC of his value. They offered him a long-term contract (seven or nine years, whichever he preferred) at £200 a season, plus 30 shillings a day match pay and a travel and hotel allowance. These were very good terms indeed and spelled security for the first ten years or so of his adult life. Yet he was a Yorkshireman who really preferred to be amongst his own kind, and he would rather play for Yorkshire than anyone else. At the same time he understood that since his county had no ground staff, conditions for a professional cricketer were quite different there. Only the capped players earned the sort of money that gave them the security MCC were offering him and he regarded himself as far from close to his cap.

So he wrote to Leeds for advice from the county secretary, now Sir Frederick Toone, who was recognised as one of the foremost administrators in the game. He had managed three tours to Australia, and after the third of these his reward was the knighthood. He was a highly respected county official and obviously an outstanding administrator, so his vague reply of just three-and-a-half lines to the young cricketer seeking guidance – which left Bill Bowes no wiser at all – seems very strange indeed: 'It is not for me to advise you to sign for a number of years. What I suggest is that your position as to playing county cricket should be made quite clear. I am enclosing a copy of our regulations.' What was Bowes to make of that? Did Yorkshire want him or didn't they? Was there likely to be any future for him in his native county or not? No matter how many times he read the letter (and the regulations) it gave not the slightest indication of anything to give him hope. The MCC's offer, on the other hand, was clear as crystal; they certainly wanted him as a contracted player. He signed a nine-year contract with them.

He was still permitted to play with Yorkshire – *when* they wanted him and *if* he was not required by MCC – but while his doubts

about his future security had been cleared there remained his own
doubts about his ability as a bowler. He worked hard to develop the
ball that moved away from the bat, but real success had not been
achieved as he went into the 1930 season with two games for MCC
against Surrey and Yorkshire. That brought him up against, successively, the two greatest opening batsmen in the country, Hobbs and
Sutcliffe, men whose pads always formed an effective second line of
defence if the bowler managed to beat the bat. The lbw Law
demanded that to get a decision in his favour the bowler had to
pitch his delivery in line between wicket and wicket, and while the
ball which came in to the batsman after pitching outside the off
stump might be effective against lesser batsmen it was not going to
be good enough against Hobbs and Sutcliffe. Bowes's first week of
the new season left him without a wicket while he had conceded 142
runs.

There was no joy for him in the next match, either, because he
was called up by Yorkshire to play against the visiting Australians
where he encountered for the first time Bill Woodfull and the 22-
year-old Don Bradman. At the end of that match his figures for the
season were none for more than 200. Then we saw something which
could probably only have occurred in the game of cricket, one of
those dramatic changes of fortunes which can make all the difference
to a career, to a life. In the next five matches Bill took 33 wickets
for 233. A thin time for MCC against Cambridge University brought
him down to earth but this was followed immediately by a telegram
from the Yorkshire captain, Alan Barber, which reached him at
Lord's: 'Congratulations on being awarded county cap.' Now he
faced a perplexing situation, especially after Sir Frederick Toone
told him: 'We shall play you just as much as we can. If you are
rested by the county you will be expected to return to Lord's and if
MCC ask for you to take part in any of their big matches you will
have to go.' And that is how his cricket progressed, playing largely
with Yorkshire but returning to the MCC fold when they formally
applied to the county. It was an odd sort of arrangement but Bill
was content, for he was now undergoing another apprenticeship in
the toughest training ground in cricket. His tutors were Wilfred
Rhodes and Emmott Robinson and his fellow pupil was a man who
became his closest friend until war separated them for ever – Hedley
Verity.

For those who recall the original film of *The Four Feathers* and
remember the scene where C. Aubrey Smith (as General Feversham)
uses the fruit and the cutlery on a dinner table to describe his
greatest battle, the operation of the Rhodes–Emmott academy of
cricket will be immediately familiar. At 10.30 each evening the two
veterans would collect the two apprentices and set a field of shaving
sticks, tooth brushes, hair-brushes and anything else that was handy
and play their war games. After Verity had taken seven for 26
against Hampshire he was taken severely to task for 'giving away' a
four to A. K. Judd and reprimanded because his figures did not
read seven for 22! Field-placing by the two experts later that evening
in the hotel bedroom proved their point conclusively.

Oh, it was a hard school, that Yorkshire team of the 1930s. But it
was probably the best cricket training ground the game has ever
seen. The two new boys were encouraged to keep a cricketing ledger
in which they not only noted, but wrote up in detail, the strengths,
weaknesses and individual characteristics of opposing players. They
learned about different types of wickets, about field-placing, about
umpires. No detail was regarded as too trivial to be considered. It
must have been rather like the General Staff preparing a First World
War offensive, and it constituted one of those traditions of learning
which were handed down from one Yorkshire cricketing generation
to another. It was still there in the 1960s; only in the next decade
did it fade away, and with it Yorkshire's pre-eminence.

Bill was ever a tolerant sort of chap. Maybe it was that early MCC
experience which muted what should have been a natural Yorkshire
abrasiveness, but now that he was capped by Yorkshire and spent
the major part of his season with them (despite his MCC contract)
he remembered with affection the games he had played at public
schools and against Service sides; he smiled gently at the recollection
of amateur captains who couldn't play but who barked orders like
parade-ground commands. It must have been an attitude which
infuriated George Macaulay – the most volatile of bowlers – and it
probably perplexed grizzled veterans of the professional stage like
Wilfred Rhodes and Emmott Robinson. But that was always Bill's
way. When he finally quit cricket for journalism, writing about
cricket and Rugby Union for first the *Yorkshire Evening News* and
later the *Yorkshire Evening Post*, his criticism – when any was voiced
– was gentle and ever constructive. I worked with him a lot in those

days and I am sure it positively hurt him to speak ill of anyone. His counterpart in later years would be Tony Nicholson, who groaned and moaned and expostulated and called upon all the cricketing gods to witness his continual misfortune, but there was a complete absence of malice and venom in the man and everyone knew it.

Bill, in the thirties, played in a side which was truly great. Thrift, rather than arrogance, dictated that in fixtures against counties like Somerset and Northants the side booked in to their hotel for two nights rather than three; experience, rather than conceit, decreed that when Yorkshire won the toss at a seaside venue the last three in the order could prepare to spend the day in deckchairs on the beach.

In August 1932, Bill bowled a number of bouncers to the great Jack Hobbs with five fieldsmen on the on-side, and the whole course of cricket was changed. Hobbs was not pleased by the method of attack and made his point by walking down the wicket to a point well beyond that where the ball had pitched and ostentatiously did a bit of 'gardening'. Bowes genially responded by indicating a spot half-way along his run-up to the wicket. 'Okay,' said Hobbs and gravely patted the turf several yards behind the bowler's wicket. Bowes unleashed another bouncer and Hobbs made no further histrionic gestures. The day's play ended with each of them satisfied that he had made his point and that the incident was closed. Not so. Far, far from it. In one newspaper the following Monday morning the correspondent wrote: 'Such "play" is not in the spirit of cricket as I understand the game and if Yorkshire are as keen as this to win the County Championship they can have it for all the rest of England cares.' Oh-ooooh! In another paper Plum Warner wrote: 'Bowes must alter his tactics . . . that is not bowling; indeed, it is not cricket and if all fast bowlers were to adopt his methods, MCC would be compelled to step in and penalise the bowler who bowled the ball less than half-way up the pitch.'

The Surrey captain was D. R. Jardine. The following winter England went to Australia with Douglas Jardine as captain. And with Plum Warner as manager!

We shall come to the bodyline controversy in a minute but first I would like to dwell for a moment on the dismissal of Bradman in the Second Test in Melbourne. He had missed the First because of illness and England had won by ten wickets. He played in the Second, where the superb bowling of Bill O'Reilly had ensured an

Australian victory after Bradman's 103 not out in the second innings. Now in 1965, when Arthur Wrigley (who took over from Roy Webber as the BBC scorer and statistician) published a book giving the scorecards of all Test matches played from 1876 to 1964, I noticed that just three times in his career Bradman had been *bowled* for no score: by Bowes at Melbourne in 1932–3, by Alec Bedser at Adelaide in 1946–7 and by Eric Hollies at The Oval in 1948. Recalling the drama of that last dismissal I wondered whether the three dismissals would make a radio programme if I could get the three bowlers to describe them in their own words. Accordingly, I arranged with my colleagues in London to record Bedser, with our Midland region to get Hollies on tape and I went to see Bowes myself. It resulted in one of the finest pieces of cricket broadcasting I have ever heard.

Now in cold print it does not make anything like the same impact. Bill had been stricken with asthma as a legacy of his years in a German prison-of-war camp – sadly this was to restrict the amount of cricket commentary he did for us (and he was a splendid broadcaster on the game) – but it enhanced the dramatic effect of the story as he told it: We were taken out there to the middle of that vast Melbourne Cricket Ground with him. This is the story as he told it:

> Every step he took from the pavilion to the wicket was cheered. He took his time and to get accustomed to the brilliant light after the shade of the pavilion he walked almost in a semi-circle to the middle. The crowd cheered him all the way. The cheers continued as he took guard; they went on as he looked carefully round at the field-placings. And as I started to run in to bowl the cheering continued. It was so deafening that I stopped in the middle of my run and before starting back I asked the mid-on fieldsman to move in closer. There was no deep-laid plot in this; really, it was just something to do, having stopped in my run. Again I started to run in; again the roar of the crowd swelled in a mighty crescendo; and again I stopped without delivering the ball. This time, I signalled the fine leg fieldsman to move in a bit from the boundary. Bradman watched carefully and suddenly the thought flashed into my mind, 'He expects me to bowl a

bouncer.' Could I fool him, I wondered. I knew (we all knew) that he was a great batsman but now I sensed that he was expecting a short-pitched ball. If I could bowl one well up to him, the line of the off-stump, it was just possible that . . . I put on the most threatening expression I could find and ran in. I saw him start to move across his stumps – he *was* preparing for the bouncer – and I let it go on a good length. He was so good a player that he started to change his shot. He got just the faintest of inside edges and the ball hit the stumps. For the first and only time in his career Bradman was out first ball bowled for a duck. Well, there was no cheering now. You could have heard a pin drop. It was possible to hear the rattle of the trams as they crossed Flinders Street down in the middle of Melbourne. Silence in the ground. Absolute silence. And it was all silence as he walked slowly back to the pavilion. And then it was broken by the sound of one pair of hands clapping. It was a woman and we could pick her out in the crowd.

Great cricket. Great cricket talk. But Australia still won the Test.

It was at Adelaide, in the Third Test, that the bodyline row really erupted after Oldfield had top-edged a ball from Larwood into his face and it was Plum Warner, as manager, who was cold-shouldered by the Australians when he went into their dressing-room to check on Oldfield's state of health. In view of his comments about Bowes's bowling at The Oval only five months earlier he was well and truly on the spot. Bill supported Jardine in his leg-theory strategy. His view was that cricket had its own evolution process and that it was up to batsmen to evolve a new technique against bowling of a type – and more particularly a speed and accuracy – which was new to them.

There is a certain grim pragmatism about that view that might owe more to the character of Wilfred Rhodes than the genial giant, Bill Bowes. Contrast it, then, with Bowes the good tourist, Bowes the good companion, Bowes the entertainer. He was 'hooked' at an early age on sleight-of-hand, conjuring tricks which whiled away the hours in dressing-rooms when rain stopped play. After seeing an amateur magician at work at Lord's, Bowes began to tour theatres in his leisure time and if there was a conjuror on the bill he was invariably accosted after the show by the tall, bespectacled young man in search of a few trade secrets. He even cultivated a Find-the-Lady crook who worked the trains going to race meetings and learned how to take a few bob from team-mates and opponents alike. The difference was that Bill donated the proceeds to charity. He went to fairgrounds and learned more tricks until he had built up a formidable repertoire, especially with card tricks. The big man had a tremendous sense of fun, and although honour demanded that he didn't cheat at cards his colleagues became wary of playing against him, especially after one episode on the way to Jamaica by sea. His partner was Arthur Wood, who found himself holding three aces when the opposition bid a grand slam. A beatific smile spread across Arthur's face as he doubled the call and when it was re-doubled he breathed, 'My, but I'd double thee ageean if I could.' Nevertheless, the Bowes deal somehow ensured that the declarers made the contract and Bill paid up rather than confess that he had 'worked' the cards. Now *that* I find difficult to credit in a Yorkie; it must have resulted from Bill's early training at Lord's!

Bill Bowes played his first game for Yorkshire (we're back to cricket now) in 1929 when they finished second in the County Championship. In 1930 they were third. In 1931, 1932 and 1933 they won the title, as they did in 1935, 1937, 1938 and 1939. He came back from a prison camp, his health impaired if not totally shattered, to help them win again in 1946. He took 1,351 wickets for the county at 15 runs apiece, 100 wickets in a season nine times. With Tests and MCC matches the total rose to 1,639 wickets. After his retirement he coached Yorkshire cricketers and after that he wrote about them. It had been a notable cricketing life. And like so many of his generation he saw great changes. In 1985, at the Headingley Test match, we had our usual chat after he had taken his usual seat in front of the commentary box and he said, 'I filled up with petrol to come down from Menston and said to the wife, "D'you know – it cost more to fill the tank than we paid for our first car".'

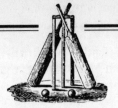

10
The Post-War Years

The early post-Second World War years were a period of part-confusion, part-rebuilding. Sellers, Sutcliffe, Leyland, Bowes, Arthur Wood, Frank Smailes, Wilf Barber and Cyril Turner soon retired from the first-class game, and Ellis Robinson went to Somerset after 1949, leaving Hutton and Norman Yardley to carry on the traditions of the thirties. The championship had been won in 1946 largely because of the off-spinning of Robinson and the appearance of a remarkable little man called Arthur Booth. He had been one of those competing for Wilfred Rhodes's place in the side sixteen years earlier but had lost out to Verity and had spent most of the intervening years in league cricket, content to be called up occasionally when Hedley was on Test duty. Even then he had to compete, usually disadvantageously, with another rival for the slow-left-armer's spot, Horace Fisher (who in 1932 achieved immortality by becoming the first bowler to get a hat-trick of lbw victims although I always felt it must have been the umpire who was the star of that particular show!). Booth, in his first full first-class season, took 111 wickets and topped the first-class averages. He was forty-three years old. He played one more season, did some coaching for Yorkshire and then joined the county committee – of Lancashire!

It was a time of change. Yardley became the new captain in 1948 but the leagues now had to be dredged for almost a full side of young players. The leagues, as they always had done, responded nobly. Harry Halliday, with just a little pre-war experience under his belt, was around to open the batting or to fit in lower down the order when required – a good trouper in difficult days of rebuilding. Into the middle order were drafted Gerry Smithson, a left-hander who sparkled brilliantly and all-too-briefly; Ted Lester, a hard-hitting right-hander from Scarborough, whose 127 against Derbyshire was the first century I saw after my own return from service overseas, scored 10,616 runs at an average of 34.02 and was always good to watch. He then led the Second XI, where he helped in the development of many of the young players who were to bring home the championship for Ronnie Burnet in 1959, and after that became an immensely influential scorer and guide, philosopher and friend to the team through the sixties and seventies, and is still doing it in the eighties. He also became my regular bridge partner on the circuit and, perhaps despite that, I like to think he also became a good friend. Alongside him came the gifted Willie Watson (Huddersfield Town and England footballer), a cultured left-hand batsman; Vic Wilson, the burly and phlegmatic farmer from the fertile plains of the east, who hit the ball hard and took marvellous catches close to the wicket. Johnny Wardle was now established as the leading slow bowler, Don Brennan was a Yorkshire rarity – an *amateur* wicket-keeper – but the opening attack was still something of a problem.

In the first six years after the war an astonishing series of permutations of fast bowlers was tried. Some of them made their mark, others may well have slipped quietly out of most memories: George Cawthray (afterwards a noted groundsman at Headingley), Ron Aspinall (destined to be a long-serving first-class umpire), Alec Coxon, Peter Brayshay, Ted Burgin, Bill Foord, Frank McHugh, Johnny Whitehead, Hubert Padgett. In view of what was to happen in the future it seems almost heresy to say that when F. S. Trueman came on the scene in 1949, serious doubts were felt about his ability to discipline himself and his bowling. And yet the leagues kept spawning ever more talent if one offering proved unsatisfactory. The record of the Bradford, Huddersfield and Yorkshire leagues in producing players in that period was incredible. Many, rejected by Yorkshire, drifted away to join other counties until there was scarcely one which did not include an exile, burning with the ambition to prove the Yorkshire Committee wrong when he came up against his fellow countrymen. Desmond Barrick, Arnold Hamer, Charlie Lee, Don Bennett, Bill Greensmith, Graham Atkinson, Gordon Barker, Freddie Jakeman, Dickie Bird were just a few

Victorian captains: **1a** Tom Emmett (1878–82) **b** Lord Hawke (1883–1910)

The great all-rounders: **c** George Hirst **d** Wilfred Rhodes

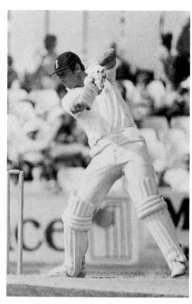

Geoffrey Boycott: **8a** on the front foot and **b** the back foot

c Yorkshire, Benson and Hedges Cup-Winners, 1987

of the players who drifted away in the fifties and sixties, but who all made the grade with other counties and were to be followed by men who went one better: Ray Illingworth, captain of England after moving to Leics; Jack Birkenshaw and Chris Balderstone, capped by England after failing to achieve that distinction with Yorkshire; Brian Bolus, a Test player after moving to Notts; Brian Close, recalled by England in 1976 at the age of forty-five after getting a new lease of life with Somerset; Barry Wood, regarded as not likely to make it in Yorkshire but capped twelve times by England after moving to Lancashire and later made skipper of Derbyshire. It's a long and impressive list which adds up to a great tribute to the productive powers of league cricket in Yorkshire. No other county has anything even approaching the same capacity for turning out first-class cricketers.

So the leagues did their stuff and by 1952 Yorkshire could turn out a twelve which read: Hutton, Lowson, Watson, Lester, Wilson, Close, Illingworth, Brennan, Yardley, Wardle, Appleyard, Trueman – not a bad line-up in any stage of cricket history. Yet for the next seven years in succession the county championship was won by Surrey. There were two reasons for this. One was the undoubted excellence of Surrey, tigerishly skippered by Stuart Surridge, with solid rather than inspired batting and a brilliant attack of the Bedser twins, Loader, Laker, Lock and Surridge himself allied to superb close-to-the-wicket fielding.

The other reason was undoubtedly provided by the divisions within the Yorkshire camp. As Shakespeare put it:

> This England never did, nor never shall
> Lie at the proud foot of a conqueror,
> But when it first did help to wound itself.

For 'England', read 'Yorkshire' and you have the situation of the 1950s in a nutshell. That side, man for man, was superior to Surrey's. It was, damn it, superior on paper to very many Test sides we have seen in recent years. But it never won a thing because of the grievous wounds it inflicted upon itself by internal dissension. Later historians have tended to place the blame on the captain, Norman Yardley, for being too easy-going with the 'hard men' in the side – and there were at least three of them, all pulling different ways – but possibly we should regard it as the first, ominous sign of changing attitudes. For nearly a hundred years the Yorkshire philosophy had been that above all *the team* was the thing, that it was bigger than any one individual. In the fifties the cracks began to show.

Bob Appleyard was a truly wonderful two-in-one bowler who could use the new ball with devastating effect, then switch to briskish off-spin with equal success if the conditions were right. He bewildered a new generation of county cricketers to such an extent that in 1951, his first full season in the county game, he took 200 wickets at only 14.14. Before he had been in the game five minutes, so to speak, he was established as a match-winner and was thus required to serve no apprenticeship of modesty and humility. Illness tragically limited his career, but he was around long enough to take 637 wickets at only 15.4 and to play in nine Tests, including four on Hutton's Ashes-winning tour of 1954–5. Appleyard did not court personal popularity and never achieved it. He was respected as a truly great bowler and he always wanted to bowl, no matter what the conditions. Appleyard was convinced that by one method of attack or another he could always take wickets – and usually he could! But he was not always helpful to the younger players in the side. Ray Illingworth recalls, with some understandable bitterness, being asked by Yardley in one game to take over from Appleyard. 'What do you want?' demanded Appleyard as he peeled off his sweater. 'T'skipper's told me to bowl,' replied young Raymond. 'Bugger off,' came the reply. 'I'm bowling here.' And he carried on. That is precisely the sort of incident which has led to the conclusion that N. W. D. Yardley (St Peter's School and Cambridge University) was too-easy going in his captaincy.

It is a view which was shared by at least some of the contemporary cricket-writers who regularly followed Yorkshire, but at the same time there has always been a reluctance to be openly critical because Yardley was a man of great charm and courtesy who earned himself considerable personal respect. He was also a fine player, scoring 11,632 runs for the county at 31.95 and taking 192 wickets with his medium-paced swingers and seamers. He captained England in fourteen Tests, was a selector between 1951 and 1954 and chairman of the panel in 1951 and 1952. He was also an all-round sportsman of high ability, excelling at squash and hockey in particular. Yardley was, indeed, a 'nice' man and remained so during his later years as Yorkshire committeeman and then President. Was he, then, too 'nice' to cope with the hard men in his side, as Appleyard, Wardle and to some extent Willie Watson (all in their different ways) undoubtedly were? There has got to be some truth in the allegation, as the results of the fifties show, and Illingworth's personal recollection of weak captaincy on one occasion is by no means an isolated instance of the sort of thing that happened. Yardley did not possess the natural toughness as captain of a Brian Sellers; almost certainly he would have been a less well-liked individual if he had. He had been brought up in a different world from Sellers, and while certainly a complete Yorkshireman in most respects he had served his cricket apprenticeship in more gently-nurtured circles than The Crackerjack.

I think it is important, however, to look at one other aspect of the matter. Yardley had been introduced to Yorkshire cricket in the mid-thirties when the side, individually and collectively, would have died for the cause. He had picked up the pieces after the war and it must have come as a total shock to someone with his background to find players in his side who rocked the boat. He had been schooled in the one-for-all-and-all-for-one tradition and any attitude within the side which showed itself as less than that was alien to him. It was simply not in the Yardley nature to have an almighty confrontation with the hard men and to tell them: 'You toe the line or else . . .' I cannot see that it diminishes him as a human being that this was so; rather, one feels, it diminishes those who rocked the boat. But Yorkies being what they are, it took a man from the leagues to sort it all out: Ronnie Burnet. But first let us look in more detail at four men who were to play major parts in cricket drama, not only for Yorkshire, but for England as well.

Johnny Wardle, like Brian Close a decade later, was a man sacked by Yorkshire in an atmosphere of the most bitter acrimony who could not, nevertheless, keep away from the county he loved. He worked hard to straighten out the problems of Geoff Cope, the off-spinner whose action was declared unacceptable by Lord's; his passion for golf and his essentially competitive nature led him back into the social fold to join with former team-mates and committee in competing for the Gibson Cup (a competition staged annually by the county for players, ex-players and Committee); and for several years shortly before his death he devoted endless hours of work to helping the Doncaster Town club sort out problems with their pitch and called in many of his friends to speak at functions to raise money for the club.

Wardle was, like almost everyone in these pages, a 100 per cent, dyed-in-the wool, no-nonsense Tyke. And yet he had two images. To the public he was a droll, a comedian on the field, a big hitter, a man who could make them laugh as well as admire his cricket. His party-piece was to hold a red-hot catch at gulley, pocket the ball in almost the same movement, and then turn to gaze ruefully down to deep third man as he convinced just about everyone on the sidelines that it had gone for four. Within the dressing-room and to those a little closer to him on the field he could have a cutting line in invective. He had come up very much the hard way through the Yorkshire ranks and he bitterly resented play from anyone which was less than the best. He was a magnificent bowler in the slow left-arm tradition, but he had had no Rhodes to coach or encourage him and the war had deprived him of the chance to study under Verity. He was, you might say, self-taught and he had done a great job on himself by the late forties. Not only could he bowl his orthodox stuff with devastating effect on helpful pitches and miraculous economy on good ones but he came to master as no one before him the Chinaman, the left-armer's wrong 'un. He could, if he felt the occasion and circumstances demanded, bowl it not merely as a surprise weapon but for over after over, 'dropping' it on perfect line and length. It was, remember, like asking a right-arm leg-spinner to do that, and few have ever been able to do so with real consistency.

Wardle was a fighter. He had to fight off the rival claims of two other bowlers of his type – Ronnie Wood and Alan Mason – after the retirement of Arthur Booth. Indeed, it was touch and go who would get the regular place; Mason was strongly fancied in some circles. But in 1948 Wardle took 148 first-class wickets and there was now no argument about it. Even so, after making his Test début on the 1947–8 tour of West Indies (and being called upon to bowl just three overs!), Johnny now found himself up against more stiff competition – from Jack Young of Middlesex, then progressively Malcolm Hilton and Bob Berry of Lancashire (even Denis Compton occasionally!) until the arrival of his arch-rival, Tony Lock. For long periods, as the forties turned into the fifties, the England Selectors declined to use a slow left-armer at all, preferring the right-arm leg spin of men like Doug Wright, Roley Jenkins, Eric

Hollies, Freddie Brown and Eddie Leadbeater. When Lock arrived, Surrey were marching triumphantly through the 1950s with seven county championships, which made it a good deal easier for Lock to attract attention. So once again it was a struggle for J. H. Wardle. Nevertheless, he played twenty-eight times for England and got 102 wickets at 20.39, not forgetting 12 catches and 653 runs with his forthright batting. In those 'good old days', before covered wickets and an adjustment to the lbw law had convinced even the most modestly endowed tail-ender that he could stay around for a long time by simply pushing down the line with bat and pad together, every side had a batsman in the lower order whose arrival signalled some form of fireworks. Wardle could not only flog the bowling with the best of them, but he batted quite well too. It was his six-hitting which endeared him to the crowd as much as his clowning as a fieldsman. He was, indeed, a highly popular figure with spectators everywhere.

But the fact that 'nobody had ever given him owt', that he had had to fight for every form of recognition, gave him an intolerance which was not always easily understood by young players starting to make their way in the side. A dropped catch would almost certainly mean a blast from J. H., and youngsters remembered them long afterwards. Mike Cowan, later to become one of the most jovial of cricketers once put one down, started to stammer a trembling apology and received the icy blast: 'It's my own bloody fault for putting you there.' Wardle left his mark on a young Ray Illingworth to such an extent that when Wardle was summarily dismissed in 1957, Illingworth was less than sympathetic to a bowler whose work he much admired.

Wardle was furious, understandably so, when the Yorkshire Committee decided in November 1957 to make Ronnie Burnet captain in succession to Bill Sutcliffe. Professional captains by this time were not new in the game; he was the senior, and very much the most experienced player in the side since Willie Watson had decided to join Leicestershire. Burnet was thirty-nine years old and had never played first-class cricket at all. Johnny simply could not accept that the Committee were trying to establish the old-style amateur captain who could stand aloof, to a great extent, from the factions within a team and deal with problems objectively. To him, it was an outrageous affront in the increasingly egalitarian atmosphere of professional cricket. Whether Johnny himself could have evoked the same response from a fairly young side as Burnet was to achieve in his second season (1959) we shall never know, but personally, as a friend and intense admirer of the late J. H. Wardle, I am inclined to doubt it. He would certainly have given everything he had got, but I am not entirely sure he could have got the best from everyone else.

He was a blunt man in the extreme at all times, unable to dissemble in the circumstances in which he played his 1958 cricket, and as Burnet struggled to learn his new trade he very quickly found he could expect no help from his senior professional. Burnet found himself forced to go to the Committee with a him-or-me ultimatum and – this time with a wretched piece of timing forced upon them – Yorkshire's rulers announced that the services of J. H. Wardle would not be called upon in 1959. Four days earlier he had been picked as a member of the MCC party to tour Australia.

Needless to say, all hell broke loose and not for the first time and certainly not the last the rest of the cricketing world wondered at Yorkshire's infinite capacity for projecting themselves from the comfortable back pages of newspapers onto the more dramatic front. At the time I was a news reporter with the *Daily Express* in Manchester, where my contract stipulated that I was to be free on Saturdays so that I could go back to Yorkshire to play cricket. The day after he had been, in effect, sacked and voiced his views publicly and colourfully I chanced to be in the West Riding on a story which 'fell down' and when I made a check call to the office I was told: 'Do you know where this chap Wardle lives? Right. You can offer him £50 for his exclusive story.' Cheque-book journalism was in its hey-day and the *Express* were the kings in this field. In this case they were clearly going to fall down and I pointed out that this was a very big story indeed and if we were going to get it exclusively we would have to think in more generous terms.

News editors generally have a fine disregard for the importance of stories involving sports personalities and, although a brilliant man in other respects, my immediate boss, Keith Howard, proved no exception in this case. He flatly refused to go a penny above £50 and, disapproving professionally of this type of journalism anyway, I drove off to Wakefield knowing that the errand would be fruitless. Johnny answered the door, listened to the offer without encouragement, but as a mate invited me in for a cup of tea. There I found, already comfortably established in the Wardle living-room, Harold Pendlebury of the *Daily Mail*, the daddy of all newsmen based in Manchester. He greeted me like a fox which has just dined very well. The *Mail* had offered Johnny £500 plus a trip to Australia to *report* the series in which he should have been playing (the MCC had withdrawn his invitation to tour after the eruption in Yorkshire).

Wardle returned from Australia to follow in Bobby Peel's footsteps and play with distinction in the Lancashire League for several years. He left behind a record in Yorkshire of 5,765 mostly flamboyant runs and 1,537 wickets at 17.67. He was the toughest of competitors and a very fine bowler indeed. He never at any stage of his career had it easy and he didn't ask for concessions. Nor would he make any, and because of that he was, sadly, lost to Yorkshire when he had many more wickets to take. Fortunately, he was not lost to cricket until his death in 1986.

II
Fiery Fred

Frederick Sewards Trueman was the greatest fast bowler Yorkshire has ever produced and, arguably, the greatest we have had in this country. He was also one of the greatest characters the game has ever known. The folklore of the game is littered with his epigrams, many of them bitingly witty, all of them caustically to the point. When the seven-sided threepenny bit was part of our currency it occupied a place in the argot of cricket to describe a batsman who lived dangerously or enjoyed more than his share of good fortune when the ball found the edge: 'He's had more edges than a threepenny bit.' Fred scorned any phrase in general usage and coined (in the context of an innings by the Warwickshire batsman 'Billy' Ibadulla): '. . . more edges than a broken pisspot'. It was brilliant in its graphic vulgarity and my friend Ibadulla, domiciled far away in New Zealand for many a year, still treasures it.

No one ever had the last word in an exchange with Fred. Richard Hutton once *thought* he had achieved this distinction, a view shared by most of the auditors of their conversation. F.S. had been describing a 'typical' spell of his bowling: 'Pitched leg and middle and whistled ower t'top of t'off stick . . . next one, came back from t'off and how it missed his leg stump I'll never know . . .' As he paused for breath, Hutton inquired loftily: 'Tell me, Fred. Did you ever bowl a ball that merely went straight?' We gasped. Surely this was the moment we had waited for? There could be no answer to that barb. Fred did not even hesitate for a second. It was as if he had left the opening for his inquisitor to feed him the line: 'Aye, three years ago. It were a full toss. It went through Peter Marner like a streak o' piss and knocked 'is middle 'ob out.' It was the perfect response. Even Hutton was silenced and that is not easily accomplished. It was twenty years later (during the Second Test against New Zealand at Trent Bridge in 1986) that I mentioned to Marner that he figured in a prime piece of Yorkshire cricket folklore. To my surprise (for, like everyone present on the occasion of Fred's pronouncement, I had assumed the story of that particular bowling success to be apocryphal), Peter recalled the occasion. He replied, 'It's right enough. But what I bet he didn't mention was that it was nearly pitch dark and F.S. was bowling like a demon out of the black background of the pavilion at Bramall Lane with no sight screen.'

It is possible to dine out on a repertoire of Trueman stories for a whole season of after-dinner-speaking engagements and many people do. Unfortunately there is a temptation to gild the lily, and I have listened to men who have never met Fred telling stories which are totally untrue. This is something which I find infuriating because it is so unnecessary; there are enough *true* stories of Fred's bowling and his repartee to keep the narrative going for hours.

During county games he spent far more time in the opposition dressing-room than in Yorkshire's, and there are those who say he got a few wickets this way. Certainly he could always count on one – that of Peter Wight, of Somerset – as a result of a personal propaganda campaign. The Guyanese-born Wight was a prolific scorer of runs and, like most West Indians, he particularly relished fast bowling. He could murder all but the very best and on occasions he could deal with that as well. But not the bowling of F. S. Trueman. Peter has (he's still around as a first-class umpire) a distinctive high-pitched voice which carries a fair distance. Fred was to bowl at him for the first time on a visit to Taunton and in the Yorkshire dressing-room before the first day's play started the voice was plainly heard exhorting the Somerset troops not to worry too much about Trueman: 'Statham, yes. He's a fine bowler, but I don't think much of this Trueman fellow.' Silence descended upon the Yorkshire legions. Fred paused in the lacing up of his boot and then strolled casually next door to exchange the time of day with one or two old adversaries. He greeted Bill Alley with the usual exchange of colourful pleasantries, went round the remainder of the side with a genial nod and 'How do', pointedly ignoring P. B. Wight, now looking a trifle apprehensive in one corner. As he left the Somerset

sanctum, Fred spun round and addressed Wight shortly but suc-
cinctly: 'Ah'll see *thee* later.' From that day to the end of a very
fruitful career, Peter Wight never scored runs against Yorkshire
when Fred was playing. He emphasised the point himself in the
most colourful way possible in 1962 (see page 172).

It was at Taunton, too, in 1963 that Fred Rumsey, the left-arm
quick bowler, playfully let go a couple of bouncers in the direction
of Frederick Trueman, who first gaped in disbelief and then warned
of the dire retribution in store for the joker. There were only a few
minutes of the third day remaining when Somerset were due
formally to start their second innings and the captain, Harold
Stephenson, decided to enter into the spirit of things. As Rumsey
prepared to change into his 'civvies' as the no. 11 batsman, Stevo
casually instructed him to pad up: 'You've had your bit of fun.
Let's see what happens now.' Rumsey duly appeared on the field
with Brian Langford (later captain, then cricket chairman of Somerset) as his partner to see Trueman waiting at the end of his run,
already pawing the ground like a French charger at Agincourt.
Anyone who had thought of leaving the ground quickly dismissed
the thought and waited in anticipation of seeing the fastest over ever
bowled in the history of the game. It ended in hysterical anti-climax
as Brian Close (who had taken over from Vic Wilson as captain at
the start of that season) refused to give the ball to the fuming and
furious Fred. Despite all entreaties, pleas, threats, fire and brimstone, Close tossed the new ball to the most occasional of all his
bowlers, Doug Padgett, dismissing Trueman to the furthest extent
of the field he could find. The livid F. S. T. watched from long leg,
bristling with impotent fury which was enhanced (if that were
possible) by the dismissal of Rumsey, bowled Padgett, at which
point the game ended. Trueman was inconsolable for weeks. If he
had not had a healthy respect for Close's physical presence we might
well have seen blood spilled in the Yorkshire dressing-room.

Apart from the natural gift of a perfect cartwheel action, Freddie
(as he was always known in his younger days) Trueman positively
radiated aggression. He was, John Arlott said, 'Never simply a
cricketer. He was purely – in method, mind and heart – a fast
bowler.' I have seen young batsmen quail at the thought of going
out to face Fred in full cry and he did nothing to dispel their fears.
The ultimate in encouragement he had to offer a newcomer was,

'Don't worry, sunshine. You'll soon be back wi' your mates.' Peter Parfitt, who was to become a close friend in later years, recalls his first encounter with the great Fiery Fred. As a young batsman trying to establish himself in the Middlesex side of Compton, Edrich and Co. he misguidedly tried to hook a short-pitched Trueman delivery and retired to the dressing-room spitting out blood and teeth. Three wickets later he returned to the fray and had to pass Fred who remarked, with menace filtering through his air of mild surprise: 'They doan't usually come back when I've 'it 'em.'

Fred loved nothing better than to be feared by the opposition. The ultimate accolade was a Roy Ulyett cartoon (the original hangs, proudly framed, in his home) of a West Indian mother urging her offspring to go to sleep 'or that Fred Trueman will come to get you'. And this was in the days when Hall and Griffith were wreaking havoc amongst *English* batsmen! He literally terrified the Indians on their 1952 tour by sheer pace. He was a 21-year-old National Serviceman in the RAF when he was called up by England at Headingley, and after returning a modest three for 89 in the first innings looked with grim satisfaction at a scoreboard which, when play ended on the Saturday, read: 'India, second innings, O for four wickets.' He had taken three of the wickets and although he bowled only nine overs altogether his figures were four for 27. Fred Trueman had arrived. At Lord's, in the Second Test, he took four for 72 and four for 110 but his finest hour came at Old Trafford in the Third: eight wickets for 31. And such was the physical dominance he had established over the Indians that he swore he could see Tony Lock, the leg-slip fieldsman, clearly in the gap left by 'Polly' Umrigar (one of the most prolific scorers in Indian cricket) between his body and the stumps: 'Ah thought he were going to end up sitting in t'umpire's lap.'

Fred hated Australians on the field and loved them off it. He was a tremendous admirer of men like Neil Harvey, Alan Davidson and Ray Lindwall – but only in retrospect. While engaged in combat with them he believed firmly in his own supremacy; the friendly exchanges over a drink or two came later. He also, as the years went by and his experience grew, began to *think* about his cricket and to introduce certain variations. At Headingley, in 1961, he pleaded with Peter May to be allowed to experiment with off-cutters bowled at something like medium pace. May was not easily convinced –

until Fred took five wickets for no runs in 24 balls to wreck the Australian second innings and give his side victory by eight wickets.

His 300th Test wicket came at The Oval on 15 August 1968. Just before lunch with skipper Ted Dexter uncertain what to do next, Trueman grabbed the ball and put *himself* on. With his fifth ball he bowled Ian Redpath, and the sixth, the outswinger which he bowled with more deadly effect than anyone in his day, saw Graham McKenzie caught at slip by Colin Cowdrey. Trueman had 299 Test wickets, more than anyone in the history of the game, and he was on a hat-trick, as lunch was taken.

Neil Hawke, the next man in (and another who afterwards became a very close friend) was left with forty minutes to reflect that if *he* went first ball in the afternoon he would figure for ever in the record books (he modestly insisted that there was no other way in which it would happen). As Dexter called up an umbrella field, Fred was given full reign to his great sense of theatre. There was not a single occupant of the bars or refreshment rooms; everyone was out to see the historic moment. But Fred bowled wide of Hawke's off stump and we had to wait until the new ball was taken before he departed: c Cowdrey, b Trueman, 14. The 300th Test wicket. The record has now been overtaken, first by Lance Gibbs, then Dennis Lillee, Bob Willis, Ian Botham and Richard Hadlee. How, then, do these players compare with Freddie Trueman as bowlers? Gibbs was, of course, a *slow* bowler, with fewer calls upon strength and stamina; he took his 309 Test wickets (against Fred's 307) in twelve Tests more and he did not have anything like the same amount of toil in county championship cricket. Lillee (a great bowler in every sense of the word), Willis and Botham have taken many more Tests than Trueman to pass his total and none of them has had to undertake the year-in, year-out task of bowling hundreds of overs more in county cricket. Fred loved Test cricket; he is intensely proud of his achievements in it. But he was first and foremost a *Yorkshire* bowler to whom the supremacy of his county was paramount.

Partly because of his own volatile temperament, partly because he made enemies in high places during his playing career, partly because of prejudice against him by men of influence and partly because the competition for Test places was infinitely stronger in his era than in later ones, he played in only sixty-seven Tests spread over thirteen years of his life. If he had bowled in even twenty more, as he might well have done, and if they had been concentrated into a relatively short number of years, then he would almost certainly have reached 400 victims. But it has to be remembered that while he was gathering in 307 Test wickets he was taking another 1,745 for Yorkshire and at only 17.13 apiece. In all first-class cricket he claimed 2,304 wickets and the cost (18.29 runs each) was lower than any other modern (i.e. post-Second World war) bowler except Les Jackson and Brian Statham. Let us look at his service to Yorkshire. In 1960, while taking twenty-five Test wickets in five Tests against South Africa he found time to take 132 for Yorkshire at 12.79. Twice in that season he took seven wickets in each innings – against Northants and Surrey. In 1963, when he took thirty-four wickets against the powerful West Indians he had seventy-four county championship wickets at 12.84.

His striking-rate was phenomenal. He was relied upon as a matter of course to knock over two or three of the early batsmen, after which it was his right to take a rest before being called upon to mop up the tail. This was a Yorkshire formality. Sometimes, if conditions were right, he'd go right through the main strength of opposition batting and then it took a very strong captain indeed to prise the ball out of his hand with the advice: 'There are a lot more games to come, you know.' If he found himself temporarily banished because it was a spinner's wicket he would chafe in the field, muttering darkly that he could bowl these bastards out on *any* sort of wicket. He made himself into a superb short-fine-leg fieldsman after putting down a simple offering at mid-on in his first appearance with Yorkshire and was immensely proud of his record as a catcher. His sense of outrage when, in a game for Combined Services during his two years in the RAF, he was despatched to long leg while an elderly Army officer was given *his* fielding position, is as poignant at the memory thirty years on as it was when it happened.

As a batsman he graduated from an uninhibited and sometimes undignified smiter of the ball to a man who accumulated 6,852 runs for Yorkshire with two championship centuries of which he was inordinately proud, against Northants in 1963 and Middlesex in 1965. Ah, but what about the *other* hundred? Fred loves nothing better than to pose cricketing quiz questions and a favourite is: where did I make 100 (not out, as well) for England? Answer: at the 1963 Scarborough Festival for an England XI *v*. Young England. It used to be one of the pleasures of watching county cricket to await the arrival of a down-the-order batsman who would entertain with some mighty hitting. Almost every county had a player of this kind and Yorkshire, in the late fifties and throughout most of the sixties, had two: – Fred and Don Wilson. Fred's concession to propriety and decorum was to play forward and sedately block the first ball delivered to him. After that, who knew what might happen? He could bat pretty well, but he loved to hit sixes and he has hit some crackers in his time. The sight of Fred and 'Wils' together in full cry was one of the great joys of my middle years.

Yet in all truth it has to be said that he was not always the easiest of men to get on with. I am probably the only person on earth who has never exchanged a cross word with him, and those who know us both will find the news remarkable. But it is so and I hope we shall never spoil that record. He has, however, had more than his share of brushes with authority, something which has tended to fade from his memory.

He had an uneasy tour of the West Indies in 1953–4 under the captaincy of Len Hutton. They were both Yorkies, but that was just about the only thing they had in common. Fred, very young in the international cricket sense, was loud, brash and believed firmly in his God-given right to call spades bloody shovels. Hutton, the first professional to lead an MCC side on tour, was quietly reflective and very much aware that a lot of critical eyes in NW8 would be focused on how he and his team conducted themselves abroad. It is one thing to skipper a side at home, another altogether to be in command on tour, and the first thing that Hutton had to explain to Trueman was that 'Len' was out for the duration of the trip and it was 'captain' or 'skipper' for the next three months. Fred who thought this stupid, nevertheless tried to remember this part of the code of conduct but did not always succeed, probably because of his lack of conviction that it was necessary. Hutton had been 'Len' during the previous summer and as far as Fred was concerned he would be 'Len' the following summer – what need for this temporary change? Fred was twenty-two years old and a very young twenty-two as well. He would learn . . . but that was in the future.

Leonard had firm views about most aspects of captaincy, and one of them was that excessive fraternisation with the opposition was undesirable. It would, he felt, lead to a less positive attitude as regards winning the Tests. This did not appeal at all to Fred, who, even at this early stage in his career, was developing the habit of spending more time in the opposition dressing-room than in his own, saving his natural aggression for the field of combat. He spent much of the tour with Tony Lock as his room-mate, and between them they did much to dispel the idea that like poles repel. It might hold good in physics but Trueman and Lock confounded the principle as far as human relationships were concerned. Both were passionate, noisy, demonstrative, aggressive cricketers; both were brilliant leg-slip catchers who liked to complement each other's bowling; both were quick-tempered, had little time for necessary formalities, were not over-responsive to party discipline. Spending much of their time together and sharing many views and attitudes, the pair of them did not make life any easier for their captain. It has to be seen, too, that there was a generation gap of formidable proportions between the younger and the more senior members of the party.

Hutton, and the senior professional Compton, were not only players whose reputation had been established in pre-war cricket (a world away from that of post-war players) but they had served *in* the war. Discipline had a meaning for them which could not possibly be shared by the young Turks of the post-1945 era. That common factor apart, Compton and Hutton were totally different from each other in character and temperament, and as the tour manager, Charles Palmer, was a man of gentle, easy-going nature Hutton inevitably felt himself isolated and lonely. He could be forgiven for feeling that life would have been a bit easier for him if Trueman had been a little less volatile and a little more like their fellow-Yorkshireman in the party – the dependable and strong-minded Willie Watson. He was aghast when, in Barbados, a lady of considerable presence complained that she had been jostled in a hotel lift by two members of his party whom she identified as Trueman and Lock. He summoned the two players to the lounge the following morning. They listened in silence to her catalogue of complaints and then offered their humblest apologies for the incident. Hutton thought they had done well, and said so. 'So do I,' snarled Fred bitterly, 'seeing that it wasn't us who had upset her.' He has never forgiven Leonard for that occasion, nor for what he has always felt was an adverse report at the end of the tour. And yet heaven help any man who utters a word of criticism of Hutton as a batsman in the Trueman presence. To this day Fred refers to him always as 'the great Sir Leonard' and he means it. It is this ability to separate his personal prejudice against Hutton as his captain from Hutton the master batsman which is one of the most endearing paradoxes of the Trueman character. He is not as tolerant with everyone.

He has long harboured deep suspicions that he was omitted from the 1954–5 tour to Australia because of Hutton. Leonard, however, insists that he wanted Trueman in his party but was outvoted, and since his strategy for the tour was based on fast bowling it seems inconceivable that he would regard Fred as surplus to his requirements. Trueman was disappointed, too, to be omitted from the tour party to South Africa in 1956–7 and it remains one of the great regrets of his life that he never went to that country as an England player.

He had problems with authority on many occasions throughout his career. In 1962–3 he was hopelessly at odds with the manager in Australia – not entirely surprisingly, since there was less than no chance of finding any common ground between England's greatest fast bowler and the Earl Marshal, the Duke of Norfolk, whose appointment stands alone as one of the most stupefying and monumental pieces of nonsense ever to come out of Lord's. (Yet, here again, we encounter another great paradox – Fred has long observed an almost idolatrous regard for members of the hereditary peerage!) He had his problems with many captains, including Yorkshire's Vic Wilson (1960–2) who did not like or understand Fred. Wilson, a sound and honest county cricketer, waited his time and chose the moment of one of Fred's most cherished occasions – his captaincy of the Players in the last match ever to be played against the Gentlemen (professionals *v.* amateurs in modern parlance) – to order him home for being late on parade when Fred reported for the next game at Taunton. He even clashed with Godfrey Evans over which end he was to use in a Scarborough Festival game of largely meaningless import.

Fred, in all truth, was never an easy man to handle for any captain or manager, yet none would ever question his burning desire to be on the winning side. He was utterly convinced that he was capable of winning, single-handed, any game in which he ever competed. In his second decade after retirement he retained this view when leading the Courage Breweries Old England side in a series of charity matches! His proudest moment came, not in a Test Match but when, in 1968, he led his beloved Yorkshire to victory over the Australian touring team at Sheffield by personal example and a shrewd tactical skill. Nothing, but nothing, in his whole playing career gave him the same satisfaction, and to do it at Bramall Lane before his own South Yorkshire folk . . . In his own special way he loved those people dearly, and very little has disturbed him more in his whole life than to see the land of his upbringing transformed by changing political conditions into the 'Soviet Republic of South Yorkshire'.

In his younger days Fred liked nothing better than to be pictured at the end of a day's toil with a pint in his hand – the archetypal product of the mining areas – and it became his gimmick. Yet he was not a good man at handling a pint and (again the paradox) he grew to resent bitterly the image so often presented of him as the beer-swilling product of the coalfields. He presented a series of programmes for Yorkshire Television in which he was perfectly happy, at the time, to be shown with the inevitable pint in his hand and the signing-off catch-phrase, 'Ah'll sithee.' And he *still* was infuriated by any suggestion that this was in any way the *real* Fred Trueman.

When in 1985, in the *Sunday People*, he criticised Ian Botham's bowling against Australia at Trent Bridge and got a return blast in Botham's ghost-written column in the *Sun*, what enraged him most of all was the suggestion that he had watched the cricket on that occasion from 'behind a pint glass'. The fact is that for more years than he or I care to remember, Fred's tipple has been a gin-and-tonic or a glass of white wine, but he will not accept that he achieved a reputation in his younger days which he was content to foster and which has lingered on.

His deposition from the Yorkshire Committee in the previous, bitter year of 1984 was the most fearful blow to his pride he has ever suffered. His opponent in the Craven district constituency polled 128 votes to just 65 for Fred, and he swore a great oath that never again would he have anything whatsoever to do with the county cricket club. He vowed he would never again wear the blazer-badge or the tie of Yorkshire, so deep was the hurt he experienced. Since Lord Mountgarret became president of the club and Brian Walsh chairman, both have tried hard to bring him back to the fold because they have felt that Yorkshire needs its heroes to continue their association with the club. So far they have failed because Fred's wounds are deep and they will not heal easily. The fact that only sixty-five of his constituents voted for him on an issue which was basically about Geoffrey Boycott hit Fred like a thunderbolt. In his own career, he was larger than life but never did he regard himself as bigger than Yorkshire CCC. He has warred with many people in his time, tilted at many authoritarian windmills, argued irrationally, quarrelled sometimes needlessly and made enemies unnecessarily. He has not reacted with delight to the eclipsing of his own records by later practitioners, and his friends have had to urge him: 'You were the first – no one can ever take that away from you.' But when viewed in context, and taking into consideration the opposition he bowled *against*, Fred Trueman's record has to be seen as infinitely more substantial than that of the two Englishmen who have overtaken his 307 Test wickets. He was the greatest personality of his day, too, in an age when the competition in all respects was infinitely keener. He fought for his Test place against Tyson, Statham, Loader, Moss and, at times, against a horde of lesser mortals.

Twenty-five years later he was forced to write about, and commentate on, an age in which any English-born player who could project the ball at more than seventy miles an hour was gratefully seized by the Selectors, thrust into the Test side and asked his name later. Fred, at ninety miles an hour, bowled the out-swinger, the in-swinger, the yorker, the bouncer, the cutter – all with devastating effect and considerable skill. Above all, he bowled that extensive repertoire with consistent and sustained hostility. No one before or since his time has contrived that versatility at high speed. He won games for Yorkshire and England which no one else in his generation could have done and he ranks in the forefront of great Yorkshiremen.

Like others in that distinguished band, his stubbornness is as great as any other's and greater than most. He was deeply wounded by the defection of his constituents in Craven and inflicts even deeper wounds upon himself by his rigid determination to have nothing further to do with the county, even though his pride in his birthright remains undiminished. He is bitter and violent in his condemnation of the men who wronged him – but let anyone at

Lord's, or The Oval, Trent Bridge, Edgbaston or Old Trafford,
when we all meet for Test match commentary, speak ill of Yorkshire
and great will be his wrath. Fred is still every inch a Yorkshireman,
and somehow we must coax him back.

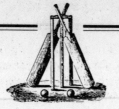

12
Illy and Closey

Raymond Illingworth played his first game for Yorkshire in 1951 and well over thirty years later, now in his mid-fifties, he remembers the reaction when he ventured an opinion in that dressing-room. He was curtly told to keep his mouth shut, unless he was spoken to, until he had been there at least a year. There was no post-war relaxing of discipline or breaches of protocol in Yorkshire cricket. That left its impression on Raymond in a number of ways.

His pedigree as a cricketer was as impeccable as it was possible to achieve: he was of the very soil and turf of the great Bradford League – in Pudsey St Lawrence's third team at eleven, Farsley's second team at thirteen and the senior side before he was sixteen. In a game which straddled his seventeenth birthday he made 148 in a Priestley Cup-tie (the League's knock-out competition). In his nineteenth year he was regularly playing for Yorkshire Colts and he was still only nineteen when he was called up to play against Hampshire in the final home game of the 1951 season. He had to work hard for his cap, which came in 1955, and he celebrated with a century at Scarborough. Originally a seam bowler, he turned to off-spin with Yorkshire. England called him up for the first time in 1958 as a spinner, and his Test career of sixty-one matches included a spell of thirty-one as captain, during which he brought back the Ashes from Australia at a time when our oldest Test opponents were a very much more formidable side than the pathetic bunch we were to see in the 1980s. In short, there was an inevitability about the whole Illingworth career. He was a professional's professional, a man who believed that first of all you learn your trade thoroughly and then continue to work at improving yourself every day of your working life. Illingworth was not only a player with talent; he was an industrious and conscientious cricketer. Nearly forty years playing the game, and thirty of those at first-class level, have given him an encyclopaedic knowledge which he now applies expertly with BBC commentary teams.

He and Brian Close have been friends for most of their lives – Close is godfather to Vicky, the elder of the two Illingworth daughters – and yet in character and captaincy they were poles apart. Close had the flair, Illingworth the application. A combination of all Close's natural gifts and Illingworth's in-bred industry must have produced the best all-round sportsman of all time. Where Close would try some often wildly improbable tactical ploy to 'make something happen', Illingworth would prefer to cut out the possibility of the batsman (or the bowler) getting the upper hand to frustrate him into making a mistake. In golfing terms, Illingworth would play the percentage shot while Close would be attempting to manufacture a miracle stroke.

Close was good-natured and easy-going; Illingworth more intense and rarely relaxed. As Yorkshire captain and first lieutenant they formed a superb team, the more so because apart from being two of the shrewdest thinkers in the game they combined a multiplicity of playing ability – as batsmen, bowlers and fieldsmen. At times Close exasperated Illingworth; they would have a furious exchange and in the next minute the row would be forgotten as they both got on with the job of winning matches for Yorkshire, which both of them firmly regarded as the job they had been put on earth to do. But while Close's relaxed nature prevented his getting too deeply involved in extraneous matters, Illy was ever a man of principle. It was this which caused him to leave Yorkshire in 1968 when he was thirty-six years old – a risk which was in so many ways out of character. But then again, he was playing the percentage shots: he *knew* he had at least three good years of cricket left, he knew he could skipper a side well, and when Leicestershire offered him the job he took it. As with Close at Somerset later, it was to prove a cataclysmic loss to Yorkshire and an immeasurable gain to his new county. Once again, with infinite sadness, it has to be said that Brian Sellers's autocratic attitude was primarily responsible.

Illingworth left, not for more money but on a matter of principle. He had had a lot of discussions with senior players about their lack of security in a world which was becoming increasingly conscious of the need for it. In asking for a three-year contract instead of the traditional, annual gentleman's agreement with his county, Raymond was to some extent firing the shots from a gun loaded by one or two of his colleagues, although he was more than willing to be the marksman. He firmly believed that his request was not unreasonable. The answer from Sellers was – and it reached him at third hand! – 'He can go and take any bugger with him who feels the same way.' It took Yorkshire an awful long time to move into the twentieth century as far as employer–employee relations were concerned. So at the end of 1968 Raymond went, and Leicestershire, for so long in the wilderness, won the 1972 Benson and Hedges Cup (beating Yorkshire in the final!), in 1974 the John Player League, in 1975 the County Championship *and* the Benson and Hedges Cup, in 1977 the John Player League. Up to the point when Raymond Illingworth arrived at Grace Road, Leicestershire had never won a thing. He and the manager-secretary, Mike Turner, got together a side which has since become a regular contributor to England Test sides.

His international reputation was not easily achieved. While he was very much an all-rounder in Yorkshire, he was generally picked by England (until he took over the captaincy in 1969) as an off-spin bowler who could bat a bit. He then had to compete with Freddie Titmus of Middlesex, David Allen and John Mortimore of Gloucs, Jim Laker of Surrey, and Martin Horton of Worcs for his Test place.

After starting with one Test against New Zealand in 1958 his international career followed something of the pattern of Close's in that he could never really feel he was established. Competition, in the fifties and sixties, was tough, very tough. He played two against India in 1959, five in the West Indies (1959–60), four against South Africa (1960), two against Australia in 1961, one against Pakistan in 1962, two in Australia (1962–3), three in New Zealand – as an opening batsman! – in 1962–3, one against New Zealand in 1965, two against West Indies in 1966, three against India and one against Pakistan in 1967, three against Australia in 1968, and he took over as captain against the West Indies at Old Trafford in 1969. England won that Test and the series 2–0, as they did the following three-match series that summer against New Zealand.

He then won, memorably, the Ashes in 1970-1 in a series where not one lbw appeal by England was answered in their favour. Managing the tour was D. G. Clark, who told a press conference before the cricket started that he would rather see Australia win the series than have all the Tests drawn! Captain and manager were always going to be on a collision course on that tour. A Yorkshire view of what was necessary Down Under was clearly different from that held in Kent. Seven Tests, instead of the scheduled six, were played, and Raymond had to cope with a threatened mutiny by strong personalities in the side for an extra fee for the extra game. Then, in the seventh game in Sydney, he had to take his team off the field when it was invaded by the crowd and the ground littered with missiles. It had not been an easy first tour as captain, but he brought back the Ashes. He was captain in twenty Tests before England was defeated – surprisingly by India – then retained the Ashes in 1972. His team beat New Zealand again in 1973 (2-0) but lost 2-0 to West Indies later in the same season. That cost Raymond the England captaincy and Mike Denness took the tour party to the West Indies that winter.

He was recalled to Yorkshire as the cricket manager at the start of the 1979 season which, by terrible coincidence, was the start of the blackest period in Yorkshire history. The Boycott revolution was just beginning, and in the mud-slinging which so horribly disfigured the county's great record he became a prime target for stupid, unreasoned and totally inaccurate insults at the hands of the Boycott faction who were in power for a mercifully brief period in 1984-5, but who were extremely vocal during the whole civil war of 1978-86. It is necessary to put a few records straight.

Raymond played 462 matches for Yorkshire, scoring 14,829 runs (fourteen hundreds) and taking 1,390 wickets, and he held 271 catches. That is all-round cricket of a high order. At Leics, in 176 matches he scored another 5,341 runs and took 372 wickets, with 84 catches. In sixty-one Tests he scored 1,836 runs (two hundreds and five fifties) and claimed 122 wickets plus 45 catches. With fifty-four other matches for representatives sides his total of first-class runs was 23,977 plus 2,031 wickets and 432 catches. That is the man in terms of figures. Now let's look at the character. Raymond gave 100 per cent to every side he ever played with, and nothing infuriated him more than a man who did less than that. He has always been blunt and outspoken because he believed that basic honesty is essential in all dealings with fellow-humans. He is less than tolerant of anyone who does not approach life in the same way. As a small boy he knew of the struggles of his parents to keep a good home in the hungry thirties, and this was to give him in his adult life a proper appreciation of money. If it didn't come easily, you didn't part with it easily. This brought him a reputation for being 'a bit tight', but then is that any more or any less than a natural Yorkshire characteristic? He applied the same principles to his bowling. He *hated* to be 'collared' and treasured a maiden over nearly as much as a wicket: the opposition had got nowt out of him in *that* six-ball period.

In this connection he learned an early lesson from Len Hutton, temporarily in charge of the side in a game against Gloucs. When Tom Graveney came in to bat, Hutton took off Brian Close and handed the ball to Raymond with the instruction: 'I want you to bowl four or five maiden overs at this chap. That's all – just make him work.' Raymond not only kept the vastly talented Graveney quiet, he took his wicket. So he was not too pleased to be taken off and Close reinstated as the bowler. Later he thought about what had happened and realised the value of the lesson. He was a *tighter* bowler than Brian; Tom was a natural stroke-player who didn't like to be tied down. QED.

He has mellowed a good deal in middle age. He is a more relaxed personality, quicker to enjoy a laugh. He has been a friend for well over a quarter of a century and I have always loved to listen to him talking cricket. Now it is possible to enjoy a much wider range of topics, but it is still one of the great delights of my working life to be working in tandem with him in the 'Test Match Special' commentary box. Just when you think you've nicely tied up a description of what is happening, in comes Raymond with a comment about something one hasn't noticed, a comment which enhances and complements the commentary but doesn't in any way point to a commentator's shortcomings. In my sixties I'm still learning; in his fifties, Ray is still teaching.

His work in the box is very much like his life-style. It is organised, disciplined, planned. Twenty-five years ago he didn't know much about the media or its operations. He could not understand that a reporter in, say Leicester, could telephone a report to his newspaper office which was basically correct and find something entirely different appearing in next morning's edition because a sub-editor, without a clue about what had been happening in the game, had taken it upon himself to do a bit of re-writing. This was a nonsense to Raymond (it was not exactly a source of great delight to those of us phoning the reports). When he joined the TV and radio teams (he has worked for both) he realised that this was something new to *him*. While he was perfectly confident that he knew the game well enough to offer valid views on what was happening out in the middle, he quickly realised that there was more to it than that. He had to learn *when* to talk and when not, when to expand on a theme and when to realise that only a couple of sentences were called for. He had to choose his words with care and make use of an extended vocabulary. He had to introduce a leavening of humour or try to dovetail with the style of his working colleague, learn when to be serious, when to be funny and, just occasionally, when to be indignant (Botham's unintelligent waste of the new ball at Trent Bridge in 1985 appalled him). He applied himself to his new work with the same conscientiousness he had used in his cricket. In both his radio and television comments, in my view, he is – and I don't throw the word about indiscriminately – brilliant.

He is the father-in-law of Ashley Metcalfe and delights in setting that gifted young batsman targets with dinner-for-four (Raymond and his wife Shirley, Ashley and his wife Diane, née Illingworth) as the stake to be won or lost. Never did I expect to see Raymond pay up so frequently and with such delight!

In a storm-tossed career, Brian Close scored 34,824 runs, took 1,167 wickets and held 808 catches (he actually brought off one stumping, too!). Those figures are, in fact, incomplete because Close (now aged fifty-six) still selects and skippers a side which plays a first-class match in the Scarborough Festival, but they will do for the purposes of our opening argument. He played twenty-two Tests for England and led them on seven occasions without being beaten. And yet he is seen in his native county as a failure (put in the starkest terms) or a player who never fulfilled his potential (in the kindest terms we can muster). Now look again at the list of his achievements and the description may be taken as a Yorkshire compliment. We demand the very highest of standards from our heroes.

Close was capped by England before Yorkshire had got round to doing so, but he never held on to anything like a regular place in the Test side *as a player.* The nearest he came to establishing himself in Test cricket was in 1966–7 when, after Mike Smith had lost one Test to the touring West Indies and Cowdrey two (with one drawn), Close took over leadership at The Oval and England won by an innings and 34 runs. Brian's personal contribution in statistical terms comprised 4 runs, no wickets and one catch. But talk to any man who played in that match and he will tell you that Close's share in the victory was immensely and deeply significant. He led England six times the following year, achieving three big wins over India, a draw and two huge winning margins against Pakistan. And he never skippered the side again.

If ever a man could claim that the slings and arrows of outrageous fortune pursued him throughout his career, that man is Brian Close. And yet at the same time it is entirely possible to see how those who make the claim that he never fulfilled his potential can justify it. He played League football for Arsenal, Leeds United and Bradford City, and officials of all those clubs claim, in school report terms, that he could have done better. He has played golf to a single-figure handicap both right-handed and left-handed – an almost incredible achievement. He has shown the highest ability at tennis, squash, snooker. If it had been possible to compete in Formula I motorracing by smashing straight through the opposition (or flying over the top) he would undoubtedly have been world champion.

What, then, is the explanation of his lack of *consistent* success? It has got to be: lack of concentration because he was too good at too many things. When he was leading Yorkshire to great prosperity in the 1960s (four county championships – three of them in succession – and two Gillette Cups) his men could point to occasions, not infrequent, when they felt 't'rudder had gone', because Close was mentally miles away, practising golf shots in his mind while the opposition got off the hook. I have been on a golf course with him when he has played sixteen holes in something like two under par and lost his ball on the other two ('I started thinking about something else'). In the middle of a bridge game he has driven his partner (the grimly intent Raymond Illingworth) to distraction by going four-down in a stone-cold certain contract because, 'I lost interest in the middle.' No – lapses of concentration have been the downfall of D. B. Close. And yet, to complete the paradox, his prime doctrine in cricket has always been: concentration. Whether you are batting, bowling and fielding, keep your concentration going. His failure to follow his own precept can clearly be seen over and over again throughout his career. A batsman of unbelievable talent, he never reached 200. But with scores of 198 and 184 in his record he clearly had the opportunity to do so.

Close was brilliant at getting the best out of others, at pointing out faults in technique, at ways of improvement. That is why he was an inspirational captain. He had an encyclopaedic knowledge of the strengths and weaknesses of opposition players, and of his own team. Rarely, one is forced to conclude, did he look at his own fallibility. If only he had been less of a subjective individual and been able to adopt an attitude of do-as-you-would-be-done-by there is no telling what heights he might have reached – and that is said with all the affection and yearning of a close friend. Nevertheless, Dennis Brian Close will leave his mark on cricket in general and Yorkshire cricket in particular because he has been spectacularly involved with it for nearly forty years. He came into the side in May 1949 with two other young players who were attempting to win their spurs against Cambridge University – F. S. Trueman and Frank Lowson. He had a sound rather than spectacular début but retained his place in the side as it turned its attention to championship cricket.

With two months of the season still to go, Close had scored 579 runs and taken 67 wickets. By the end of the season he had done the double (1,000 runs and 100 wickets) and played for England against New Zealand at Old Trafford. Close in those days was a two-in-one bowler: he could bowl fast-medium seamers in an opening spell and switch to off-breaks if required. From the first he was determined to be involved in all departments of any game he played. In the England side, as third seamer to Trevor Bailey and Les Jackson, he took his first Test wicket – and it was a good one, that of Merv Wallace. Batting at no. 9, and England leading comfortably on the first innings when he went in, his instructions were to have a look at a couple, then give it a go. Close took this quite literally, played back two deliveries and attempted to hit Tom

Burtt for six! He was caught at long on by Geoff Rabone, and in what was to become characteristic fashion complained: 'If he hadn't been t'bloody tallest man in t'side I'd have started my Test career with a six.' It did not occur to him to respect, perhaps, a refinement of the slow left-arm bowler's art or to reflect that he hadn't been able to form a reasoned view of the pace and bounce of the pitch when he essayed that ambitious launch into international cricket. He was eighteen years and 150 days old at the time. Thereafter, his Test career coughed and spluttered through the years: one against Australia on the 1950–1 tour, one against South Africa in 1955, two against West Indies in 1957, one against India in 1959, one against Australia in 1961, five against West Indies in 1963, one against West Indies in 1966, three against India and three against Pakistan in 1967, three against West Indies in 1976. Twenty-two Tests spread over twenty-seven years – what sort of a Test career is that, you may ask? Storm-tossed and star-crossed would have to be the reply, as Close has in turn been hero and villain.

At Old Trafford in 1961, for no other obvious reason than that he was D. B. Close, the controversial Yorkshireman, he was singled out not only for special mention but public ridicule in the popular press for being just one of Richie Benaud's six second innings victims when England, after looking certain of a spectacular win, finally lost by 54 runs. Close has always been fond of the sweep shot (the lap, as it is known in the trade) and he has always been a great theorist. With Benaud bowling leg-spin *round the wicket* into the bowler's rough, Close worked out to his own, if no other's, satisfaction that to sweep him 'with the tide' was practical cricket. Getting no response from his captain, Peter May, to his suggestions, Close decided to work out his own salvation. He had, to be perfectly fair to him, worked it all out with a mathematical precision (as explained in detail in his autobiography, *I Don't Bruise Easily*, Macdonald and Jane's, 1978), but it came unstuck and he was caught on the leg side. The following morning it mattered not a damn to the national paper cricket-writers that after a brilliant innings from Ted Dexter which had given England a chance to win by scoring 256 at 72 an hour, Raman Subba Row had been completely bogged down by Benaud's round-the-wicket attack, nor that May had been bowled round his legs for nought. Close was made the scapegoat, and in unequivocal terms.

Having just been brought back into the side after two years he now went out again for another two, but this time to return as a hero. It is not without significance that of Close's twenty-two Tests, half have been played against the West Indies, and while the all-out pace attack of the last ten years has been the most formidable in history because it has gone on non-stop all day (if an innings lasted that long), the 1963 pairing of Wes Hall and Charlie Griffith was the most potent English Test batsmen had faced since Lindwall and Miller in 1948. At Lord's, Close certainly saved and very nearly won the match by scoring 70 in one of the bravest innings ever seen. Balls which couldn't be hit he took on the body and when he arrived at Bramall Lane, Sheffield, the following day to play for Yorkshire against Glamorgan the right side of his body was a mass of purple bruises – so much so that there was a pre-match photo-call for the press so that the battered torso could be pictured in all its technicolour glory. Close went out into the field, bowled 25 overs and took six for 55. He then batted and scored 61; next, he bowled another 16 overs, taking four for 19 and Yorkshire won by ten wickets. He laughed at all the fuss about his bruises.

Whatever faults may be found with D. B. Close, no one, anywhere in the world, has ever questioned his courage. His 808 catches were taken either at slip, short leg or silly point, and occasionally in suicidal positions of his own invention. He has seen men caught at second slip off rebounds from his forehead, standing at short leg. He has stood at silly point with blood pouring from a gashed shin, blasting the bowler for not 'getting on with it' as the whole side waited for the leg to crumple under him. Close has always regarded himself as utterly indestructible and spent most of his cricketing life trying to prove the point.

His side of the sixties, though occasionally exasperated when he went off on one of his mental walkabouts, sometimes moved to laughter at his fixations, nevertheless regarded him in affectionate wonderment and professional respect. As a captain in the field he had, above all, flair. He would bring about a bowling change or switch a fielding position where there was absolutely no reason in the world for doing so, and nine times out of ten it came off. He was an implicit believer in his ability to *make* something happen in the field when nothing seemed likely. He was far-sighted in terms of situations which might arise to the extent that his anticipation at times seemed uncanny. Early in the career of Ted Dexter, the most naturally gifted batsman of his day, Close fortuitously got his wicket with a full toss and firmly believed ever after that Dexter was susceptible. Close's 'tactical full toss' helped Lord Edward to a lot of runs after that – but somehow Close brought about his downfall a lot of times, too. It was this sort of fixation which alternately drove his team to distraction and wonderment as, first, a stream of fours would result and then a wicket would fall for an outlay of runs which was acceptable.

He convinced a mystified Don Wilson, fairly early in his slow left-arm bowling career, that a leg slip was a necessary part of his attacking field on the grounds that even if Wilson could not turn a ball the 'wrong' way the batsman would *think* that he could. Closey was an innovator. When Yorkshire were trying to winkle out a side on a good wicket, with the odds all against them, it was an entertainment in itself to watch him searching for a means to accomplish the unlikely. Somehow a wicket very rarely seemed unlikely. Yorkshire played some marvellous cricket in the 1960s.

Close believed 100 per cent in Yorkshire and it is not in any way an exaggeration to say that he would have given his life for his side. There is no doubt at all that he would have if it had been necessary. He lost the England captaincy when, for once, he was firmly established because he regarded the needs of his side in the County Championship as paramount. It happened at Edgbaston in August 1967. Yorkshire went into the game needing to beat Warwickshire to take over from Kent at the top of the table, and towards the end of it Warwickshire were left to make 142 in 102 minutes to win. Close's view of the situation was quite simple: 'If we can't win the game we have to do our damnedest to make sure the opposition don't.' There is no doubt at all that Close firmly believed in that policy, but his efforts to keep Warwickshire at bay were not seen in the same light by either spectators or the cricketing press. The following day he was pilloried throughout the land for slowing down play to prevent Warwickshire from getting the runs. As a result, he was called upon to face a panel of former county captains to answer criticism of his tactics. He made out what he considered a cast-iron case in justification but the panel unanimously decided that he was responsible for using unfair delaying tactics. He spent the following weekend avoiding the national press (having to go to some rather undignified lengths to do so) and during the Final Test at The Oval was informed that he would not be leading the tour party to the West Indies that winter.

Close was not the first captain to slow down an over-rate – even though to this day he insists that he did not consciously do so – and most assuredly he was not the last. The Edgbaston incident led to the Law that a minimum of twenty overs had to be bowled in the last hour of a first-class game, but by no means has it ensured an acceptable bowling-rate in the preceding hours of a game. Indeed, Cowdrey went to the West Indies as captain instead of Close and infuriated the normally imperturbable Gary Sobers by slowing things down. In the 1980s a Test over-rate by the West Indies of between eleven and twelve an hour has become the norm, and they resist all attempts by the International Cricket Conference to improve this. In India, I have seen Doshi and Shastri – two slow left-armers – reduce the rate to nine an hour with the most ostentatious and cynical co-operation of their captain. Yorkshire at Edgbaston in 1967 were in their *sixteenth* over, with a wet ball, in a drizzle and three fast men operating, when the first hour passed by. But Close was ever an innovator, and now he had lost the England captaincy for alleged tactics in the field which were to become commonplace in the future!

Misfortune in its highest form continued to dog the footsteps of D. B. Close, and the worst day of his life came on 25 November 1970, when he was called to Yorkshire headquarters, confronted by Brian Sellers and John Nash, and given ten minutes to decide whether to resign or to be sacked. The reason given for this astonishing ultimatum was Close's public criticism of the limited-overs game. We had had the Gillette Cup since 1963, with teams playing knock-out cricket for sixty overs a side, and the Sunday afternoon John Player League (forty overs) had begun in 1969. Close was far from being alone in expressing disquiet at the effect the Sunday afternoon frolic in particular was having on young players trying to learn the first-class game – fast bowlers who had to operate from a stipulated length of run and bowl without slips or short legs, batsmen who were forced to play across the line to score runs against defensive fields. Everyone who cared for first-class cricket saw the advance of 'one-day' cricket as a serious danger to the 'proper' game. But it brought in the crowds – (as did the open bars on Sunday) – and counties who looked apprehensively at their balance sheets knew that it had to stay. Yorkshire, who were expected by members and committee alike to be in close contention for *every* title, had won the Gillette in 1965 and 1969, but they had made little or no impression in the first two years of the Player League's existence. Perhaps what made matters worse was that the first two Sunday championships had been won by *Lancashire*! Somehow, it seems, the Committee had mixed up this lack of success with Close's criticisms and come to the conclusion that Yorkshire were not winning because the captain didn't think much of the competition. It is staggering to realise how little that Committee knew of their captain. They dismissed him from the leadership and appointed in his place Geoffrey Boycott. Close's philosophy of captaincy was that it was all about giving – to the Club, to the side, to every individual member of it. Boycott's approach was somewhat different, as the Committee were to find to their cost.

Close's sense of personal grief at his dismissal was overwhelming. I went to play golf with him at Bradford Golf Club, to offer my profound sympathy and to talk about his future. He said he had already had an approach from Leicestershire with generous terms and I advised him not to accept it. 'Why?' he asked, curiously. 'Because,' I said, 'Ray Illingworth was a marvellous lieutenant to you in Yorkshire [Illy had gone to skipper Leicestershire in 1969] but I doubt very much if you could be a good lieutenant to him. You always want to lead from the front and you know perfectly well that Raymond is very much his own man. It wouldn't work. Think about it. So what about Somerset – a marvellous opportunity there?' So off he went to the West Country, where Brian Langford generously made way for him to take over the captaincy in 1972, and the greatest period in Somerset's hundred-year history began. It is, of course true that during the next six years the county saw the arrival of a brilliant young West Indian called Vivian Richards and the emergence of an English prodigy named Ian Botham, but it is equally true that Close played an important part in the development of both of them. And before they arrived on the scene my good friend Brian Langford had already noted a different attitude to the game in men alongside whom he had been playing for years. That Close was an inspirational leader there can be no doubt whatsoever.

That he is a great Yorkshireman is equally clear from the way he returned to try to help, at Committee level, in the midst of the revolution of 1984. Given the circumstances of his departure from Yorkshire cricket, one can only marvel that he wanted to be involved again at any price.

He allowed his name to be put forward as a candidate for the 1984 elections, and the group of Boycott supporters who achieved a landslide victory in the poll did not oppose him in Bradford no. 2 District. No doubt they felt that after the scandalous way he had been treated fourteen years earlier he would be a formidable ally in opposition to the Establishment of the county club. In the event they were totally mistaken. Close put aside any sense of grievance he might have felt (and been readily forgiven for feeling) and set about trying to put matters right in a club experiencing its bleakest period since the beginning of Lord Hawke's reign. He was quickly frustrated by the Boycott brigade; it took less than a year for him to resign rather than sit idly by while the new force in the club ran it in a way he regarded as absurd. He started from scratch the following year, standing again for election and putting forward a vote of no confidence in the Boycott-orientated committee. He won the election, though lost the no-confidence vote, but the winds of change were now blowing through the ranks of the Yorkshire membership and at last Close began to feel he could make some progress. He still believes that, while recognising that it is a long road back to the point where he left the county in 1970.

The Yorkshire team of the sixties were the happiest bunch of cricketers I have ever known. It was my privilege to be closely associated with them as both newspaperman and broadcaster, and without doubt it was one of the best periods of my life. It was the last link with the golden age, and then what J. M. Kilburn has called the silver age, leading up to the Second World War. It was the end of the era when young players joined the Yorkshire first eleven with humility, feeling that they were entering into a very special way of life. There the heritage of a hundred years was not something which was consciously taught; it was essentially an atmosphere which was absorbed. But it was by far the most powerful force in English cricket. Although Trueman, Taylor and Binks had retired and Illingworth had moved to Leicestershire, Close at the end of the 1970 season still led a strong enough nucleus of the old brigade to retain the traditional atmosphere of the Yorkshire dress-ing-room: Padgett, Sharpe, Hutton, Wilson, Nicholson, Hamp-shire. Old and Cope had fitted well into the pattern, Bairstow was just one of two leading candidates for the wicket-keeper's job and was unlikely to rock the boat. In fact no one thought in terms of *anyone* rocking the boat. Yorkshire were in a transitional period and had lost more experienced players in a short space of time than was usually the case.

Boycott, who had been in the side for eight years, had certainly proved to be an odd-ball in that gregarious and fraternal dressing-room but he was regarded as just another character (of a strangely different type) in a side full of them. Fred Trueman had never spent much time, socially, with his team-mates but on the field he was essentially a Yorkshire player of huge professional stature. Under the Close type of captaincy no one in that dressing-room was, in Orwellian terms, more equal than anyone else and there was not the slightest reason to believe that Boycott was an exception to the unwritten rule. The departure of Close and the appointment of Boycott as captain changed all that almost overnight. Suddenly, from a captain who believed his job was all about *giving*, the team found itself with a leader who believed it was about *taking* – taking every opportunity to enhance his personal reputation. And York-shire cricket has never been the same since that day.

So the fact that Close's reign as a successful skipper came to an abrupt and miserable conclusion was most certainly not his fault, but within the broad context of a long career it has to be seen as yet another instance of genius unfulfilled. If he had been able (or allowed) to complete that period of transition the last seventeen or eighteen years of the county's history might well have seen the dawning of another golden or silver age. Instead, it heralded the blackest period in a hundred years.

13
A New Lease of Life

Ronnie Burnet's appointment to the captaincy in 1958 was as much of a surprise to the man himself as it was to Johnny Wardle, the rest of the Yorkshire team and the county in general. Within the Bradford League, Ron was a well-known player with Baildon, as he was within the county club itself, but I think it is fair to say that he had never aspired to the higher realms of the game above Minor Counties level. He was a pleasant, cheerful and popular cricketer who was known to be quite capable of cracking the whip when necessary but preferred, on the whole, to enjoy his cricket in the company of men who enjoyed it similarly. He was certainly aware that factional interests and groupings within the first eleven had caused his predecessor, Bill Sutcliffe, a lot of difficulty and he was equally aware of the Committee's view that these had been primarily responsible for a lack of success throughout the fifties. The side was full of talent and ability, but spirit and attitude were clearly wrong.

Now times were changing. Willie Watson, the senior professional, had joined Leicestershire and ill-health was forcing Bob Appleyard out of the game (he played for the last time in 1958). Sutcliffe's retirement as a player as well as captain meant that Burnet would have a nucleus of experience – formed by Wardle, Vic Wilson, Close, Trueman, Illingworth and Jimmy Binks, the wicket-keeper – leaving four places (when all the senior men were fit or not on Test duty) to be filled by young and relatively inexperienced men. There was an exciting challenge about the job which had to appeal to the new captain. On the other hand, he recognised that he was thirty-nine years old, that his work in the field would not be spritely and might indeed be an embarrassment at times. There was the transition to make from league and Colts XI (two-day) cricket to the long-term strategic issues of the first-class game, as well as the day-to-day tactical operations. Most of all, he faced the task of encouraging and 'bringing on' the younger players while harnessing the goodwill and co-operation of the more seasoned campaigners. It was a very tall order indeed, and it says a good deal for Burnet's strength of character that he was willing to take on the job at all.

That he and Wardle were on a collision course from the start, there can be no doubt. Johnny, understandably, felt slighted at having been passed over when he had pretty firm grounds for expecting to be made Yorkshire's first modern professional captain. Burnet was in no doubt about Wardle's feelings, but he had been given a job to do by the Committee and he was a steely enough character to be determined to see it through. He simply had to face up to Wardle – twelve years a Yorkshire player, with twenty-eight England caps and four tours – or lose face completely with the remainder of the side. Even the experienced players were divided in their loyalties between captain and senior pro: Illingworth, still scarred by comments Wardle had made to him and other youngsters seven years earlier, believed that Burnet should be given every chance; Close thought it an absurd appointment. Before one season had gone by, Burnet had to tell the Committee: 'It's either Wardle or me. The dressing-room is not big enough for both of us and I can't do the job I think you want me to do while he is there.' In the meantime, Yorkshire's position in the County Championship had slumped from third in 1957 to eleventh in 1958 as internal strife tore the side apart. Wardle went. And in 1959, Burnet in his second and last season as captain, led Yorkshire back to the top for the first time since the 1949 shared title with Middlesex. It had been the longest period without a championship in the twentieth century and it didn't matter twopence to any Yorkshireman that in those ten years they had been runners-up four times.

It was a summer which might have been born out of controversy and bitterness but it was to give Burnet memories which bring back smiles of pure delight nearly thirty years later: 'Derbyshire at Chesterfield where Donald Carr delayed his declaration until we had to get 304 in 170 minutes. We were hopping mad – so mad that we got 'em and I'll never forget Ken Taylor's 144 as long as I live . . . Essex at Colchester where we scored 86 off eight overs and five balls to win before time ran out . . . Hampshire at Hull where we got the last 105 in ten overs. . . . The facts and figures roll lightly from the tongue as if it all happened last week. And the greatest memory of all stems from the day the championship came back to Yorkshire again, 1 September at Hove.

To win, Yorkshire had to score 218 in ninety-five minutes on the last day of the season to beat Sussex. They did it with seven minutes to spare and five wickets in hand to complete one of the most heroic days in the county's history. The miracle of their achievement was matched by the miracle of the transformation Burnet had wrought in team-spirit in the course of one season. Of his side at Hove that day, Close, Illingworth and Trueman were already Test players; Brian Bolus (with Notts), Doug Padgett, Ken Taylor, Jimmy Binks, Don Wilson and Jack Birkenshaw (with Leics) were to reach Test status in the future. The exception, apart from the captain himself, was Bryan Stott who retired in 1963 when he was only twenty-nine because he was needed to help in the family business. He had scored 9,168 runs in 290 innings for the county. My outstanding memories of Bryan Stott will centre on his opening partnerships with Ken Taylor and their magnificent running between the wickets. Both were superb athletes and when they took five short singles in the first over of a Roses Match I felt (reared on those awesomely dour pre-war encounters) that cricket would never be the same again. One could visualise dear old Emmott Robinson, then in his eighties, shaking his head in bewilderment and chuntering away to himself: 'Dear, oh dear. Wotivver is goin' on?' Emmott, whose unforgettable description of the social graces of a Roses match was, 'We say "Ow do" on't first morning and then nowt else but "Ow's that?" for t'next three,' would never have understood.

Ken Taylor, like Willie Watson before him and Chris Balderstone after him, was a Huddersfield Town footballer. He was, in fact, an all-round sportsman of high ability and a gifted artist who had studied at the Slade. Clearly he had something of the artist's restless nature because after retiring as a Yorkshire player he enjoyed cricket and football in New Zealand and in South Africa (where he coached both at the highest level) before returning to England. This characteristic was obviously inherited by his son Nick, who bowled fast for Yorkshire, then Surrey, then Somerset!

Ken was an out-fieldsman of the highest quality, especially at cover point, and his medium-paced bowling was of something better than stand-breaking standard. He hit 12,864 runs for Yorkshire and took 129 wickets, many of them in crucial situations. His Test appearances were limited to three – two against India in 1959 and one against Australia in 1964 – all of them as a batsman. But as a county cricketer he was an exceedingly useful man to have in the side. He got rid of a nerve-racking habit of his youth, when still a Colt, which somehow demanded that he take one hand from the bat-handle and touch the peak of his cap in the period *between the bowler starting his run and delivering the ball*. My lasting memory is of Ken batting for Yorkshire II against Notts II in Nottingham in the early fifties and going through this maddening ritual to the bowling of Freddie Stocks. As Stocks was an off-spinner whose approach to the wicket was just two paces, the mannerism reduced me to a gibbering wreck. What it did for the batsman himself – or indeed the bowler! – we can only conjecture, but thankfully he had rid himself of it by the time he established himself in the first team.

Doug Padgett, a real Bradford lad, was technically the most polished and correct of the fifties–sixties batsmen and so it was a fairly orthodox appointment which made him the county coach after his retirement in 1971. He batted for Yorkshire for twenty years, starting when he was seventeen, and scored 20,306 runs. As a Bradford League player in his teens he had every shot in the book. Later, he reduced his repertoire but retained that most graceful of strokes, the late cut, which he played better than anyone of his day. There were times when I thought he looked more like Hutton than Hutton! Following a tradition which went back a full century, Doug was a great connoisseur of beer and for anyone searching for the best pint in any town where the game was played, the man to follow was D. E. V. Padgett. He was an inveterate talker – and walker – in his sleep, causing never-ending anguish to his room-mate and travelling companion, Ray Illingworth.

As Padgie spent most of his twenty years in the outfield, appealing to the umpire was not, strictly speaking, in the natural order of things. Perhaps it was a sense of frustration, then, which caused him to leap to his feet (still in bed) in the middle of the night, roaring 'How's that' in the most vociferous Tony Lock style. The heart-rending lamentations of Illingworth (who prized his eight hours a night above almost anything else) at breakfast usually ensured that the team started the day on a note of high mirth. A great character, a beautiful batsman, Padgett's finest hour (although he hit 29 centuries) was probably in the championship-winning match at Hove in 1959 when he hit a dazzling 79 and shared a partnership of 141 with Stott.

Brian Bolus was a highly intelligent man, articulate, witty and humorous, who did some surprisingly unintelligent things in his time. He theorised a great deal about his batting and worked out a method which ensured he went a remarkable number of innings without ever being bowled out. It was fairly late in the day when it was pointed out to him that he was rapidly approaching a record number of lbw dismissals! He was one of a number of batsmen who had to fight for a place in Yorkshire's side of the middle-to-late fifties – Stott, Taylor, Sharpe, Dickie Bird – and scarcely had he established himself as a regular first-teamer than he was released by Yorkshire in 1962 when the Committee decided that there were too many capped players on the books. He had scored more than 1,000 runs in 1960 and 1961 but his reputation was as a fairly stodgy accumulator of runs rather than an elegant stroke-maker. He was offered a contract at Notts, and, typically, he confided his latest theory: 'My method doesn't seem to have done me much good. I shall now start to crash the ball to all parts.' And he did – to the extent of 2,000 in his first season at Trent Bridge.

It brought him an England call-up for the last two Tests against the West Indies in 1963, and I remember when I telephoned my congratulations asking what his policy was to be. 'Well,' he said, 'the new method has got me there. I'd better stick with it.' He drove the first ball he received in Test cricket to the long-on boundary for four! As this was the hey-day of Hall and Griffith it provided a remarkable start to a Test match (and career) but it was unlikely that it could last. With innings of 14, 43, 33 and 15, however, Bolus earned himself a winter tour to India, where his ability to find something amusing in the direst situation made him a good companion. His theories worked out well, too: 88 and 22 in the First Test, 25 and 57 in the Second, 39 and 35 in the Third, 58 in the Fourth and 67 in the Fifth.

By the summer of 1964 England had acquired a new opening batsman who looked likely to be around for some time – one Geoffrey Boycott – but although he fractured a finger in the First

Test (and missed the Second), England called upon four other opening batsmen in that series, two of them makeshift, without finding a place for J. B. Bolus. He had batted just seven times for England, never failed completely and averaged 41.3. What did *he* do wrong?

Don Wilson is the only Yorkshire player to have come out of the heart of The Dales, and such is the shortage of the big grounds necessary for a slow left-armer to develop his art successfully in the uplands of north-west Yorkshire that he could never have made it if he had not moved from his native Settle to play in the Bradford League. But of course he had to have the natural ability in the first place, and it had to be recognised, so there is no reason why the more remote fastnesses of the county should not produce more players of class. Wilson, like Bolus, was a Character, though by no means in the same way. His first close friend in the county side, where he had the unenviable task of following the great Wardle, was Jack Birkenshaw, the fledgeling off-spinner who understudied Illingworth. After Birkenshaw had moved to Leicestershire Wilson became especially matey with Philip Sharpe, and when Richard Hutton came into the side via Repton School and Cambridge University, the three of them formed as unlikely a trio of musketeers as one could expect to find on the circuit. Today, a quarter of a century on, they are still great friends.

Wilson was not a great spinner of the ball and by no means had the thoughtful application of a Verity. But he was ever a competitor, always an enthusiast. Tall and angular (a good badminton player), he got bounce on firm wickets and this, allied to shrewd field-placing by his captains and a lair of close catchers just as good as those of the 1930s team, brought him a haul of 1,104 wickets for the county between 1957 and 1974. He played in six Tests and enjoyed (literally) tours to Australia, New Zealand, India and Ceylon. Wils has enjoyed – still does – every minute of his cricketing life; in fact it is difficult to think of a player who ever got more obvious delight from following his chosen trade than Wilson, D. His expectancy as a bowler was wonderful to behold, arms flying up into the air in anticipation even when the ball had contacted the middle of the bat most resoundingly. He was a vastly entertaining hitter of the ball and an electrifying fieldsman. Taylor at cover and Wilson at mid-wicket would die rather than let the ball through.

Early in their travels with Yorkshire, Wilson and Sharpe became seriously addicted to The Black and White Minstrels stage shows, and whenever they were playing either at Lord's or The Oval they became the most regular pair of Stage-Door Johnnies the Victoria Palace has ever seen. They developed close friendships with the company and became adept at staging a two-man version of the Minstrels routines. Twenty-five years later they can 'sing' for a full hour, non-stop and word perfect, the medleys which made the Black and Whites so immensely popular. (The quotes around sing are because while Sharpe has a pleasant voice, Wils's was once described as resembling that of a corncrake with laryngitis). But they are a hugely entertaining pair and their joint rendering of 'She's Only a Bird in a Gilded Cage' is one of the funniest party-pieces I have ever seen.

Wilson, like Sharpe, Hutton and others too numerous to mention, did not 'get on' with Boycott and after the 1971 appointment of a new captain he did not linger too long. He coached with tremendous success in the native township of Soweto in South Africa, and when the Indoor Cricket School was opened at Lord's in 1977 Wilson became the chief coach, a post he still retains and of which he has made the most tremendous success. I must confess to being surprised at the appointment, not because I had the slightest doubts about Wils's ability but because it seemed utterly anachronistic to find a Yorkshireman put in charge of *anything* at Headquarters. It is, good, very good, to report that Don not only is damn near worshipped by the MCC Young Cricketers on the Lord's ground staff and the kids who simply go there for coaching, but has a good relationship with the junta of colonels who preside over matters on the other side of the ground. He has taken Dales cricket a long way.

Jimmy Binks earned his place in history by keeping wicket in 412 consecutive County Championship matches between 1955 and 1969 but, that apart, he was not only a superb 'keeper but an indispensable member of the High Command in the field. He was the man consulted by Burnet, Vic Wilson, Close, Illingworth and Trueman on such matters as the pace of the wicket, strengths and weaknesses of batsmen (real or imagined), lines of attack, fractional adjustments of field-placings. Binks not only kept wicket magnificently, he *noticed* everything that was going on around the bat. He kept on 'keeping with a multitude of injuries – including broken fingers –

and certainly in the sixties the team would rather have seen him standing there with ten broken fingers inside his gloves than anyone else with a full complement of intact digits. It has always been fashionable in Yorkshire to believe that *any* of our specialist players ought to be in the England side as of right, and it is undoubtedly true that Jimmy was unlucky to have been capped only twice. Even those modest honours came when he toured India in 1963–4 as second wicket-keeper to Jim Parks, a good batsman who, *behind* the stumps, was scarcely fit to lace Binks's boots. In his second Test, in Calcutta, Binks was called upon to open the innings with his former team-mate, Brian Bolus, an occasion which both of them recall with wry amusement. 'At least,' mused Binks, 'if I never do another thing I've opened for England before a bigger crowd than most players see in a lifetime.'

At his peak, Binks was rated the best in England by the man who kept him out of the Test side for most of his career, Alan Knott. In his best year (1960) Binks claimed 107 victims, and he forged a most distinguished link in the chain of Yorkshire wicket-keepers which started with David Hunter in 1888 and continued through Arthur Dolphin, Arthur Wood, Don Brennan and, since Binks, has been stretched further by David Bairstow from 1970 to the present. Broadly speaking, the county has had six regular wicket-keepers in a hundred years! One of the small but notable bunch of county players to come out of Hull, Binks could be outspoken and didn't suffer fools gladly; in many years of happy association with him I took these as manifestations of his basic honesty. He was a good companion, if a terrible dominoes partner!

Occasionally – and it had to be in the absence of Close, Illingworth and Trueman – he skippered the side, and a strange lack of belief in himself prevented his doing it terribly well. Once I gave him a bit of stick in the *Daily Mail* for what I considered tactical shortcomings. Having read this the following morning he asked me over breakfast what I would have done in the same situation. He listened without interruption to a perhaps not entirely convincing policy statement, then grinned, 'Oh well. If you're so bloody good you can buy the beer tonight.' That's the sort of relationship I treasure. On another occasion when Jimmy was in charge in Bristol the evening festivities in the hotel got a bit out of hand, largely due to the press gang rather than the players, but it resulted in a complaint to

Headingley. Jimmy need not have worried about it; the Committee hauled in F. S. Trueman and administered a severe reprimand to him as the acting captain. Fred had been busy at the time taking eleven West Indies wickets for 152 at Lord's!

In the fifties and sixties, the number of bowlers who had partnered Freddie Trueman soared even higher (try working out the full list some time if you want an interesting little exercise) and the three most notable additions were Mike Cowan, Bob Platt and Melville Ryan. Cowan, in line of descent from Abe Waddington and George Hirst, was a left-arm quick bowler who looked to have the potential to be one of the best of his kind when a back injury forced him to return from a tour to Pakistan in the winter of 1955–6. He was never quite the same bowler after that and he struggled for the remainder of his career against injury and illness which caused him to miss whole seasons of cricket. Nevertheless, he had a heart as big as a pumpkin and his passion for playing cricket for Yorkshire brought him back time after time when most of us thought never to see him again.

He was rarely to be seen without a smile, despite all his misfortunes, and he could always be relied upon to cheer up the gloomiest gathering. Early in 1960 – just back after another debilitating illness – he was struggling to take a wicket but laughing, as ever, as he staggered about the dressing-room with a stump tucked under his arm, as though impaling him. It was his 'It-only-hurts-me-when-I-laugh' sketch but Don Wilson turned it round on him. 'Ow, Mick,' he inquired, pointing to the stump, 'Has ta ever *hit* one o' them?' Given the circumstances of his career at that moment, it was the sort of cruelly humorous remark which was a speciality in the Yorkshire camp and for a moment I saw the smile flicker and almost die on Cowan's lips. But he had the last laugh that season – nine for 43 against Warwickshire at Edgbaston – and he went one better: his usual score line, Cowan, 0, was actually 0 not out in his only innings there! He missed most of 1961, again with injury problems, and finally had to call it a day in 1962. He took 263 wickets for Yorkshire (93 more than his total of runs!) and we shall never know how good he might have become but for that injury in Pakistan. I like to think that he would have been very good indeed. Although Mike was born in Leeds he has always been by residence and inclination a South Yorkshireman from Doncaster, where he claims the fish-and-chips are as good as those in the Leeds–Bradford area – a nonsense of course. But he still smiles and makes others smile too with a brilliant after-dinner speaking routine. A sales representative for Penguin Books, it is difficult to imagine any bookseller being able to resist his blandishments.

Bob Platt came from 'The Last of the Summer Wine' country, Holmfirth, but had none of the characteristics of any of that amusing trio of Clegg, Compo and Foggy. Platt was always the best-dressed man on the cricket circuit, his high-quality Huddersfield worsted immaculately tailored, a man of great charm and polish. His cricketing ancestry would come from Billy Bates, through Herbert Sutcliffe, and as a bowler he was almost unique in county annals because he was a purveyor of in-swing. His variations lay in change of pace and his most potent ally was short square leg, now known as the bat-pad position, where Bryan Stott in particular took many catches from his bowling.

It was not, as we have learned from Bill Bowes, the most fashionable form of attack for a Yorkshire bowler, but Platt commanded line and length so well that he was never easily 'collared' and gathered 281 wickets for the county before retiring and going to help out Northamptonshire. But he was soon back, running Yorkshire's Second XI and working as a Committee member. As a batsman, he always showed that he possessed all the strokes but somehow seemed incapable of imparting any strength to them. Thus, the most perfect cover drive would trickle gently into the hands of cover point, an exquisitely timed cut would require third man to come in to meet it. It exasperated Robert that he could not score more runs while his efforts to do so caused wild hilarity within the dressing-room.

Mel Ryan, from Huddersfield, took 413 wickets by dint of consistent effort and industry and a modest degree of outswing and medium-fast pace. He was the Paul Getty of the dressing-room of his day, the wealth accumulated not from oil but from the family chain of newsagents and tobacconists shops strategically placed around the centre of the town. Having a bit of brass in his pocket meant to Ryan that one had to be all the more careful in guarding it. Thus I once found myself being fiercely harangued by my partner on Finchley Golf Course for joining the opposition pair in laughing when my wretched tee-shot ricochetted from the tee-box, over Mel's head and out of bounds. 'Come on, Bull [his Yorkshire CCC name in tribute to an outstanding physical attribute]', I protested when his tirade lost momentum. 'We're only playing for half a crown and only last night you were telling us how much you've got in the bank.' The fury returned. 'That's how it got there,' he stormed, 'by taking care of the half-crowns.' And he meant it. A gentle and genial bear of a man off the golf course, he was transformed into a raging tiger on it. Although the books show his best performance as six for 33 against Leicestershire, his best for me was in the Old Trafford Roses match of 1960. Lancashire needed only 78 to win on the final day but Ryan took five for 50 in making the ancient foes struggle to reach their target with just two wickets left. It was one of the most thrilling afternoons of cricket I have ever seen and it was Melville Ryan, junior partner, who caused panic in the opposition ranks rather than the legendary Trueman.

It is as one of the greatest slip-fieldsmen of all time that we tend to remember the cricket of Philip Sharpe, forgetting, perhaps, that in twelve Tests he averaged 46.23 with the bat. He held a total of 617 catches in first-class cricket, and in 1962 he held 71 of them – the season in which he also scored 2,201 runs. Thus it seems incredible that he did not go with England to Australia during the following winter and had to wait until the Third Test of 1963 against West Indies before being called up for the first time. There is no real line of descent for P. J. Sharpe except from Norman Yardley, or more probably from one of the captains in the period between Lord Hawke and Brian Sellers, when the skipper's destiny was to toss up and then be dismissed to the outfield while the joint dictatorship of Wilfred Rhodes and Emmott Robinson dictated the course of events. This was more a matter of character, certainly not a comparison of playing ability. Sharpe had – still has – a mild, easy-going nature which abhorred dispute or confrontation. Perhaps it was the background of Bradford Grammar School and Worksop College which gave him a temperament more suited to playing his cricket at Hove or Canterbury than Leeds or Bradford. And yet no one has ever worked harder for Yorkshire, on the field or in the Committee Room. He has always believed 100 per cent in the county pre-eminence over so many years, always given 100 per cent to sustaining it. A man for all seasons, Sharpe played hockey for Yorkshire, the North and very nearly for England and it is impossible to imagine that he ever made an enemy in his life. On the other hand, he has made a very large number of friends.

Purely in the catching sense, his forebear would have to be Long John Tunnicliffe. In his own era, the only possible rival was the Australian Bobby Simpson, but Ray Illingworth, who played with both, rates Sharpe slightly higher:

> His concentration was incredible. He could stand for five-and-a-half hours with nothing coming his way and then, in the last thirty minutes, pull off the most breathtaking catch. In 1969 at Lord's he had been fielding at slip all day with nothing happening and then, five minutes from close of play, John Shepherd pushed hard at a ball, aiming for the covers and there was Sharpie, diving full length to take the catch right-handed. That's slip fielding.

A generation reared on limited-overs cricket loudly claims huge improvements in fielding standards because of the one-day game. This is the sheerest, most arrant nonsense. Athleticism, speed about the outfield, is certainly of a higher standard than it generally used to be, but the *real* fielding, the artistry of the close-catcher, has all but disappeared, so it is worth taking a close look at the art of P. J. Sharpe. By the time he was two years old, he was already getting catching practice from his father! A lovely man, Bert Sharpe, who gave up his own cricketing life early and then regretted it, but later, like most of us, got more pleasure out of watching his son do well than he could ever have derived from his own sport. Bat and ball went everywhere with father and son (and let's not forget mother, who was an enthusiast too) and catching practice was always a part of any day. As Bert pointed out to his son, with sound Yorkshire common sense: 'If it comes to a choice between two batters or two bowlers who are just about as good as each other, the verdict will always go to the one who fields better.' So young Philip had hours of practice, first to the right hand, then the left, some sharp chances, some tantalisingly lobbed almost out of reach. Father's reward was to have his son picked to play for England virtually on his slip-catching ability alone, though, as we have seen, he made his mark with the bat as well.

Like everyone else he was made to realise very early in his career that in playing for Yorkshire he was entering a hard school. He was twelfth man at The Oval in Eric Bedser's Benefit match of 1958 and was called on to the field as emergency fieldsman and stationed in the junior's position at short-leg – 'Boot Hill'. Ray Illingworth bowled a full toss (a rarity in itself) and Peter May cracked it square, straight on to Sharpe's knee. As he hopped about in agony, insult was literally added to injury by Illingworth's grinning comment to Ronnie Burnet: 'I thought you said this bugger could catch.' Raymond, in fact, became Sharpe's greatest fan, not least of all because the man who was to become the world's best slip-catcher held more of them off his bowling than that of anyone else. He took them as they were about to sail over his head or hurtle past his ankles; he took them via Close's head at short leg and Trueman's boot at leg slip. If P. J. Sharpe ever missed a catch it was the immediate signal for every man in the Yorkshire press gallery to make a note in his book. He raised slip-catching not only to an art form but to a geometrical science by working out the optimum place to stand after taking into account the pace of the pitch, the type of bowling, the positioning of the wicket-keeper and the known technique of the batsman. Yet, laconically he listed the requirements to be a top-class slipper as (1) being able to judge the speed of the ball as it comes to you, (2) naturally quick reflexes, (3) concentration and (4) a reasonable amount of luck. The latter point in itself ensured that there would never be any point of intellectual contact between Sharpe and Geoffrey Boycott, who believed with passion that good fortune played no part in the game of cricket. To him, it was an exact science. He did, however, come to believe that *bad* luck could be an influence!

Playing for Yorkshire in the sixties was Sharpe's idea of heaven, as it was to the whole side. When, occasionally, something went wrong he would be far from the raging arguments which ensued, though just as deeply concerned that things *had* gone wrong. But to him, tomorrow was another day – and another chance to put things right, preferably without fuss, certainly without bother. There was a lot of *un*Yorkshireness in P. J.! He shunned the Close-–Illingworth–Binks inquests on the evening of an unsuccessful day, searching instead for companionship in a few quiet beers and a lot of noisy singing. He was (and is) an accomplished light baritone who is today one of the most enthusiastic members of the York Light Opera Company. They sang at his wedding a piece called 'I will walk with God', which provided John Hampshire with the one-liner of the year: 'Does that mean he's going to open t'batting wi' Boycott?' Sharpe left Yorkshire after the 1974 season, played forty games for Derbyshire, then devoted himself to skippering Norfolk's Minor Counties side and the Manningham Mills team in the Bradford League. In 1983 he became a Test Selector and when he gets to heaven he will undoubtedly become immediately involved in the cricket team there, standing at first slip and teaching St Peter how to effect a compromise. He is my very good friend but I have always found it difficult to think of him as a 100 per cent, dyed-in-the-wool Yorkie. He's too damned reasonable!

John H. Hampshire was another man of the sixties who was the son of a devoted, cricket-loving father. Father John played three games for Yorkshire in 1937, brother Alan one for the county in 1975 but young John Harry was involved in 456 of them between 1961 and 1981 until, sickened to the depths of his soul by Boycott and his support group, he left to join Derbyshire and then became a first-class umpire. Hamps grew up in South Yorkshire as a contemporary of G. Boycott. He was as popularly gregarious as Boycott was introvertedly solitary. Boycott made more runs, Hampshire played more strokes – and made more friends. But each of them influenced the life and career of the other to a degree which neither of them really understood. I have dealt with that matter at some length in another book (*Boycott*, Methuen, 1985) and this is not the time or place to repeat it.

Let us instead look at Hampshire as the considerable Yorkshire cricketer he was in his own right. He averaged 34.61 in scoring just short of 22,000 runs for the county, almost all of them attractively accumulated with powerful strokes, particularly on the on-side. There was a lot of Arthur Mitchell in John Harry Hampshire and yet, paradoxically, they were opposites. There was a grim resolution about both of them in dealing with the opposition, and they would have died rather than let the enemy have any sort of easy passage. But whereas a smile from 'Ticker' was a rarity, nothing delighted Hampshire more than an opportunity to enjoy a laugh – a great, full-throated laugh in his booming bass. Conversationally, he loved to indulge himself in the Rotherham vernacular, conjuring up vowel-sounds which are impossible to translate into the written word and which must have rendered him incomprehensible in his coaching winters in Tasmania.

His initiation into the special freemasonry of Yorkshire cricket companionship was carried out by F. S. Trueman, in whose car he was a passenger until capped-player affluence enabled him to buy his own (no sponsored vehicles for the fledgelings of the sixties) and this was a character-forming influence. It taught him very early in his career that there is no point in buying rounds of drinks in pubs when there is always some silly sod standing at the bar willing and anxious to buy them for Yorkshire cricketers. This would, of course, be in pubs *outside* Yorkshire! It also gave him a rich store of anecdotes about life on the road with the greatest of cricketing characters, for a quarter of a century later Fred is still the player around whom most of cricket's folklore is built.

Hampshire started life as a leg-spin bowler, a branch of the game which has rarely enjoyed a vogue in the higher echelons of the county's cricket, and consequently never had much chance to practise his special skills at county level. One rare opportunity came at Cardiff in 1963 when, with Close on Test duty, acting-captain Illngworth took soundings of the turf, called up the Met. Office for a weather report, checked with every known reference book and threw the greatest of Yorkshire caution to the winds: he asked Hampshire to bowl leg-spin. Close, the great exponent of flair, would have had apoplexy if he had known what Illingworth, the arch-pragmatist, was about on the sunny afternon in July 1963 at the old Arms Park ground. Hampshire returned 13–2–52–7 and Yorkshire had beaten Glamorgan by a quarter to twelve on the third morning. And he wasn't even a capped player at the time. On his return to the camp, Close demanded: 'What the hell were you bowling – 52 runs off only thirteen overs?'

At the end of the season Yorkshire won the championship by just 20 points from Glamorgan, and since that day Hamps has been able to dine out on the occasion when his leg spin brought home the title to Yorkshire once again. As for Ray Illingworth, when anyone has put the point that Close had all the flair: 'What about Cardiff in '63?' Sadly, that year – in other ways such a happy season – was the one in which John was felled by a ball from Charlie Griffith, the highly suspect West Indian fast bowler, at Middlebrough and he still feels pain and suffers sleeplessness because of it. Nevertheless,

when he was called up by England for the first time in 1969 and
went to the wicket with a scoreboard reading 37 for four (after a
night wandering around the streets of Maida Vale) he became the
first England batsman to score 100 on his début at Lord's. And he
did it while suffering hairline fractures of both his forearm and a
finger! Physically powerful and possessing great reserves of mental
toughness, Hampshire never acquired Boycott's depths of concentration and he got out too often when, solidly in his forties and
fifties, he should have been well and truly entrenched. That is
undoubtedly why he did not play more than his eight Tests, but as
a county batsman he was most certainly better than average and his
run-scoring invariably had colour and character. Above all, he was
a 100 per cent team-man and thus dovetailed beautifully into that
happy band of pilgrims who were the best and most attractive side
in the country.

Completing it, we had Tony Nicholson, known universally as the
best opening bowler never to play for England. Freddie Trueman
rated him the best of his great collection of opening partners and he
was the longest-serving of them. A real son of the Heavy Woollen
district, from Hanging Heaton, he was, in many ways, an unlikely-
looking practitioner of the art of away-swing bowling. He had big
shoulders and a deep chest, but his approach to the wicket and his
delivery contrasted starkly with the smooth menace of F. S. T.
when he was called up in 1962 to take over from the ailing Mike
Cowan. Nevertheless, he produced a prodigious out-swinger which
brought him 15 wickets (and a no. 11's batting average of 49!) in his
first part-season. The following year he took 66 wickets and the fear
was, after a full summer of bowling, that the thoroughly professional
batsmen of the county circuit would have 'worked him out'. But
Nick was a pro, too. He produced an off-cutter variant which took
a lot of people by surprise in 1964 and more than one experienced
opener returned to the dressing-room shaking his head and muttering, 'I didn't know he bowled that one.' Tony Nicholson, like Don
Wilson, was an engagingly expectant bowler who could not believe
it when batsmen played and missed altogether. How could they
have failed to get an edge?

With infinitely more hope than faith he believed every shout for
lbw would be answered affirmatively and whenever one was turned
down he would stand, gazing disbelievingly down the pitch, one

hand tucked into his ribs in what became known as the teapot stance. There was a touch of George Macaulay about Nick, but he lacked Mac's aggressiveness. He bowled and shouted with ferocity but without the naked loathing directed at the man at the other end. Everyone feared George Macaulay; everyone loved Tony Nicholson. Even a batsman who had just gone through a torrid over of playing and missing would be unable to resist a friendly exchange with him at the end of it. The appeals might have point and indeed poignancy but there was an absence of malice. Nick kept in his head a league table of the number of 'shouts' turned down by every umpire on the circuit, convinced that there was a massive plot to deprive him of a hundred wickets in a season. The umpires knew this and Tommy Spencer, the Kent veteran, was aware that he was usually at the top of Nick's black list. In 1965, after one plaintive but abortive appeal, Tommy inquired genially, 'How many's that I've refused, Nick?' Tony, who hadn't realised the umpires were in on the act, answered without thinking, but with some bitterness, 'Twenty-bloody-seven.' 'Well, there'll be another twenty-seven,' came the response, 'if you go on shouting for balls missing the leg stump.'

The following year Nicholson reached the coveted 100 wickets, and again the following year, but then he began to encounter serious health problems. He very nearly died in 1969 but when I sat at his bedside in hospital in Leeds he made out that it was simply part of a plot to keep him off the golf course. He never stopped smiling, never stopped joking until his tragic death in 1985. He was my regular golf partner for many of his years in Yorkshire cricket and I observed with much interest his philosophy that while it was wrong to cheat, it was all right to give yourself an even-money chance. Thus, whenever Mick sprayed a shot into the thickest of forests it was usual to find the next one hurtling high over the treetops to somewhere adjacent to the flag. He had, it transpired, found his ball conveniently sitting up on a tussock of grass in a clearing. It used to drive Mel Ryan, one of our regular four (with Ted Lester as the other) into a frenzy of fury so that in later years Nick was not allowed to play any shot from anywhere on any course without The Bull standing over him. All the same, he left us with a standard piece of terminology in cricket/golf circles. Any shot falling any-where from the depths of the jungle to the bottom of a lake is known as a Nicholson lie, as nice a piece of double-entendre as one can find anywhere in the language. He was only forty-seven when he died. The funeral was something like Roy Kilner's had been.

One of the more shadowy figures of this period was a player who was later to win world renown – but as an umpire. Harold Dennis Bird, from Barnsley, is today known universally as 'Dickie' and there is little doubt that he is respected as the best umpire in the world. As an uncapped player with Yorkshire he made around a couple of dozen appearances over a period of four years in the late 1950s before moving on to Leicestershire, where he *was* capped very quickly and where he spent the next five summers. He scored 613 runs in his twenty-three innings for Yorkshire, 181 of them in just one innings against Glamorgan at Park Avenue in 1959. This has given rise to a legend that he hit that big hundred (he was not out as well and, in point of fact, carried his bat through the innings after opening with Bryan Stott) and 'never played for Yorkshire again'. It is a story trotted out, sometimes as a quiz question, more often as an indication of how tough it was to make one's mark in the Yorkshire side of those days. It is, however, untrue. Dickie played against Hampshire at Bournemouth six weeks later – batting at no. 7 and still contriving to score 26 and 68 – against Derbyshire at Chesterfield, Essex at Scarborough, Gloucs at Headingley and in the return match at Bristol, and finally in the Scarborough Festival match against MCC. More than half his innings for Yorkshire came in that championship-winning season of 1959, and more than half of his runs for Yorkshire too. He was by nature and personal preference an opening batsman, and with competition from Stott, Taylor, Bolus, Sharpe and Padgett, who were all perfectly at home in the no. 1 or 2 position, he took the sensible course of accepting a contract with Leicestershire. He was a dour and dogged type of batsman rather than a stroke-player, but he later developed into a good coach and in 1970 joined the first-class umpires' list.

It was then that he proceeded to astonish his friends and, in some ways, still does. A bachelor and a rather nervy, excitable individual, he can be seen before start of play on any Test occasion as very nearly a nervous wreck. He has a natural gloom and pessimism which inevitably suggests that calamity and disaster are always at hand. Then he goes out to the middle and takes charge in a way which commands the respect of players wherever the game is played. Few of his decisions are ever questioned; rarely, if ever, does a batsman, or a bowler, return to his dressing-room muttering, 'Dickie had an off day today.' His authority on the field is in stark contrast to his diffidence and uncertainty off it. He has a wry sense of humour and in odd moments when the natural gloom lifts loves to chuckle at some exchange which has taken place on the field.

After only three years on the first-class list, Bird was appointed to the Test panel in 1973 and has now 'stood' in more Tests than any other umpire. He still retains a keen coach's eye for an outstanding talent and is always quick to draw the attention of club officials and cricket-writers to promising young players he has spotted in his travels. If his umpiring had not won his world renown, his farmyard impersonations might well have done. My colleague Brian Johnston, learning that Dickie's sleep was being disturbed in the early morning by the cry of a peacock, lured him into the commentary box to give listeners an example of the sound which awakened him each morning. It made 'Pick of the Week' as a piece of original broadcasting and when, the following season, Brian learned that Dickie's peacock (it was, one hopes, a pea*hen*) was sitting on a clutch of eggs, the cricketing world waited through a whole Test for news that they had been successfully hatched. Finally, B. J. was able to announce, 'Dickie is the proud father of three peachicks.' I have been asked in both Australia and New Zealand for reports on the progress of the 'family' and so, I am sure, have both Brian and Dickie himself.

His marvellous South Yorkshire accent and the exaggerated seriousness of his approach to the most light-hearted aspects of his cricketing life all help to make Harold Dennis Bird one of the great characters of the game – and one of the best-loved. Even his over-cautious approach to allowing play to resume after stoppages by the weather has become the subject of topical jest. On the brightest July day, with cricket progressing serenely, it is not unusual to hear the comment, 'Dickie would have had 'em off for bad light an hour ago.' Now that's fame for you.

One major figure remains to complete our story of the sixties – Vic Wilson. The big, burly, weather-tanned farmer from those fertile plains east of Malton was Yorkshire's most successful captain ever when you look at the record of his three years at the helm: Yorkshire were champions in 1960, runners-up in 1961 and champions again in 1962, after which he retired. He inherited from

Ronnie Burnet an enthusiastic, well-balanced and happy side, but his own contribution must not be under-estimated. Vic was a fairly stolid and phlegmatic character who usually disappeared in pursuit of his own interests at close of play, while the remainder of the team tended to stay together, with F.S.T. the only other notable exception. He was regarded in some quarters as a trifle unimaginative but while it was wrong to expect spectacular tactical innovation from Vic he certainly did not do much that was wrong in getting two firsts and a second place. He was a sound left-handed batsman and his huge hands rarely missed a catch at leg slip, from where he liked to direct operations. He had come through the dramas of the 1950s without being obviously caught up in any particular one of the various factions, and he remained very much his own man, skippering in a relatively aloof manner. This was not indicative of any form of stand-offishness, however – it was simply his way.

He was a physically strong man and could be tough when he thought it necessary, as when he dropped Freddie Trueman and ordered him home from Taunton for being late on parade in 1962. And in the fast bowler's benefit year, too! Fred's fury was on a Wagnerian scale but Vic stood his ground, refused to be involved in debate and F. S., with much wailing and gnashing of teeth, had to wend a solitary way home. He did it in his own time, of course, but he went. Peter Wight, the Guyanese batsman whose scoring for Somerset was prolific against all bowlers in first-class cricket except Fred Trueman, duly hit 215, which gave the absentee just as much satisfaction as the batsman, but the Yorkshire Committee backed their captain. Vic Wilson played 658 innings for Yorkshire and scored 20,539 runs. He hit 1,000 in a season fourteen times and topped 2,000 in 1951. He toured Australia in 1954–5 without playing in a Test, thus following in the wake (to quote one of the game's oldest jokes) of Captain Cook: 'Which Yorkshire captain toured Australia but never played in a Test?'

And so finally we come to Geoffrey Boycott.

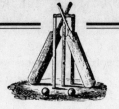

14
The Dark Ages

Geoffrey Boycott, the most controversial figure in 124 years of official Yorkshire CCC cricket, scored more runs and more centuries than anyone in the county has ever done, more runs for England than any other batsman and more than anyone in the world apart from Sunil Gavaskar. It is probably true to say that he was more difficult to dismiss than any batsman in modern cricket except Bradman, but he lacked Bradman's ability to take an attack to pieces. He scored two more centuries than Herbert Sutcliffe (151 against 149) but apart from the Gillette Cup final of 1965 never played one which excited or appealed to the imagination in the way that so many of Sutcliffe's did. He scored twenty-two more centuries than Len Hutton, but never with the grace and poise and charm of Hutton's stroke-making. And, despite all the protestations of his 1987 autobiography, the controversies surrounding Geoffrey Boycott brought Yorkshire cricket to the very brink of total destruction.

There was no hint of revolution ahead as he made his way through the Colts, forcing his way into Yorkshire's first team – successful as it was in the early sixties – in 1962 by the sheer weight of his scoring in the second team. He was a Test player by 1964 and for the next seventeen years could regard himself as England's first-choice opening batsman. He reached a hundred hundreds at Headingley in 1977, the first player to reach that personal landmark in a Test match. He overtook Gary Sobers's record of Test runs (8,032) during the Third Test in New Delhi in 1981 to lead the batsmen of the world until Gavaskar crept up behind him. He captained England in Pakistan (one Test) and New Zealand (three) after the tour skipper, Mike Brearley, had broken a forearm, but was then passed over for the leadership of his country by, successively, Bob Willis, Ian Botham and Keith Fletcher, just as he had earlier been passed over by Mike Denness and Tony Greig when he had legitimate claims to the position.

In 1971 he was made captain of Yorkshire and that season hit 2,197 runs with an average of 109.85. By the time he had done it he was a hero with the public and cordially detested by his colleagues. To the public the issue was quite straightforward: Boycott was a great player and the rest of the side were not good enough. Within the cloisters, however, it was all seen rather differently: Geoffrey was obsessed with achieving targets and records of his own, was not concerned with helping younger players and did not seem greatly concerned with what happened to the side as a whole. It took rather a long time for the county membership to realise just what was happening within the team – indeed, there still exists a small minority which has never realised it – but by 1978 the Committee at least had come to the conclusion that his appointment had been a mistake.

They deposed Boycott from the captaincy and gave it to John Hampshire, and there followed eight of the most depressing and disgraceful years in the county's history. After two years Hampshire was driven out by Boycott's noisy and unintelligent support group. Chris Old took over and was quickly forced to flee to Warwickshire. Ray Illingworth, recalled from Leicestershire to manage the troubled county, found himself having to captain the side at the age of fifty. David Bairstow was next, but still the membership was in uproar and the team in turmoil. The Committee found themselves voted out of office in March 1984, and Boycott's supporters now achieved a majority on the county club's governing body. There followed a year which made the legislation of the Brent, Islington and Lambeth Councils seem strictly orthodox and Boycott, a contracted player with the county, was now on the Committee as well.

Gradually the tide began to turn. At last the county membership began to understand that the involvement of Boycott with the unrest of the last thirteen years was not merely a coincidence and that skippering a county side requires something more than scoring lots of runs. Some of Geoffrey's most devoted supporters began to leave the ranks. At the 1986 election for Committee membership he lost his majority of followers; in 1987 he lost more, and by this time he had lost his contract as a player. That was ended in September 1986, and after flirting briefly with the idea of joining Derbyshire he retired to write his memoirs. It was suggested, perhaps unkindly but with reasonable justification, that they should be entitled *They Were All Out Of Step Except Me*. As I have written elsewhere, 'Geoffrey set himself goals which demanded total application to the exclusion of all other considerations. He achieved them, but somewhere along the road he lost his way as a person because he lost sight of what life is really all about – even in Yorkshire.'

The autobiography, published in June 1987, was launched with massive publicity and copious interviewing on radio, television and in the newspapers. It was the one chance Geoffrey had to make his critics understand that they had been mistaken about him, that they had never fully appreciated what he was *really* all about. He missed the boat – completely. Instead of pleading a case which would have cleared him of major responsibility for the turmoil which had beset his county for seventeen years he quite simply established the case for his critics beyond all shadow of a doubt. Page followed page of claims that everyone had made mistakes except Geoffrey himself. Few, if any, of his associates over twenty-five years in the first-class game escaped censure for having at some stage conspired to deprive him of his rightful place in history. Here we saw his singlemindedness at work again, and with terrible emphasis. He was never wrong; everyone else was wrong, all along the line, but not Geoffrey. His ghost-writer, Terry Brindle, who is an intelligent man, must have writhed with embarrassment as he churned out line after line of whining self-justification on behalf of his principal. If he had been allowed just once or twice, here and there, to write that there was a faint possibility of fallibility in Boycott's attitude to fellow professionals, the story might have had some credibility. As presented to the world, it had none. Many of those who had clung to Geoffrey's oft-repeated claim, uttered in those world-weary, little-boy-lost tones, that 'all he ever wanted to do was his best for Yorkshire', now winced as they read a pitiful, pathetic attempt to bolster the claim.

The tragedy of Geoffrey Boycott is that his batting was always going to entitle him to a place in cricket's Hall of Fame. His scoring achievements were prodigious. It has always been impossible even for his most trenchant critics to fail to respect the way in which by sheer determination and Yorkshire cussedness he made himself into a batsman whose wicket was the most prized by bowlers all over the world. Rejoicing was unconfined whenever he fell, whether it was at a crucial stage of a Test match in Australia or a one-day knockabout during the Scarborough Festival. The fielding side's delight was out of all proportion, but so was Geoffrey's dejection and despair. With every dismissal he died a little death. He never allowed himself to feel that tomorrow was another day; he dwelt on the loss of his wicket with a brooding intensity which had never been seen in the whole history of the game.

This was one of the characteristics which created the uniqueness of his reputation in the game. He saw the rejoicing of the opposition simply as a tribute to his ability. It never occurred to him to think that while that was undoubtedly true, it also contained more than a faint element of relief that an alien feature of that particular game of cricket had been removed. For – make no mistake about it – he was so often regarded as an alien. Even in the most intense of exchanges between professional cricketers, even in the midst of the most dramatic of life-or-death situations, there has always been an acceptance that 'life or death' was a figure of speech, a newspaper headline. It wasn't to Geoffrey Boycott; dismissal, at whatever stage, was stark tragedy, utter disaster. He could no more have said 'Well bowled' to the man who had claimed his wicket than he could have returned to the dressing-room with a smile and a professionally natural comment that 'he won't fool me with that one again'.

The consequence of all this was that over a period of twenty-five years he *created for himself* an aura of dislike, not only amongst opposition but amongst his own colleagues as well. He never came to understand that professional acceptance of a moment of superiority by the opposition was a right and decent and wholesome attitude to take. To him it was defeatism, an acceptance of standards which were less than the highest. In Geoffrey Boycott's perfect world he would never have been out; he would have batted for ever. He would have thought it a case of throwing in the towel when Boris Becker left Wimbledon in June 1987 with a comment which was a model for the sporting world, 'I lost a tennis match. I didn't lose a war. It is not the end of the world.' Geoff couldn't do that, and while Yorkshiremen must admire him on the one hand for bringing together all our best and worst traits into one personality and refining them to an incredibly high degree, so we must accept that it all went too far. His obsessiveness with personal achievement affected not only the results of the Yorkshire teams he led in the seventies and played with in the eighties. Inevitably it affected his relationships with his colleagues as well, and subsequently with his employers and, ultimately, many of his erstwhile supporters. Even at Test level (and in five-day Test matches his dedication to not getting out was a bonus for most sides) he alienated his team-mates. In Pakistan, for instance, in 1977 he infuriated fellow tourists anxious to find some form by 'hogging' the opportunity to get practice 'in the middle' all one afternoon. Geoffrey's viewpoint was beautifully simple: 'I am the best batter and the most important thing for this side is that I am in good nick.'

It was the truth. It was not, however, the whole truth and nothing but the truth. Lesser batsmen could argue most cogently that their smaller talents required them to practise more assiduously than G. B. needed to do, and who could argue with that? Geoffrey could, and did, because he saw every game in which he played through an intensely subjective eye – it was all about what part *he* had to play in it. And so, through seventeen long and miserable years, two generations of young Yorkshiremen watched their chances of winning matches (and making some personal mark themselves) recede and finally disappear as Boycott inched his way towards another career landmark. Did he, one wonders, ever ask himself what a team of eleven Geoffrey Boycotts could have achieved? He affected an intolerance of – indeed, there was a complete failure to understand – players less dedicated than himself, players with different attitudes. But let us for a moment assume that such a Boycottian Shangri-La could have been discovered – what would have become of the game of cricket?

Len Hutton received, as we have seen, criticism for slow scoring in the early days when he was working on perfecting his defensive technique as the necessarily sound base for making big scores. What did he become? There was no more pronounced strokeless wonder in the game than Glenn Turner, the great New Zealander, when he first came to this country. How did he develop at Worcestershire? Geoffrey operated in reverse. The one innings of his which is remembered was the 146 in the Gillette Cup Final – of 1965! He did play great innings apart from that, of course, notably on difficult wickets when he was the most accomplished player of his day, but fewer are remembered because they are seen in context, and that, all too frequently, meant a drawn game. No one can take away from Geoffrey Boycott his place in the record books, and no one would seek to do so. His run-scoring achievements stand uniquely in the county's and country's records. But when one starts to think of 'great Yorkshiremen' in the cricketing sense one is talking about something more than individual achievement. That is where his supporters and critics come to the parting of the ways. Yorkshire cricket has always been about something more than personal accomplishment.

On 9 May 1987 I went to Headingley to watch Yorkshire play Lancashire in the Benson and Hedges Cup. We (and I had thought never to say 'we' again) had started the sunny season by winning a championship match at Lord's and another against Hampshire at Leeds, a Benson and Hedges tie and a Refuge Assurance Sunday League match at Edgbaston. I saw a Yorkshire team transformed from the hang-dog, bickering, demoralised bunch of previous years into a side with a spring in its collective step, a glint in the eye. The boys looked positive and sharp; they looked as though they *wanted* to win and knew how to do it. The Club chairman, Brian Walsh, QC, a potent Boycott supporter in 1984, asked, 'Well, what do you think?' I replied, not without a certain emotion, 'I haven't felt as happy for seventeen years.' And, by God, I meant it.

In the following weeks I saw them set out to try to score 160 off seventeen overs against Somerset. Ashley Metcalfe aimed to drive the first ball he received and was caught at deep third man! Could we have thought to see Geoffrey Boycott do that, I was compelled to muse. Martyn Moxon, having moved to the other end, hit the first ball he received there into the pavilion for six. What would have been G. B.'s reaction to that, I wondered. That particular bid failed, but not through want of trying. There followed defeats in Glamorgan and Northampton as Yorkshire went for targets; there followed victories against Derbyshire at Harrogate and in Kent, where they were given nothing and had to fashion their own salvation. Not only were the side playing like Yorkshire again but they were being treated like Yorkshire: 'give them nothing' by way of declarations. After the Derbyshire win Michael Austin in the *Daily Telegraph* brilliantly captured the essence of the new Yorkshire in the phrase 'a players' co-operative'. That is what it had been in the heady days of the sixties. The difference was that that side had been made up of great players all the way through the ranks. The new Yorkshire, under the sane, sensible and experienced leadership of Phil Carrick, was largely composed of men seeking to make their way in the world of cricket. Moxon, who had been picked by England at a low point of his form, was, by the end of June, looking the most accomplished opener in the country. The glorious batting eloquence of Ashley Metcalfe was expressing itself more fluently in the one-day games than the championship matches, but the massive talent was so clearly visible. At twenty, Richard Blakey was fashioning centuries of rare technical expertise. Behind them stood the greater experience of Kevin Sharp and Jim Love, the inventive genius of David Bairstow and the solid dependability of Carrick himself. As July dawned, Yorkshire found themselves leading the County Championship and with a place at Lord's in the Benson and Hedges Cup Final.

On 11 July at Lord's they won the Benson and Hedges Cup for the first time in a marvellously exciting finish: Northants 244–7, innings closed; Yorkshire 244–6, the victors by virtue of losing fewer wickets. Benson and Hedges had not had their fair share of luck in sixteen Lord's finals, either because of the weather or because the excitement of close finishes was lacking. Here, they had ample compensation for previous misfortunes. The sun blazed down all day; there was good cricket, heroic cricket and the usual quota of run-out dramas, which can be very amusing if you are not immediately involved as player or partisan supporter.

Yorkshire, substantially the less experienced side, played with great character and, while it was impossible not to feel sympathy with the Northants boys who played just as whole-heartedly as their opponents, it was a specially emotional moment for the vast Yorkshire contingent in the packed house. Nevertheless, it was an impeccably well-behaved and well-mannered crowd. It was as if they sensed that a new era was dawning and they had to show that Yorkshire once again could win, as well as lose, with dignity if not with light hearts. In the commentary box my colleagues asked me to describe the final over and I couldn't do it. I just couldn't. All the professionalism in the world would not have helped me get through that over without a break in my voice. It was a feeling which I am quite sure none of my colleagues could fully understand (although Brian Johnston would have got pretty close to it). But no one who had not been brought up in Yorkshire cricket and had gone through the previous seventeen years could fully have appreciated just what that moment meant to all of us. Those young men out in the middle, a good half of them relatively inexperienced and not one of them having played in a final at Lord's, were our Sutcliffes and our Huttons, our Veritys and our Bowes, our Closes and Illingworths, our Truemans and Nicholsons. It was a sublime moment in itself when Jim Love calmly blocked the last ball of the match to complete the victory, and yet it was part of all that had gone before. The pattern of Yorkshire cricket history which had been so miserably and unworthily broken during the previous one and a half decades, was in that moment, somehow restored.

A great party took place in Don Wilson's garden in the far corner of Lord's. Trueman and Close were there, Stott and Platt, Illingworth and Richard Hutton. So were Phil Carrick and half his merry men, while the remaining half partied elsewhere. There were friends and relations. And the friends of friends, those who were not truly of the blood, hurried from group to group with half-anxious, half-apologetic smiles, saying, 'My wife's uncle came from Yorkshire . . . originally.' In the middle of it all, Don Wilson turned to Richard Hutton and said, 'This is the day we buried *him*.' And no one had to ask who 'him' was.

Looking at the bowling in 1987, it was not realistic to say that it looked capable of bowling out a good side twice on a good wicket. *But it clearly believed that it could*, and that was what was important. When four seamers – Jarvis, Sidebottom, Peter Hartley and Fletcher – bowled line and length and the fielders hung on to the catches everything looked possible. If the quicker men struggled, then Carrick was capable of bowling marvellously economical spells. Rarely did we see any bowler returning figures of seven or eight wickets, but so often were the ten shared by three and sometimes four bowlers – a players' co-operative indeed. Waiting in the wings were the explosive batting of Philip Robinson and the steady all-round ability and brilliant out-fielding of Neil Hartley. There were more batsmen of high promise on hand and a group of young bowlers learning their trade under Duggie Padgett and Steve Oldham.

Most of all there was the spirit of the side and a new attitude amongst the Committee. The handsome new indoor school was operating across the road from the ground and, though its half-million pound cost would take a lot of covering, Brian Walsh was now leading a determined campaign to raise the money. Yorkshire cricket, in all its many facets, was pulling together again. Of Geoffrey Boycott there had been no sign since the previous September; Committee meetings took place without him and their work was none the worse for his absence. Metaphorically and meteorologically the clouds had rolled by; God was in his heaven and the sun was shining at Headingley. When the southern press arrived to voice their annual criticism of the pitch for the Test match we were ready to take them on again: 'Yorkshire can do all reight on it, why can't England?' Things were starting to come right again at long, long last.

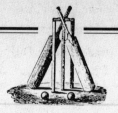

15
Home-Grown Cricketers

As Yorkshire's period without success (save for an isolated John Player League win in 1983, achieved by default rather than the team's own efforts, a title which must be seen as an embarrassment rather than a distinction for a side traditionally geared to chasing the County Championship) extended from the seventies into the eighties we began to hear the lament that we were at a disadvantage compared with the sixteen other counties because tradition demanded that only Yorkshire-born players were allowed to wear the county's colours. The import of talented overseas players by every other county had certainly improved results in many quarters and had resulted in a levelling-up of standards throughout the country. Honours now went where they had previously been unknown. We began to hear the cry that must have caused Wilfred Rhodes and Emmott Robinson to turn in their graves (mercifully, neither of them lived to see the chaos which descended upon their county after 1970): 'We are at a disadvantage because *we* do not use overseas imports.' It was a heretical cry we heard from both Geoffrey Boycott and David Bairstow, captain in 1984, 1985 and 1986. Including Lord Hawke and Geoffrey Keighley (whose lineage was undoubtedly Yorkist, an amateur who played thirty-five games between 1947 and 1951), around a couple of dozen players who were *not* born in Yorkshire had slipped through the screening net over the years – 24 out of more than 500, and only a few had made any impact, major or otherwise on the game. Exceptions could still be made at the discretion of the Committee, but they would have to involve men with very definite Yorkshire family connections. By and large, Yorkshire cricket was very definitely for Yorkshiremen.

Yet now we found two captains of Yorkshire bleating that other counties had an unfair advantage because they imported expensive mercenaries from overseas to bolster their own home-grown talent! The Yorkshire membership did some rather strange things in the early eighties (probably for reasons which it may well have thought best at the time) but surrendering its cricketing birthright was, thank goodness, not one of them. When a referendum was conducted amongst the membership in 1982, the voting was just about nine to one against a surrender, and Yorkshire's side has remained a team of Yorkshiremen. And so it must. If we cannot find a winning team from the vast breeding-grounds of the Broad Acres, either the talent-spotting system has failed or playing standards in the leagues have deteriorated to a sorry state. Whichever is the case, the problem can be sorted out.

It is entirely possible to sympathise with counties like Northants, Leicestershire, Hampshire, Sussex, Gloucs, Somerset and Glamorgan over their lack of an extensive system of league cricket to develop talent. Lancashire, Middlesex, Surrey, Warwickshire/Worcestershire (the Birmingham and other leagues overlapping), Notts, Derbyshire and to some extent Essex have a certain amount of good league cricket within their borders. Kent, in recent years, have shown what a well-organised system of talent-spotting and developing can do. But nowhere is there anything like the abundance of league cricket that is to be found in Yorkshire, ranging from evening 'workshop' leagues to the best of Saturday/Sunday afternoon cricket. I am indebted to Ian Chappell, honorary secretary of the Yorkshire Cricket Association for a list of affiliated leagues and the number of clubs they represent:

*League**	*Number of clubs*
Airedale and Wharfedale	24
Airedale Junior League	17
Barkston Ash and Yorks Central	35
Barnsley and District	20

* Some of these leagues spill over into other counties. In such cases we have counted only the Yorkshire-based clubs. Some leagues have just one club from Yorkshire playing all its away games on foreign territory, like, for example, Todmorden in the Lancashire League. Some clubs are not in any league at all, simply playing 'friendly' fixtures, and forty-nine

League	Number of clubs
Bradford	30
Bradford Central	32
Bradford and District Evening	20
Bradford Mutual Sunday School	40
Bradford Junior	30
Bridlington and District	24
Central Yorkshire	25
Cleveland and Tees-side	24
Craven and District	24
Cricket Pennant Alliance	10
Dales Council	20
Dales Villages	8
Darlington and District	12
Derwent Valley	15
Dewsbury and District	40
Doncaster and District	58
Doncaster and District Evening	20
Doncaster and District Infirmary	20
East Riding Amateur	45
East Riding Independent	15
East Riding Sunday	10
East Yorkshire Cup	12
Eskdale	12
Esk Valley Evening	6
Feversham	8
Foss Evening	10
Halifax	28
Halifax and District Association	20
Harrogate Amateur Evening	38
Heavy Woollen Junior	20
Howdenshire Evening	12
Huddersfield	30

of these are affiliated to the Yorkshire Cricket Association; others are
not. There are nomadic clubs who play all away fixtures like The Hawks,
The Saints, The Owls and the delightfully named Honourable Society of
Gentlemen Troughers.

League	Number of clubs
Huddersfield and District Association	16
Huddersfield Central Association	35
Huddersfield and District Evening	15
Humberside Federation	8
Humber-Don	20
Hull WSA	35
Langborough WRD	16
Leeds and District	18
Leeds and District Junior	20
Jack Gahan (Sunday)	14
Mexborough and District	15
Middlesbrough Mid-Week	10
Mirfield and District Evening	6
Newland Evening	10
Nidderdale and District Amateur	40
Northallerton and District	4
North Humberside Junior	10
North Humberside Sunday	10
North Yorks and South Durham	20
Norton and District	54
Old Malton Evening	8
Pickering Evening	8
Pilmoor Evening	9
Pocklington and District Evening	10
Pontefract and District	20
Pudsey and District	12
Rotherham and District	20
Rydedale Beckett Evening	10
Saddleworth	1
Scarborough Beckett	30
Scarborough and District Evening	20
Selby Evening	10
Sheffield	45
Sheffield Alliance Mid-Week	20
Sheffield and District Junior	20
Sheffield Works	28
Sheffield Indoor	10

League	Number of clubs
Sime Memorial Evening	10
Snaith and District	8
South Riding	45
South Yorkshire (and Rotherham)	12
Spen Valley Workshops	12
Sugg Evening	8
Tadcaster Evening	20
Thorne Mid-Week	5
Upper Airedale Junior	25
Wakefield and District Union	12
Wath and District	12
Wensleydale	12
West Riding	36
West Riding Sunday	12
Wetherby and District	36
Whitby Evening	10
Wrelton Evening	8
York and District Senior	40
York Saturday	20
Yorkshire	16

Now, if those figures involve a certain duplication in that many cricketers will play for one team on Saturday and perhaps another in mid-week or on Sunday, this is more than balanced by the fact that we are looking at many clubs which field two and three sides each. It all adds up to an awful lot of cricketers playing every week in Yorkshire. In terms of recruitment to the county side, the primary leagues would be Yorkshire, Bradford and Huddersfield but they, of course, recruit in turn from the more modest leagues so it is all part of a continuous process of development. No other county, even allowing for the greater concentration of population in the London area, in Birmingham and Lancashire, can look to such fertile nurseries of cricket. *Of course* we should be able to find enough good players who, properly groomed and encouraged and developed, could take on the best from other quarters.

The Yorkshire county side has, over the years, beaten the full might of touring sides from Australia (six times), India (five times), West Indies (three times) and New Zealand, Pakistan and South

Africa once in each case. Why then do we find it necessary to whimper about unfair advantages because Hampshire, for instance, field Gordon Greenidge and Malcolm Marshall from the West Indies Test side or Somerset for some years turned out with Vivian Richards and Joel Garner? At Middlesbrough, in 1963, Yorkshire beat West Indies by 111 runs in a game in which Freddie Trueman took ten wickets for 81 runs; he was backed up by Mel Ryan who was never even close to getting a Test cap, yet he did a great job for Yorkshire for ten years. Yorkshire players used to *look forward* to taking on full-strength touring sides, not merely county teams with a couple of overseas Test players in their ranks. There has been no reduction in the amount of cricket being played throughout the county since those days; on the contrary, the number of clubs has increased. What has happened is that with the county club in disarray there has been less of a burning desire on the part of talented league cricketers to become a part of it.

Those dark days, one hopes, are now at an end, and by far the most important task confronting Yorkshire's Committee today is to convince not only cricketers all over the ridings but those in the very county side itself that they are a part of something extra special, an outfit which played an outstanding part in championship cricket for a hundred years when Yorkshire CCC was light-years removed from the stumbling, fractious and, let's face it, *tatty* organisation we have seen in the last ten. We have never played our cricket simply for fun; the most distressing part of the last decade has been that we have become figures of fun to everyone else. A county which produced the characters seen in the previous pages of this book is entirely capable of finding others. The nature of our native character has not changed. When we decided upon self-destruction we set about it with an energy which no other county could have matched. Now it requires the same energy to rebuild, and a look back at some of the men who made Yorkshire the most powerful cricketing unit in the world is not a bad way to start. At least their stories provide us with the inspiration.

Yorkshire Leagues 1986

Yorkshire League not indicated

0   10   20   30 km

CENTRAL (Leeds)

1 Nidderdale
2 Whixley Evening
3 Ryedale Evening
  York Evening
  York Saturday
  York Senior
  York U16
4 Claro Junior
  Harrogate Evening
5 Tadcaster Evening
6 Wetherby
7 Barkston Ash & Yorks Central
8 Leeds
  Leeds Junior

9 Howdenshire Evening
10 Osgoldcross Junior
   Pontefract
   Pontefract Junior
   Wakefield Union
   West Riding

NORTHERN (North Yorks)

11 Cleveland & Teesside
   Cleveland U13 & U15
   Langborough WRD
   North Yorks &
     S. Durham

12 Darlington
13 Esk Valley Evening
   Eskdale
   Eskdale Junior
14 Wensleydale
15 Northallerton Evening
   Wath
   Wath Junior
16 Feversham
17 Pickering Evening
   Ryedale Becket
18 Pilmoor Evening

EASTERN (East Yorks)
19 Derwent Valley & Junior
   Scarborough Becket
   Scarborough Evening
20 Old Malton Evening
21 Bridlington
22 Pocklington Evening
23 East Riding Independent
   East Riding Sunday
   East Yorkshire Cup
24 Foss Valley Evening
25 Cricket Pennant Alliance
   East Riding Amateur
   Hull WSA
   Humberside Cricket Fed.
   Newland Evening
   North Humberside
   Sunday & Junior

SOUTHERN
(Doncaster, Sheffield,
Huddersfield & Halifax)
26 Snaith
   Thorne Midweek
27 Humber–Don
28 Doncaster
   Doncaster Evening
   Doncaster Infirmary
29 Mexborough Evening
   Rotherham
   Rotherham & S Yorks
30 Barnsley
   Barnsley Junior
31 Norton
   South Riding
   Sheffield
   Sheffield Asian
   Sheffield Indoor

   Sheffield Junior
   Sheffield WSA
   Sime
   Selby
   Sheffield Midweek
   Sugg Thursday
32 Bassetlaw
   Worksop Junior
33 North Derbyshire
   Yorks & Derby
34 Mirfield Evening
   Quaid-I-Azam
   Spen WSA
   Spenboro' Evening
   Sunday League
35 Huddersfield
   Huddersfield CA
   Huddersfield Central
   Huddersfield Evening
   Huddersfield Junior
   Huddersfield U13
   Kirklees Junior
36 Halifax
   Halifax Dist Assn
37 Saddleworth

WEST ONE (Bradford)
38 Bradford
   Bradford Central
   Bradford Evening
   Bradford Junior
   Bradford Sunday School
   West Riding Sunday
39 Dales Council
   Pudsey
   Sports Bag Evening
   Worthington Sports
40 West Bradford Junior
41 Airedale & Wharfedale
   Senior
   Airedale Junior
42 Dales Villages
43 Craven
   Upper Airedale Junior

WEST TWO (Heavy Woollen)
44 Batley & Dewsbury Boys
   Central Yorks
   Dewsbury & District
   Heavy Woollen Cup
   Heavy Woollen Junior

16
The Press Gang

Yorkshire's personal press corps is something which other counties have envied for a hundred years. The value of having as many as ten or eleven newspapers regularly covering county matches is something the Northants and Hampshires of this world would dearly love to enjoy. Middlesex, Surrey and Essex, of course, have had the close attention of the London papers but with large circulations and early edition times it is impossible for the evenings, at any rate, to do justice to a day's play beyond a point about an hour into the afternoon. The London morning papers are 'nationals' and therefore must be expected to cover the whole range of championship matches, concentrating on selected ones only in terms of regional editions.

Yorkshire have long had the personal, undivided attention of their own newspapers plus the special attention of the 'nationals' at certain times. The peak time was probably in the 1960s when, in addition to the *Yorkshire Post*, the *Yorkshire Evening Post*, the *Yorkshire Evening News* (until it closed), the *Sheffield Telegraph*, the *Sheffield* (evening) *Star* and the (Bradford) *Telegraph and Argus*, who had their own cricket correspondents, games were covered on a regular basis by the northern editions of the *Daily Mail, Daily Express, Daily Herald, Daily Mirror* and *Daily Telegraph*. This was saturation coverage with a vengeance, and there could be scarcely anyone in the North of England who was unaware of the county side. In terms of publicity the county lived in a rich vein of the free variety; its value was incalculable. It is fair to say that the county has appreciated this, and the association between its Committee and the Yorkshire-based press was an extremely cordial one until the

Geoffrey Boycott controversy shattered that harmonious relationship (amongst many others).

The first correspondent of note was A. W. Pullin, who wrote for the *Yorkshire Evening Post* under the nom-de-plume of 'Old Ebor', and how appropriate that was because his contemporaries swore that to him the game in Yorkshire was life itself. He covered much of cricket's golden age but, not content with this, also sought out many of Yorkshire's original players of the 1860s and his reminiscences with these now grand old men was published in book-form in 1898. It is very much a collector's item. When he died in 1934 he was mourned by several generations of Yorkshire cricketers who respected him as a journalist and a friend. One young admirer who had followed Yorkshire through his writing was Len Hutton: 'Lots of us in Yorkshire had been brought up on his writing and commentaries and every cricketer, star and colt alike, was in some way his debtor.'

The pseudonym 'Little John' masked for many years the identity of John Bapty, who had to wait until after the war to be given his own by-line. For the first few months it appeared in the *Evening Post* as 'By John Bapty ("Little John")' to make the transition clear to readers. His style was based to some extent on the old-world prose of Old Ebor and he had a number of phrases which one could expect to see worked into his description of a day's play with some regularity. In 1950, the West Indian spin-twins, Ramadhin and Valentine, so mesmerised English batsmen that a Trinidadian calypsoist composed a work in their honour, each stanza ending, 'With those little pals of mine, Ramadhin and Valentine.' This combination of circumstances prompted a talented young copy-boy on the *Evening Post* to write a parody, incorporating many of Bapty's most-used phrases and each verse ending, 'John Bapty or Little John.' The boy was Keith Waterhouse, later to become a distinguished playwright, author and columnist, and those who worked for the *Evening Post* in Albion Street, Leeds, at the time like to think of the calypso as the first blossoming of a great literary talent. But I hope that light-hearted digression does not suggest that Bapty was anything less than highly respected by players and readers alike. He was accurate in his facts, fair in his criticism, honest in his views – and those, surely, have always been the basis of the best journalism?

Little John was succeeded by Bill Bowes after his move 300 yards across central Leeds from the *Yorkshire Evening News* where he had learned his trade. Bill was, of course, a former player who had no basic training in newspaper-writing, but with the same energy and conscientiousness that he had employed in his quest for the outswinger he set out to learn the job from top to bottom. He brought with him general respect for his knowledge of the game as a Yorkshire and England bowler, as well as for a man who had endured years in a prison camp. He added to this reputation by his reasoned and reasonable writing, his willingness to help anyone in any way, his gentle humour and his equable temperament. A thoroughly nice man, Bill Bowes and, of course, a fine cricket writer.

Frank Stainton, who served Kemsley's provincial newspapers, is credited with the first Freddie Trueman anecdote on record. In London with Yorkshire he encountered young F. S. one evening slumped in a chair in the team's hotel, his face as black as thunder. On inquiring the reason for this melancholia he learned that Fred had spent the evening in a West End cinema watching *The Snake Pit*, the film about a mental institution for which Olivia de Havilland won an Oscar. What had upset Trueman was, first, the price of his seat – seven shillings and sixpence, an enormous sum for 1949, at least to someone more used to prices in Maltby – but, worst of all, 'There wasn't a bloody snake in it from beginning to end.' Frank was one of the first journalists to use a typewriter in the cathedral-quiet of the cricketing press box, an innovation which was received with some anguished surprise in the South of England. It was at Lord's that the South had the laugh on him on one occasion when he asked a Post Office telegraph boy to bring him back a slab of press forms – the sheets on which he knocked out his reports to a wide variety of newspapers. The boy returned with a package and told Frank, 'That's sevenpence.' 'What's sevenpence?' demanded the mystified Stainton. 'The slab of pressed pork you asked for.'

J. M. Kilburn was a superb essayist with a deep knowledge and love of the game who wrote for the *Yorkshire Post* before and after the war. He was influenced by Cardus but he developed his own particular style which reflected in every syllable how much he *cared* for the game. Some examples of his delightful prose have occurred in various parts of previous pages. He had started his working life as a schoolmaster and this showed in certain aspects of his personality. As a founder-member of the Cricket Writers' Club he believed implicitly in the preservation of the dignity of the press box and he never came to terms with a new generation of occupants for whom non-stop merry quip and jest formed an essential part of their six hours a day together. He once rebuked me at Bramall Lane for making too much noise when others were trying to collect their thoughts. I argued. I was rude to him. It's a long time ago but to this day I feel shame at the memory because Jim was absolutely right and I was totally wrong. The last few words of J. M. Kilburn's autobiography (*Thanks to Cricket*, Stanley Paul, 1973) tell us all we really need to know about the man. He had seen Geoffrey Boycott, as Yorkshire's captain, embroiled in a bitter and public quarrel at Old Trafford after which 'provocative journalism had mercilessly given quotation precedence over social conventions'. Kilburn was dismayed and 'took his pessimism for a walk'.

By chance he stumbled on a club cricket match taking place.

It was clearly a club of substance, the playing area extensive and well tended. Pavilion and scoreboard shone with fresh paint. The boundary line was neatly marked and accentuated with foot-high flags. The batting on soft turf was to slow bowling of a right-hander and a left-hander and though I could not read the scores from my distance the concentration of the players suggested a critical stage in the match. An on-drive sent a fieldsman in pounding pursuit towards the boundary, the stroke assuring a comfortable two runs but a hazardous three. The third was attempted and the scampering batsman raised a hand in acknowledgment to the umpire's signal of dismissal and turned to walk briskly to the pavilion. He was passed on the field by his successor and the fielding side were in position, the bowler ready to run up as soon as guard had been taken. For all who were playing and watching there was nothing in mind beyond the next ball, the challenge of the moment, the absorption in good-natured contest. Time stood still in a distillation of delight. People and place and circumstance gave visual representation to a meaning, a conception, an ideal. Cricket was itself again and all was well with my world.

C. R. Williamson could more easily have bridged the gap between cricket and journalism, for he was a chameleon-like personality. As a man involved with the quick-fire, deadline-catching business of writing Yorkshire cricket for the *Telegraph and Argus* evening paper in Bradford, Dick Williamson made no pretensions to be a writer in the Kilburnian mould. His preoccupation was with facts, which were dispensed with speed and accuracy. From the early 1920s through to the 1970s he followed Yorkshire cricket with devotion, chronicling the great deeds of one generation after another but, more importantly, storing *the facts* in an incredible reference library in the spare bedroom at his home in Heaton, a Bradford suburb.

Dick's idea of off-duty heaven was to browse through this mass of cuttings, seeking a new way to catch out a newcomer to the Yorkshire press box with 'a modest wager'. No one knew more about the records of the county and its players; no one could turn up more speedily the most abstruse detail of a long-forgotten match. He was a CHARACTER in capital letters. He could be the merriest of companions one minute, the bitterest of foes the next; his armoury a torrent of words dripping with vitriol. Of all Yorkshire's idols of the twenties, thirties and beyond his idol, significantly, was George Macaulay, of the acid tongue and volatile nature. When he retired from the *Telegraph and Argus* he carried on reporting Yorkshire games for Exchange Telegraph news agency. When he died, in 1986, the mourners represented a massive public and huge circle of professional acquaintances. We shall not see another like Dick Williamson.

When Jim Kilburn retired, his *Yorkshire Post* role was taken over by Terry Brindle, a very different type indeed. Terry was a gifted writer with a splendid wit and he enlivened the pages of the *Post* in an entirely different way from Jim Kilburn. He was an apostle of a different creed of journalism, for the cult of personality was upon us and the biggest personality in Yorkshire cricket from 1971 onwards was Geoffrey Boycott. Brindle was Boycott's 'ghost' in a number of publications, and when Geoffrey reached a stage of open warfare with the Yorkshire Committee Brindle was his spokesman. The *Yorkshire Post*, for so long allied to the Establishment of Yorkshire cricket, now poured forth a steady stream of pro-Boycott bulletins which were a powerful force in the toppling of the Committee in 1984. He left to work in Australia but returned when

Boycott decided to publish his autobiography in 1987. Geoffrey was badly in need of a sympathetic ghost.

The *Yorkshire Evening Post* is represented today by John Callaghan from Huddersfield, who got a thorough grounding in journalism with the *Huddersfield Examiner*, the *Yorkshire Evening News* and the *Halifax Courier* before starting to write cricket for the *Evening Post* in 1972. He has been a Yorkshire cricket follower since he was a small boy, is the author of several books and a contributor to *Wisden* and cricketing magazines.

David Hopps, Leeds-born and a graduate of Hull University, played his own cricket in the Wetherby and Airedale and Wharfedale Leagues, and trained in journalism in Essex. This gave rise to certain perhaps understandable but unworthy suspicions when he took over as cricket correspondent of the *Yorkshire Post* in March 1984. 'You were *born* in Yorkshire, weren't you?' was the first question addressed to him by the first Yorkshire CCC member to whom he was introduced. With the dry humour which characterises his conversation and writing he observes of that occasion, 'I had not realised until then that the Yorkshire-born restriction applied to the press as well.'

He entered cricket-writing at a difficult time. The Boycott brigade had just taken over the Yorkshire Committee and almost the first story he wrote for the *Post* was Ray Illingworth's sacking. 'I was taken aback to find that half the people in Yorkshire cricket circles were not talking to the *Yorkshire Post*,' he recalls – an inevitable legacy from Terry Brindle's term of office. Of the half who *would* talk to him, some blamed the newspaper for 'the mess you've got us into'. Sensibly, Hopps took a non-aligned stance but his early experience was an uneasy one. Happier days were to come in 1987.

At the Bradford *Telegraph and Argus*, the legendary Williamson was an impossible act to follow; his successor had to do things his own way. This was David Swallow, who had been at school with Ray Illingworth and played alongside him in junior cricket. He travelled the country with Yorkshire from 1967 to 1974, a sad period for him in many ways because it covered the break-up of the great championship-winning side and the beginning of the controversy which raged around Boycott from the start of his period as captain. During the development of this the *Telegraph and Argus*'s cricket correspondent, still filling the post, was and is David

Warner, from Baildon. For the past twelve years he has watched the ebbing and flowing of the great oceans of Yorkshire anger, and his outstanding achievement has been to hold the respect and confidence of both sides in the Boycott debate – a position very few people could have attained. He has twice won the Yorkshire Sports Journalist of the Year Award and has received a commendation in the Sports Council awards.

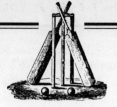

17
Cricket Societies

The county's passion for cricket is also reflected in the number of cricket societies which meet in the winter months and keep the memories of summer ticking over. Some are purely social, others involve themselves in the provision of facilities for youngsters who do not get the help in schools which should be a Yorkshire boy's right. Some provide trophies and awards which are an incentive to young players, and others provide practical help for the parent county club. One way and another, they are an excellent back-up to the county club itself, along with the personal press corps. It is an area of support which, if not unique to Yorkshire, is stronger than that of any other county.

The Boycott era saw great volumes of opinion and support for different factions appear and, as the period did in every other context, this caused some deep rifts to occur. This was in the natural order of things since we have, as a county people, tended to view things as either black or white with very few grey areas. But in the last analysis one has to take the long view that cricket societies exist to promote and foster a feeling for the great game and to provide a means of enjoying it in a spirit of good companionship.

Wombwell Cricket Society was formed in 1951 and up to 1986 still had its original President (Dr Leslie Taylor) and honorary secretary, Jack Sokell. Dr Taylor, a brother-in-law of Roy Kilner, died in that year but secretary Sokell soldiers on with a passion for cricket which even in a game which produces more than its share of zealots is remarkable. The society's motto is 'My song shall be cricket and cricket my theme', and letters with those words over the top of the letterhead have found their way into clubs and households, dressing-rooms and commentary and press boxes all over the world. No opportunity – absolutely none – to promote cricketing matters in general and those of Wombwell in particular escapes the eye or the pen of Jack Sokell.

The society lists as its patrons John Arlott, Keith Miller, Sir Brian Rix, E. W. Swanton, Colin Cowdrey, Freddie Trueman and Geoff Boycott, and has a membership world-wide of 600. More than 2,000 celebrities have been guest speakers at its winter meetings and dinners, the very first of them being Johnny Wardle, who was a good friend to the Society in its early days. The new president is Miss Jean Swift and the headquarters (after years in a Wombwell pub) are now at the Oaks Working Men's Club in Ardsley – appropriately enough, Wardle's birthplace.

In a nice mixture of sentimentality and practicality the society makes awards to promising young cricketers in the name of famous first-class players, so we have the Jack Hobbs, Learie Constantine, Maurice Leyland, Arthur Wrigley (former BBC scorer and statistician) and now the Johnny Wardle trophies. It also runs under-fifteen and under-seventeen sides and winter coaching classes with a view to sending a continuous stream of young players into the local clubs and leagues and beyond. As we have seen in an earlier page, this has produced positive results.

Secretary: Jack Sokell, 42 Woodstock Road, Barnsley.

Blackley Cricket Society started out in October 1974 with a guest speaker, followed by a meal of cold meat and pickles, cheese and biscuits and a *barrel of beer*. This was the entirely laudable idea of a good cricketing evening worked out by Roy Chappel, a local baker who was connected with Blackley Cricket Club. It worked well at first, but when the early novelty had worn off the attendances dwindled a little and so finishing off the barrel presented a few problems, at least in terms of time. Obviously, no bunch of good Yorkshiremen were going to *leave* any ale undrunk so the meetings tended to last rather long into the night!

Blackley is a small village on the hill between Halifax and Huddersfield, and the name is pronounced in perfectly orthodox fashion. But there is a Blackley in north-west Manchester which calls itself Blakeley (a typical bit of Lancashire nonconformism!) and Cedric Rhoades, invited as a guest speaker during his time as the Lancashire CCC chairman, got a few old-fashioned looks from the locals when he asked the way. Roy Chappel did the catering himself in the society's early days but ill-health forced him to quit after the 1985–6 winter and for a time there was something of a crisis: it looked as though it might be necessary to move meetings from the Blackley Cricket Club pavilion. Then one John Hudson came to the rescue, an experienced caterer from the Dewsbury League, and now the members can choose their menu from such exotic delights as curry, lasagne, stew-and-dumplings, meat-and-potato pie. Clearly the nosh is a rather important factor in Blackley C. S. meetings but their speakers have included Bomber Wells (Gloucs/Notts), Jack Robertson (Middlesex), Norman Graham (Kent), Chris Balderstone (Yorks/Leics), Peter Roebuck (Somerset) and David Frith, Editor of *Wisden Cricket Monthly*. Current membership is fifty-one (all male, which is a bit unusual in cricket society circles) and average attendances around forty, which makes Blackley probably the smallest society affiliated to the Council of Cricket Societies. Meetings take place on the second Tuesday of the month.

Secretary: Dennis Butterfield, 7 Bayswater Terrace, Halifax HX3 0NB.

Heavy Woollen Cricket Society was founded in 1974 and one of the original members was Peter Hirst, the Dewsbury district representative on the Yorkshire CCC Committee. Sadly, he died the following year so the society provided a trophy in his name which goes to the members' choice of Yorkshire player of the year. The first speaker was Norman Yardley and since then the guest list has covered players, cricket-writers, TV personalities, coaches, managers and 'cricket maniacs'. These have been roped in by the enterprising Mollie Staines, for six years a lone, symbolic female figure on the Yorkshire CCC committee and speaker-finder for the society since its inception. Meetings are held at Cleckheaton Cricket Club on the second Wednesday of each winter month (October to April).

Secretary: Gordon S. Cooper, 27 Milford Grove, Gomersal, Cleckheaton.

The *East Riding Cricket Society* started operations in the winter of 1966–7, but the seeds had been sown in the previous decade. Sidney Hainsworth, chairman of the Hull manufacturing firm of J. F. Fenner and Company, and a great friend of cricket and cricketers, had brought a number of notable figures to speak at Fenner Sports and Social dinners. Only a few guests, however, had the opportunity to hear them and it was Charles Wildblood who suggested to Mr Hainsworth that it would be nice to give a wider public the chance to listen to cricket talk from men like Trevor Bailey and Brian Johnston. And so the ERCS had Sidney Hainsworth as its first chairman and Charles Wildblood as the first secretary. One of the strengths of the society is the continuity it has achieved with officials – the present president, for instance, was the original assistant secretary – and it has an understandable pride in the work it does for junior cricket, especially at schools level where it is most urgently needed.

Winter meetings with guest speakers remain an integral part of the society's social programme, four in the first season, up to nine and ten in later years. In the fact the total of speakers in twenty-one years is over 130 and only one meeting has had to be cancelled because of bad weather. Membership is now over 200.

Secretary: Ray P. Thompson, 151 Park Avenue, Hull HU5 3EX.

Rotherham Cricket Society had as its first speaker, in 1959, Norman Yardley and he is now the patron of the society, which meets eight times a year in the winter months. This is strictly a society for listening to cricket talk on the long, dark evenings between September and April and there is no involvement in coaching or other activities. The chairman is Charlie Lee, a former Derbyshire captain and Yorkshire Colt, and the president is Athol Carr, a Rotherham hotelier and one of the more colourful characters amongst Yorkshire supporters. I remember him driving to Scarborough Festival matches in an open landau with his great friend, the late Charlie Andrassi, the two of them waving regally to the crowds of summer holidaymakers. David Welch, a former Yorkshire CCC treasurer, is their speaker-finder.

Secretary: Robin Atkin, 15 Gallow Tree Road, Rotherham. S65 3EE.

The *Halifax '13' Cricket Society* was founded by Tom Hyland after he had enjoyed a pleasant meal and an evening of cricket talk with a group of members of the League committee in Huddersfield. It seemed to him an excellent way of spending a winter's evening, so Tom asked four Halifax district enthusiasts to join him for dinner at the Fleece Hotel in Barkisland and put his ideas to them. The four guests each nominated one other member and *those* four in turn added one nomination each. With secretary and speaker-finder Hyland that resulted in a circle of thirteen cricketing friends. Tom quoted to that initial band of brothers the words of Andrew Lang: 'There is no talk, none so witty and brilliant that is so good as cricket talk, when memory sharpens memory and the dead live again – the regretted and the unforgotten – and the old happy days of burnt-out Junes revive.' His notes of the first meeting, more than twenty years ago, show the aims of the society: limitation of numbers to keep it small and friendly: informality at dinners (the speaker remains seated); no press present; nothing confidential to be discussed *outside* the meeting.

Their guests have ranged from club cricketers and personal friends, through league officials to stars of the international cricket scene, but the essential informality is retained. Tom Hyland took the trouble to write out for me a complete list of 117 guest speakers and then added an appendix: 'The list includes one Indian, one Australian and thirteen English Test players; thirty-two county cricketers; four Yorkshire captains, one from Notts, one Derbyshire, one Surrey and one England; ten cricket authors, one batmaker, three Test umpires; groundsmen, journalists, radio and TV personalities; even an artist and a Lord Mayor!'

And the society plays a New Year's Day match annually at Centre Vale, Todmorden, to prove that there is life in some of the old dogs yet.

Two societies failed to respond to my invitation to say something about themselves, which I found extremely distressing after enclosing a stamped, self-addressed envelope! I do not take any more kindly to wasting 36p than any of my fellow-countrymen. Let me from my personal knowledge, therefore, record that the Northern Cricket Society, based in Leeds, was founded by Ron Yeomans, at one time a colleague of mine on the *Yorkshire Evening Post*, who designed a very handsome tie incorporating (and for this I never forgave him) the red rose of Lancashire with the white of Yorkshire. Meetings are held at the Griffin Hotel in Boar Lane, Leeds, and the secretary is R. S. Marsh, 113 Crossgates Lane, Leeds LS15 7PJ. No response was received from Sheffield Cricket Society.

There is a world-wide co-ordinating body, the Council of Cricket Societies (with membership ranging from Australia to Zimbabwe) whose secretary is John Featherstone, 205 Hyde Park Road, Leeds LS6 1AH.

By the end of the 1987 season, even though the momentum of the first two months had been impossible to sustain, membership was increasing not only of the county club but of the cricket societies as well. With this sort of back-up surely we could never allow ourselves to descend once again to the gloomy depths of the preceding seventeen years?

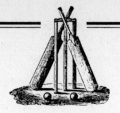

Index